The Loss of Virtue

The Loss Of Virtue

Moral Confusion and Social Disorder in Britain and America

edited by
Digby Anderson

Published by
The Social Affairs Unit

A National Review Book

British Library Cataloguing in Publication Data
A catalogue record for this book is available from the British Library

Library of Congress Catalog Card Number: 92-062219

ISBN 0-907631-50-9

Printed in the United States of America

Contents

The Authors

Mark Almond is Lecturer in Modern History at Oriel College, Oxford and a Fellow of the Institute for European Defence and Strategic Studies. His publications include *The Rise and Fall of Nicolai and Elena Ceausescu*; and *Retreat to Moscow: Gorbachev and the East European Revolution.* He has contributed articles to a number of newspapers and journals, including *The Times* and *The Spectator.*

Dr. Digby Anderson is Director of the Social Affairs Unit in London and a member of the Council of the Economic and Social Research Council and of the Health Services Committee of the Council for National Academic Awards. His numerous publications include *The Kindness that Kills: The Churches' Simplistic Response to Complex Social Issues* (ed); *Taking Thought for the Poor* (series ed); *The Moral Dimension of Social Policy* (series ed); and *Full Circle: Bringing Up Children in the Post-Permissive Society* (ed). He also contributed widely to newspapers, periodicals and to television and radio debates of current affairs.

Dr. Christoper Dandeker is currently Senior Lecturer in War Studies in King's College, London, having previously taught at the University of Leicester and Sheffield City Polytechnic. His main research interest is the armed forces in their social context and his publications include *Surveillance Power and Modernity*; and *Structure of Social Theory* (joint author). He has also contributed numerous articles on social theory, political and military sociology. He is joint founder of the British Military Studies Group.

Professor Christie Davies is Professor of Sociology at the University of Reading. He has been a visiting lecturer in India and Poland and

'Distinguished Scholars Interdisciplinary Lecturer' at the Institute for Humane Studies, George Mason University, Virginia. His most recent book is *Ethnic Humor Around the World: a Comparative Analysis.* He has contributed a number of articles on the sociology of morality to edited books and journals including *American Journal of Sociology* and *Policy Review.*

Jon Davies is a Lecturer in Religious Studies at the University of Newcastle upon Tyne where he is Head of the Religious Studies Department, lecturing principally on the liturgies, theologies and sociologies of marriage and death. His publications include *The Evangelistic Bureaucrat, a Study of a Planning Exercise in Newcastle upon Tyne* and *Asian Housing in Britain.* Forthcoming publications are *The Family under Christianity and Capitalism* and *The Sociology of Sacred Texts* (co-editor). He also has a book in progress on 'War and War Memorials'.

Professor Antony Flew has been Emeritus Professor of Philosophy, University of Reading, since 1982. For the past six years he has spent part of the year at the Social Philosophy and Policy Center, Bowling Green, Ohio. His many publications include *Crime or Disease?*; *Sociology, Equality and Education*; *The Politics of Procrustes: Contradictions of Enforced Equality*; *Power to the Parents: Reversing Educational Decline*; *Equality in Liberty and Justice*; and *Thinking about Social Thinking.* He has also contributed very many articles to newspapers and journals.

Professor Adrian Furnham is Professor of Psychology, having previously been Lecturer in Psychology at Pembroke College, Oxford. He has lectured widely abroad and held scholarships and visiting professorships at, amongst others, the University of New South Wales and the University of the West Indies. He has written numerous scientific papers and books including *Culture Shock* (with S. Bochner); *The Economic Mind* (with A. Lewis); *Lay Theories*; *The Protestant Work Ethic*; *Personality at Work*; and *Consumer Profiles* (with B. Gunter). He has also contributed articles to newspapers and popular magazines. He is a Fellow of the British Psychological Society.

Dr. Robert Grant is Lecturer in English Literature at the University of Glasgow. He has taught at the Universities of Sussex and Cambridge, where he was a Fellow of Trinity Hall. He has also lectured widely in the U.S. and in Eastern Europe, where he was involved in the work of the 'underground universities' run by the Jan Hus and Jagiellonian Foundations in Czechoslovakia and Poland during the Communist period. He is the author of *Oakeshott* and of many articles and reviews on literary, philosophical, and political topics.

Dr. John Gray has been a Fellow of Jesus College, Oxford, since 1976 and has had visiting professorships at Harvard, Emory and Tulane Universities. His books include *Hayek on Liberty*; *Liberalisms: essays in political philosophy*; *Mill on Liberty*; and *Post Liberalism*. He is currently writing a history of political thought. Work on the essay included in this volume was done during a period of residence as Stranahan Distinguished Research Fellow at the Social Philosophy and Policy Center, Bowling Green State University, Ohio.

Simon Green is a Fellow of All Souls College, Oxford, and a Lecturer in History at the University of Leeds. He is the author of numerous articles on various aspects of 19th and 20th century British history, contemporary political philosophy, and public policy.

Professor Richard Lynn is Professor of Psychology at the University of Ulster, having previously held appointments at Exeter University, the Neuro-Psychiatric Research Institute, Princeton, and the Dublin Economic and Social Research Institute. His publications include *Arousal, Attention and the Orientation Reaction*; *The Universities and the Business Community*; *The Irish Brain Drain*; *Personality and National Character*; *Introduction to the Study of Personality* (ed); *The Entrepreneur*; *Dimensions of Personality*; *Educational Achievement in Japan: Lessons for the West*; and *The Secret of the Miracle Economy: Different National Attitudes to Competitiveness and Money*. He has also contributed numerous papers to journals of psychology.

Professor David Martin is Emeritus Professor of Sociology at the London School of Economics and was recently Scurlock Professor at Southern Methodist University, Dallas, and Visiting Professor (and F. D. Maurice lecturer) at King's College, London. His most recent book is *Tongues of Fire* which represents research undertaken in association with the Institute for the Study of Economic Culture, Boston University, into the rapid expansion of Protestantism in Latin America. He is also a non-stipendiary assistant priest at Guildford Cathedral.

Patricia Morgan is a sociologist who has specialised in criminology. She has written widely in the field of family matters as well as crime and penal policy. As well as being the author of a number of books, she has been a frequent contributor of newspaper and magazine articles and to television and radio debate. Her most recent publications include *Facing Up to Family Income* on the economic status of the family in Britain today; *The Hidden Costs of Childcare*—a review of research on the effects of early day care on children and what the provision of adequate care involves; and *Families in Dreamland: Challenging the new consensus for state childcare.*

Professor Anthony O'Hear is Professor of Philosophy at the University of Bradford. He is the author of many books and articles on philosophy, including *Karl Popper*; *Experience, Explanation and Faith*; *What Philosophy Is*; and *The Element of Fire: Science, Art and the Human World.* He contributes regularly to *The Daily Telegraph* and *Modern Painters.* He is a member of the Council of Accreditation of Teacher Education.

Dr. Dennis O'Keeffe is Director of the Truancy Research Project, and Principal Lecturer in the Sociology of Education, at the University of North London. He is a specialist in the economics and sociology of education and has published widely in this field as well as in economic history, the socio-economic aspects of development, and political theory. His most recent theoretical critique of British education is *The Wayward Elite.* He is also a linguist; his most notable work of translation is Alain Fienkielkraut's *La Defaite de la Pensée*, rendered in English as *The Undoing of Thought.*

Foreword

John O'Sullivan

S ome years ago I commissioned an article on the contemporary standing of ideals such as courage and self-sacrifice. When Leon Klinghoffer defied the terrorists on the *Achille Lauro* and was murdered by them, I was struck by the fact that almost the first hostage to express such defiance of his captors had been an elderly, crippled man with a heart condition. Why had younger, fitter, and apparently more suitable people not been prepared to risk and sacrifice their lives in this way? At my request, a reporter telephoned various philosophers, historians and sociolgists to obtain their judgements on whether Klinghoffer had behaved rightly and, more broadly, whether such heroism remained a moral ideal in modern liberal consumer society.

The reporter—a young Jewish woman who had been inspired by Klinghoffer's self-sacrifice—returned somewhat shaken. Only one respondent, a classical historian, had taken a favourable view of it. Another had expressed a calculating Benthamite half-approval: self-sacrifice was always pointless but other forms of courage were to be judged by their results. Several had refused comment altogether, some professing not to understand the question. But most of those questioned had condemned both Klinghoffer and heroism itself. Klinghoffer had thrown his life away for no good purpose, they argued, and heroism was a crude, primitive, macho, even sexist, ideal that society would have to demystify if it was ever to base itself on the higher ideals of justice and cooperation. One philosopher, detecting the reporter's sympathies, told her that she simply wanted to persuade young men to go out and get themselves killed.

It is, of course, possible to think Klinghoffer's act of heroism an unwise one while continuing to admire it. I myself would have counselled him against it, but at the same time I wish I had the courage to behave as he did. It may even be that his self-sacrifice, though it apparently achieved nothing then and

John O'Sullivan, who joined National Review *as its editor in 1988, writes principally about politics, both current and historical, and about world affairs. In addition to his regular column for* NR, 'From the Editor', *he contributes book reviews and essays, and he writes for numerous other publications, in the U.S. and in Britain.*

there, has ultimately saved other lives by illuminating the vindictive viciousness of the terrorists and thus weakening political support for them. Even if that had been demonstrated, however, I suspect that it would not have undermined the disapproval of his critics. Couched though it was in terms of rational choice and hedonistic calculus, that disapproval struck my young colleague as plainly deriving from deep and instinctive feelings. What she had blundered up against was hostility to one element of traditional morality.

We should not have been altogether surprised. After all, other traditional virtues have been coming under attack in one way or another since the Second World War. Chastity was described by the sexologist Dr. Alex Comfort in the mid-Sixties as 'no more a virtue than malnutrition'. And though such candour is less fashionable in the age of AIDS, that is plainly the governing outlook of modern-minded people. They become irritated to the point of frenzy with arguments that anti-AIDS programmes should emphasise chastity or marital fidelity rather than 'Safe Sex'. Some critics even argued that such advice was tantamount to murder since it sacrificed young lives on the altar of an unrealistic religious doctrine. And Congresswoman Patricia Schroeder went to considerable trouble to eliminate modest funding for a programme that would have evaluated the success of sex education in promoting teenage chastity.

Or again, when Charles Murray published *Losing Ground,* he was accused of reintroducing the Victorian distinction between the deserving and undeserving poor. What was significant here was not so much whether the accusation was true or false but that such a distinction should be considered a disgrace. Diligence, sobriety and honesty are better than idleness, drunkenness and thieving—indeed, it is almost a tautology to say so—and those who display the (former) virtues have a greater claim on us than those who exhibit the (latter) vices. It may be difficult in practice to distinguish between the deserving and undeserving, or to construct a system of charity that will reward the former and punish the latter without harming such innocents as children of feckless parents. But such a system, if it were possible, would unarguably be an advance on our present arrangements. Yet such arguments seemingly struck the modern liberal imagination as self-righteous ('judgemental'), inspired by callousness ('uncaring'), and intended to penalise certain groups from whom the poor are disproportionately drawn ('racist').

Indeed, as Digby Anderson and his fellow contributors establish in later pages, an avalanche of promiscuous moral criticism overwhelmed almost all of the traditional virtues—self-control, marital fidelity, diligence, manliness, fortitude, self-sacrifice, honesty, trust, respect for authority, even toleration itself (because of what John Gray describes as its 'offensive implication' that the behaviour tolerated was in some sense bad). These virtues were not, of course, frontally assaulted. But the mitigating truth that circumstances alter cases became a central tenet of morality with the foreseeable result that no one could be held to account for anything. The criminal, the adulterer, the drunken driver, the dishonest employee, the negligent professional, the corrupt official could always attribute their faults of behaviour to some broad social cause. As Dostoevsky foresaw: 'They have this "social" excuse for every nasty thing they do'. That done, the virtues which constituted the morality could be, and generally were, presented in a pejorative way: judgemental, self-righteous, repressive, conformist. Indeed, as certain virtues began to look stuffy and prudish, so certain vices were suddenly seen to have a lively and attractive side: disrespect for authority became independence of judgement, promiscuity a robust love of life, selfishness a necessary self-assertion, and so on.

What was happening was that one morality was being challenged and gradually replaced by another. While this process was in its early stages, we had only a very dim sense of it. For instance, when the phrase 'the new morality' came into vogue in the mid-Sixties, it referred almost exclusively to sexual morality. The phrase signified that traditional Christian teaching on sex, seen as rule-bound and uncharitable, was rightly being superseded by a new but still Christian morality in which guidance would be provided by a loving sense of responsibility for others, unconstrained by narrow dogmatic regulations. Whether such a flexible standard could ever be a sufficient guidance in matters of passion to those notoriously self-deceiving animals, human beings, must be doubtful. But also moot. For the 'new morality' developed rapidly from this starting point. The sexual actions it was prepared to sanction soon went far beyond what even the most flexible Christianity could encompass. Simultaneously, it spread outwards from sex to cover work, public affairs, international relations, family obligations, welfare policy, crime, etc., etc. In short the entire range of human experience.

Eventually, two very different antagonists squared off against each other. Traditional morality was religious, duty based, rooted in individual responsibility, governed by objective rules, self-controlled, ascetic, guilt-forgiving, repentant, hierarchical, patriotic, and stern. The new morality was secular, rights based, rooted in social causes, governed by subjective interpretation, self-asserting, hedonistic, guilt-denying, therapeutic, egalitarian, universalist and indulgent.

Somewhat surprisingly in view of these contrasts, the old morality was not immediately vanquished. It conducted an orderly retreat and a long campaign of resistance, and it even clung on to a number of social strongholds in the popular press, the 'respectable working class', the Army, and the rank-and-file of the Tory Party (in Britain); in the married Middle Class, small towns and suburbs, Asian immigrants, the Moral Majority, and the conservative movement (in America); and among Catholics, fundamentalist Protestants, and Orthodox Jews (in both countries). But in the public sphere—the arena of official policy, bureaucratic regulations, academic scholarship, media debate, cultural transmission, legal judgement, even Hollywood sitcoms—the new morality carried all before it. What Frank Johnson has called the 'chattering classes' were instinctively on its side (without ever really reflecting on it). Even institutions that were supposed to defend traditional ways, such as the Conservative and Republican parties, or the mainline Protestant churches, were divided and embarrassed about doing so. Their leaders did not wish to seem repressive, conformist, judgemental or self-righteous. And all the clever people seemed to be on the other side.

But this triumph in public debate concealed a failure at the level of private behaviour. A morality, after all, is supposed to guide our actions in everyday life. Under the old morality, all was clear and generally agreed. A good man was a loving husband, a provident father, an attentive son, a helpful neighbour, a reliable employee, an active member of his local community in peace and a patriotic volunteer in time of war. No ordinary human being, of course, could be a paragon of all these virtues, and certainly not all at once. But most people had a concept of good behaviour against which they could, sometimes ruefully, measure their own. Indeed, as Christie Davies has pointed out elsewhere, a worker in the 19th century would often carry his 'character' about with him, namely a letter from a former employer or someone else in authority, testifying to his punctuality, sobriety, decency and diligence.

But what would constitute a 'character' under the new morality? As contributors to *The Loss of Virtue* point out, this is a matter of constant discussion and very little agreement. A good man must do no harm—no direct and obvious harm, that is, since he cannot be held to account for the harm that may arise from his refusal to accept social obligations he did not choose voluntarily and which infringe upon his liberty, such as the duty to support parents financially in old age. Society at large must fulfill such obligations. He *is* bound to live up to the obligations he undertook voluntarily such as marriage and parenthood—or at least to make a good faith effort to do so for a reasonable period of time. But he also has an obligation to himself, and when that clashes with other obligations, he will recompense any injury with a reasonable financial settlement. A good man, recognising that values differ, will refrain from any moral disapproval of the actions of others that do not directly inconvenience him—and expect them to ignore his violations of their moral standards. And a good man will treat others equally and without discrimination—but, as we have seen, that will not necessarily mean treating them well.

To put it in concrete terms, a good man under the new morality is a husband who does not break his marriage vows without his wife's consent, a father who pays generous child support, a son who regularly contacts the social services to ensure that his parents are being properly looked after, a neighbour who ignores the drug parties next door provided that the level of noise remains tolerable, an employee who is prepared to work extra hours on an emergency project in return for generous overtime, a law-abiding citizen in time of peace, and an impartial judge of his country's case in time of war.

Unfortunately, not everyone is good. Deprived of both clear moral guidelines and the incentive of his neighbour's moral disapproval, the ordinary sensual man—the Sancho Panza of the suburbs—will find his everyday conduct deteriorating. That is exactly what has happened. Perhaps the single most dramatic finding in a fascinating book is Christie Davies's evidence that one can actually trace a decline in self-control among the British in the post-war world— and that this decline marches in lockstep with the decline in attendance at Sunday School. And in both countries the signs of such loss of virtue are to be found in increases in crime, illegitimacy, drug abuse, family breakdown, and welfare rolls.

The spread of such social evils leads inexorably to the growth of another—bureaucracy. The decline in honesty in commerce forces government to resort to regulation, and businessmen to law, with greater frequency. The rise in crime compels the employment of more police and the building of more prisons. The increase in illegitimacy requires more welfare spending and more social workers. And the rise in alcoholism and drug abuse adds to the use and cost of health services in the public sector. More significantly, it also opens the way to government propaganda programmes against popular pleasures, such as social drinking, on the shifty neo-puritan grounds that good health is a moral obligation upon citizens. All of this, of course, was foreseen by Burke in 1791:

> Men are qualified for civil liberty in exact proportion to their disposition to put moral chains upon their own appetites—in proportion as their love of justice is above their rapicity—in proportion as their soundness and sobriety of understanding is above their vanity and presumption—in proportion as they are more disposed to listen to the counsels of the wise and good, in preference to the flattery of knaves. Society cannot exist, unless a controlling power upon will and appetite be placed somewhere; and the less of it there is within, the more there must be

without. It is ordained in the eternal constitution of things, that men of intemperate minds cannot be free. Their passions forge their fetters.

Yet although government grows, it is unable to solve, by technical measures, problems that are moral at root. We thus get the worst of both worlds: a vast, intrusive and costly government presiding impotently over a disorderly and decaying population. A precise description of the current state of New York City.

Some at least of these truths are now accepted by intelligent liberal commentators such as Mickey Kaus who, in *The End of Equality*, seeks to revive the work ethic as an essential component of liberal social policy. He would replace most forms of welfare with a government programme that would make available jobs to the able-bodied poor at a rate of pay slightly lower than the private sector minimum wage. Mr. Kaus's book, and the generally favourable reception that liberal critics have given it, mark a worthwhile advance.

But these liberal second thoughts need to be supplemented by the harsher conservative insights of this book. The human costs of requiring the poor, the work-shy, the drug addicts, the alcoholics, and all the other denizens of the underclass to support themselves are likely to be more painful and protracted as long as they remain, quite literally, demoralised in other respects. Welfare reform, moreover, addresses only the problems of the underclass. The social problems of the middle class—family breakdown, illegitimacy and drugs—may be less threatening in scale, but they still wreck promising lives. And perhaps the most subtle damage caused by this moral vacuum is that it deters successful middle class people from giving that moral leadership to the poor that has hitherto been a necessary part of every social movement that has significantly reduced poverty and its accompanying social evils. Indeed, insofar as middle-class people such as social workers and politicians are missionaries of the new morality, preaching the gospel of social causation and the futility of individual moral struggle in the ghetto, they make matters infinitely worse.

In the end we have no alternative but to return to the Gods of the Copybook Headings, to the hard virtues of fortitude, diligence, economy, thrift, honesty, fidelity, duty and all the rest, that alone see people through the hard moments in life. And we have to do more than recommend them to the poor; we have to try to uphold them in our own lives. That will no doubt be difficult, and we shall often fail. The assembled authors between them (and I include myself here) have probably broken all the Ten Commandments with the possible exception of 'Thou shalt do no murder'. But if upholding virtue were left to the virtuous, the world would be in an even more distressing condition than it is. Besides, as *The Loss of Virtue* demonstrates on almost every page, at least the clever people are on the side of the Angels this time.

Introduction and Summary of Contents:

The Moral Poverty of Contemporary Social Analysis

Digby Anderson

Successful economies are no proof against crime, family collapse, and disorder

The U.S.A. and Britain, societies with free-market, if heavily regulated economies, democratic governments and the rule of law, have soaring rates of crime, truancy, drug abuse, illegitimacy and welfare dependency. This book analyses these and also urban riots, divorce, abortion, homosexuality, inter-cultural conflict, environmental pollution and family collapse. Behind these obvious social problems are others of loss of social allegiance among the young, cultural disaffection among 'minorities' and urban decay. The 1980s saw the increasing acceptance of the free market as the best, or perhaps, the only economic order to ensure a prosperous and free society. A democratic polity with the rule of law won wide approval rather earlier, but even both together are clearly not sufficient to ensure an orderly or cohesive society.

Throughout the same 1980s, the opponents of the free market gradually moved their grounds of opposition from allegations of the market's inefficiency to its immorality. As it became clear that the market was indeed the most efficient or least inefficient economic order, new accusations were made of lack of compassion or care, injustice and the destruction of 'community'. And the successful supporters of the free market, themselves, started to talk of the need for a gentler, kinder society. There is a wider acceptance of the rather vague assertion, for example of the current Pope, that there is a third leg to social order, not just an economy and polity but, well, 'culture'.

The return of a moral language?

The language of morality is back in political discourse and social policy. Or is it? In one sense, it never went away. Although Marx claimed a scientific and non-moral basis for his socialism, in practice heroes and villains have been the stuff of the socialism-capitalism battle. Blaming people never went out of fashion. What did happen is that the morality changed. The standard sociology texts used to recognize morality as the centre of social order beside which the polity was comparatively trivial. Informal social order, that of habit, tradition, example, praise, stigma and support was the cement of society mediated and perpetuated by the family, the church or synagogue and the local community. This made possible an orderly polity. The informal system's self- and social control made most people law-abiding and orderly most of the time leaving the police and the courts to deal with the few exceptions. Kin and then the nuclear family were the main sources of welfare leaving the oddments to the state.

Clearly the new genuflections to morality do not, at least yet, go anywhere near accepting this vast and central role for the informal and moral order. But the new morality is not only comparatively marginal, it is pathetically unelaborated. The old moral understanding saw society sustained by an interplay of honesty, patriotism, service, self-control, respect, civility, perseverance and a host of other virtues. It was aware of the dangers of sloth, gluttony, pride, and a list of vices. The new pathetic morality consists in the bleating repetition of the same few overused and hence now largely meaningless words—care, compassion, justice or even worse, social justice. The old vocabulary had precise and explicit meanings so that the virtues could be weighed against each other and ranked to analyze or judge any piece of behaviour. The system for combining and applying them was casuistry, that of finely separating according to morality was discrimination. Now, the skill of casuistry is gone and the word pejorative. Discrimination has become itself a vice in the modern vocabulary.

The new moral vocabulary: restricted, sentimental and obsessed with 'rights' at the expense of obligations

It is readily obvious that the few virtues which the new morality can deal with are highly sentimentalized or romantic. They are about human beings being rather nicer to each other. There is no room for the harsher virtues—such as fortitude in adversity, putting up with pain

xviii

or degradation uncomplainingly or fidelity, loyalty to a spouse despite his or her continual disloyalty. More important, there is little room for the old understanding that the now sentimentalized virtues such as love require 'nastiness', that true love for children requires punishment not indulgence. Nastiness, the role of sanction, fear, trepidation, and stigma, in maintaining social order among fallen men and women with capacities for considerable wickedness and harm to others, is ignored or shunned.

The romanticism shows in yet another characteristic of the new quasi-morality, its endless demand for rights and its neglect of obligations. Modern political life consists largely in the discovery of new minority groups and their rights—women's rights, homosexuals' rights, non-smokers' rights, smokers' rights, Spanish or Bengali speakers' rights, welfare rights, animals' rights and more generally citizens' rights. Especially in Britain the idea of citizen has been re-discovered and used to create huge lists or charters of rights which, it is asserted, the state should recognize—and pay out for. Rarely is it remembered that the idea of citizenship historically was as much a source of obligations as rights, including obligations to the state.

In sum, the new morality is scarcely worthy of the name. Scan American or British newspaper coverage of truancy, family breakdown, crime or poverty and look at the use of moral language there. Do the same for politicians, for Presidents and Prime Ministers: and the same again with many social scientists' analyses. What you will see, among much sophisticated technical exposition in economics or whatever, is moral illiteracy.

The recognition of the moral dimension or social disintegration?

Two related themes run through the chapters of this book. The first is the restoration of the old understanding that social problems are in part, perhaps large part moral problems. The second is that to understand them we have to learn again to deploy a discriminating moral vocabulary. We have to learn again to use words such as 'service', 'respect' and 'diligence', and with some precision. Most of the authors do not argue either case directly: they simply each take a virtue or cluster of virtues and use it to show the potential it has for understanding the social problems that plague the United States and Britain.

The objections will be obvious: morality is not the only aspect of social order. We nowhere claim it is. The book has not taken all the virtues. It certainly has not. Some of its virtues are not really main virtues at all but virtues which act as means to other more important virtues. True. The book is a mixture, a shop window of samples. It shows the sorts of analysis which can be done, if society, social scientists and political commentators are willing to learn again the rich but forgotten language of the virtues. If they are not, if society persists in ignoring the wide and complex moral basis of social order, then, not a few of the authors offer a vision of social disintegration.

Rates for crime and disorder vary, and change in 'character' can explain why

Professor Christie Davies suggests that those in the U.S. and elsewhere seeking an explanation for the huge surge in crime, self-destructive behaviour and social disorder of the last fifty years should consider the lesson of Great Britain. Its recent rise in disorder was preceded by a half century or more in which crime and disorder *fell* dramatically. The experience of the last 150 years is thus of a U curve. The explanation for the subsequent rise in disorder cannot be sought in social conditions such as poverty or housing, which were worse in the low crime years than now. It lies in a change of national moral character, an increase in the number of aggressive, self-destructive people, the reduction of conscience and self-control, and the provision of moral excuses. This movement, promoted by 'progressive' intellectuals, has dismantled the workable moral order built up by previous generations. The example of Britain is a pointer to the centrality of morality in the preservation of social order.

Manliness and civility: lost sources of self-restraint and order

Liberal societies, capitalist societies, do not have an automatic or natural affinity for the traditional virtues but they can and have been developed and restrained by two quasi-virtues discussed by Dr. Simon Green, manliness and civility. Both are unpopular today, the first because it is seen as male aggression, the second because it seems to be less than adequately virtuous, a formalistic accommodation with others. In fact the two go together. Manliness is the character that makes civility possible. Manliness is, or was, not the opposite of femininity. Women could be manly. It was the opposite of animality. It was a state in which the innate was recognized but controlled, a virtue of ordinariness. It sought the modest cultivation and improvement of the common sum of man's attributes. It aimed not at heroism or saintliness, still less at priestliness, but at determined cultivation of the best of what is human. Civility too was an unheroic virtue, not sacrifice to others but a quiet and limited recognition of their rights, each going his own way. It is the bourgeois virtue recognizing both privacy and a limited publicness. Civility could not sustain itself. It needed a certain character and that was manliness. In jettisoning manliness and hence civility, modern society has thrown away the central sources of both self- and social control.

Toleration and its currently offensive implication of judgement

It is crucial to distinguish between two very different ways of responding to social problems. Dr. John Gray identifies them as toleration and neutrality. Abortion, homosexuality, cultural variations and other matters which divide modern societies can be responded to by the traditional virtue of tolerance or the more fashionable dogma of radical neutrality. Toleration is unfashionable for two reasons. It assumes human imperfectibility, while modern society believes only the ill will of others or the wrong social conditions prevent perfection. Also, toleration assumes evils to be tolerated and thus is inherently judgmental. Toleration has been replaced by the idea that all or most cultures are of equal worth and have equal rights. The state should be neutral to them. This is the legal disestablishment of morality. It further replaces the individual—to whom toleration was due—with the collectivity, homosexuals, blacks, women, who must have equal rights. Neutrality assumes multiculturalism. Toleration assumes a basic single culture embodying the ideal of toleration itself. Neutrality has the higher project of abolishing prejudice, incorrect thinking. Toleration, while concerned at some expressions of prejudice, will tolerate it. Neutrality is both incoherent and likely to lead to intolerance. It leads to chaos. Toleration promotes the basic condition of liberty, security. It leaves people alone and in peace.

Domestic economy: improvidence
and irresponsibility in low-income families

Low income families can do something about their condition. Their poverty, says Dr. Digby Anderson, is not simply the result of their low incomes, but is affected by how skillfully they budget, who spends what (especially whether the bulk of the income is in the wife's or husband's hands) and the extent to which and ways in which they borrow. Often it is domestic incompetence or irresponsibility that turns temporary poverty into long-term welfare dependence. And the families that manage well display not only skills but moral characteristics; perseverance, a willingness to go without in the short term to stay out of debt, meticulous stewardship and, especially in the wives' cases, self-sacrifice. Yet the poverty lobby persists in ignoring the moral aspects of poverty and treating it as merely a matter of income. Raising income alone is not an adequate solution: indeed it can hinder a solution. A change in education and incentives to promote moral change is required.

Duty and self-sacrifice for one's country: the current disparagement of public ideals

The ultimate in duty—self-sacrifice—is a pointer to the changes which have occurred in public obligations, says Jon Davies. The contemporary age justifies wild behaviour such as urban riots on the grounds of the oppressive conditions in which the rioters live. It justifies the abandonment of spouses and children when someone is not happy or fulfilled. This emphasis on the rights of individuals to instant happiness is in striking contrast to the idea of self-restraint and obligations to the long term public good, which is *duty*. And the highest form of this duty is death in war. War memorials spell out the nature of duty, the publicness of this virtue, the voluntariness of the sacrifice involved, the sacrifice so that the community, be it the country, mankind or other comrades, may survive. The memorials stand as a reproach to the current disparagement of public ideals and a lesson in the consequences of that disparagement.

Service, national service and the obligations of citizenship

Dr. Christopher Dandeker focuses on a remarkable imbalance in the recent revival of 'citizenship'. Discussions of it have dwelt far more on the citizen's rights than his duties. Yet the development of citizens' rights over the past two centuries was accompanied by and balanced by a notion of and actual imposition of duties. Such civic duties make for social cohesion, reduce government abuse of power and sustain the moral basis of individualism. In the past the chief such duty was national military service. This cannot be the centre of a new civic service because of changes in the structure and functions of armed forces. But national service could and should be civil involving care for families (creches and the elderly), work with criminals and the environment. Despite problems such a service should be compulsory, not voluntary, and comprehensive, not selective—if it is to be a proper public duty.

Fidelity: once inviolable and sacred, now another 'choice'

At the heart of the family and society is fidelity. Modern society of course recognizes obligations in the family but the obligations it recognizes, argues Dr. Patricia Morgan, are not those of fidelity. They come from legal and other sources and mean different things, the most obvious of them being contract. The obligation of fidelity is unconditional, unnegotiable and indissoluble. And it springs from the bond between family members and the requirement for them to sacrifice individual interests to it. This obligation was bolstered by custom, morality and law because it was recognized that one could not rely on mothers and still less on fathers to care for children purely out of impulse. The turning of the bond of fidelity into a re-negotiable contract of individuals free to choose, free to walk out and free to engage in adultery when it suits and without sanction or stigma is destroying the basis for the protection and security of children and breaking up society at its very heart.

Self-control: whether expressed in moral or psychological terms it is crucial for avoidance of social problems

Recently the reaction to phenomena such as urban rioting has been to blame social conditions. But, Professor Richard Lynn points out, the traditional response in Western religious systems would have been to see the problem as, at least in part, one of deficient self-control. And social science has extended our understanding of self-control, notably in psychopathy—absence of guilt or conscience, impulsiveness, inability to control behaviour in the light of possible consequences although these are known and understood. Psychologists of varying schools have explained how fear of consequences, parental example, parental conditioning, socialization and genetic inheritance can result in the development of more or less self-control and moral reasoning in children. Scope for reduction of social problems and disorder through increase in self-control lies primarily in the home.

Fortitude: contrasted with the modern tendencies to narcissism or blame someone else

Why, asks Dr. Adrian Furnham, has another virtue, insisted on in so many societies, all but disappeared in contemporary analysis? The diverse troubles of the age—cancer, discrimination, natural disaster—

have at least this in common, that they are adversities to be endured. The virtue of enduring adversity is fortitude and it is out of fashion, even to be disapproved of. It has all but disappeared because the work ethic in which it was valued has been replaced by a leisure and welfare ethic. Especially in the U.S., the culture of competitive individualism with its emphasis on taking individual responsibility and self-improvement is being replaced by a pursuit of happiness, the admiration of others and narcissism. Fortitude has been replaced by self-indulgence. In this culture fortitude looks like fatalism or a masochistic glorification of pain.

Insofar as adversity affects the modern man it does so not as a personal failing but as an injustice imposed by someone else. The exception is sport. Yet while misplaced fortitude is unwise and harmful, the loss of it from the moral lexicon is worrying, testifying as it does to the diminished sense of personal responsibility.

Honesty, honour and trust: the decline of self-policing in society

This cluster of three deeply related virtues is the very root of virtue. Robert Grant contrasts it with its equally fundamental vice, fantasy and disrespect for reality, the belief that the world and others are there to be bent to one's selfish desires. Honesty is socially useful, for instance in business relations, but it is not just functional. Honesty is essential for honour, a proper valuation of oneself and one's obligations and it is the lack of honour and the lack of coherent public obligations on the individual which explain so much crime and disorder. Honour today is denigrated but the regulation and policing of commercial affairs or crime cannot compensate for the self-policing effected by honour. Indeed the modern mania for regulation is both caused by the breakdown of trust and honour and itself furthers that breakdown. Extreme regulation—as in Communist systems—destroys honour. In other forms, such as the Politically Correct Movement, it destroys honesty and free speech. Nor are modern institutions likely to foster honesty, honour and trust. The undermining of the family, the false moral education of television and the corruption of punishment, that mainstay of moral defence, have produced a decline in virtue, which will, like all mockery of reality, exact a great revenge.

Respect and the dangers of an unrestrained 'critical spirit'

Professor Anthony O'Hear identifies two groups in modern society—the revolutionaries and libertarians—who share one quality. They are untied from, not rooted in, unidentified with, the life of society. They are not 'bound to life': the libertarian, because there is no value he acknowledges which he does not choose; the revolutionary, because of his commitment to wholesale change. Educationists have helped produce this detachment among the young encouraging an endlessly 'critical' spirit or the cultivation of 'reasoning skills' or 'powers of expression' without any shared cultural allegiance or content. Education is also about learning respect for the wisdom, morality and beauty of the past which makes up society's identity. Aesthetic education is the counter to the remorseless and empty criticism and the way of re-attaching the young to society.

Diligence abandoned

In the U.S.A. and Britain there are widespread problems of truancy, illiteracy and school failure, this despite the economic success of these countries. The extent of this failure is increasingly recognised. It is also widely seen that it has something to do with 'styles' of teaching and learning. What has failed, says Dr. Dennis O'Keeffe, is the child-centred or 'progressive' method which is taken to be some sort of technique. It is true that 'progressives' use different techniques to teach reading or mathematics. But the most important difference between progressivism and tradtionalism in schooling is not technical but moral. Traditionalism called for competition, application, obedience, fear, humility. Progressivism offers the quick fun, the easy way, self-indulgence and neither blame nor recognition of difference in talent. Only a return to the traditional morality in teaching can halt the decline in schools.

Discretion

Discretion has two meanings—discrimination among people on the basis of their deserts and self-restraint in behaviour or speech. Neither, comments Dr. Mark Almond, is fashionable today. The mass media flaunt matters which once would have been private and contradict the dogma of rights and equality. Discrimination is especially unfashionable in welfare policy where the refusal to identify the genuinely unfortunate and subsidise them rather than the lazy, self-indulgent or wasteful is in the true interests of neither. This refusal to moralise about welfare claimants is especially odd at a time when there is so much moralising about other people's lifestyle in, e.g., smoking or drinking. There are in fact strong arguments for distinguishing the deserving and undeserving poor, not least the increase in the ageing population, which will make welfare choices inevitable. Discretion in the sense of quietness also has a role to play in removing the incentives to welfare dependency created by loudly announcing benefits. But both discretions can only be incorporated in a fairer and remoralised welfare system if the illusions of universal and comprehensive welfare rights are abandoned.

Self-improvement and its neglect by the contemporary mainstream churches

One may seek to make the world better, points out Professor Antony Flew, by individuals improving themselves as well as by collective action. Those who suffer poverty and ill-health are not always helpless victims. Once the churches insisted on the importance of self-improvement. Now they demand government action as a cure for all ills. On truancy, for instance, they are obsessed with the importance of government spending on schools rather than on the attitudes and behaviour of teachers, children and parents. On family problems, they treat children and parents as victims, never as responsible victimizers. On 'minorities', they bracket together Afro-Caribbeans and Asians as blacks and victims, obscuring the vast differences in, e.g., school success between them. Systematically they confuse injustice and inequality of outcomes, again not distinguishing those in difficulty through no fault of their own and those justly in poverty or whatever. In fact, the requirement of equality of outcomes, to be secured by income redistribution, is corrupting of justice and just deserts. At the heart of the matter is a (wilful) misportrayal of the conditions of the criminal or pauper as determining his crime or poverty, leaving him no choice. This misportrayal is wrong. It also is a reversal of the traditional Judaeo-Christian understanding of man having choices and the ability to improve himself.

People can be made good—again—if society will deploy deterrents and examples

Despite the weakness of contemporary moral understanding and some conflict about particular virtues, there remains considerable moral consensus, suggests Professor David Martin. People rarely call for more evil and less good. Goodness is still widely popular. It is true that moral relativism and selectivity have eroded the consensus about what is good but there is still a consensus against lying, cruelty and exploitation. Why then are there not more calls for people to be made better? Partly because of the liberal notion that the way to more goodness is not by more goodness but by engineering changes in the conditions which, liberals claim, make people good or bad. Partly because of the contemporary obsession with the victims of badness which subverts more positive steps to promote goodness. Partly because of the notion that goodness is 'natural' and cannot be encouraged. In fact, goodness does not come naturally. Weak, tempted humans need authority and fear to promote their goodness. These do not create goodness but together with rules and examples of good conduct they create an order in which people can indeed become better and society reduce its problems, damage and disorder.

CHAPTER 1

Moralization and Demoralization:

A Moral Explanation for Change in Crime, Disorder and Social Problems

Christie Davies

Crime and disorder fell at the end of the 19th century but have soared in the last 50 years

During the last century and a half there have been two marked successive shifts in opposite directions in the moral character of British society. During the last half of the 19th century there was a marked fall in the crime rate with a substantial decrease in both crimes of dishonesty and violence, and in the illegitimacy rate, and the beginnings of a fall in the incidence of drug and alcohol abuse. It was a period of striking moral reform in personal behaviour which transformed Britain from being a violent, dishonest and addicted society into a peaceable, law-abiding, respectable and essentially moral realm that endured for much of the 20th century.

During the last 40 to 50 years, however, the earlier trend towards a moral and respectable society has been reversed; demoralisation has set in. There has been a marked growth in crimes of violence and dishonesty, a rising illegitimacy rate,[1] more alcohol abuse than previously and a rise in the number of drug addicts from being a sad but negligible band of individuals to a visible social problem.[2] Even British crowds at sporting events who used to amaze foreigners by their good-humoured and disciplined behaviour, are now known throughout Europe as thugs and hooligans.

This alarming U-curve in deviant behaviour, though of greatest concern to the British themselves, is also important for the citizens of other countries and perhaps especially the United States whose institutions and culture have from their very inception been closer to those of

3

that other English-speaking democracy on the other side of the Atlantic than to those of any other country. More is to be usefully learned by Americans from the moral success followed by moral failure of the British than from a study of, say, Japan, Italy or Russia, however important these countries may be in their own right. It is easier and more relevant to draw a moral for America from once moral and now amoral Britain.

The recent growth of crime in Britain has been so great as almost to wipe out the memory of past successes in combating it. Even in 1959 Sir Leon Radzinowicz, perhaps Britain's most noted criminologist, wrote of the criminal statistics for England and Wales as 'grim and relentless in their ascending monotony'.[3] In 1977 he and Joan King noted that:

> In 1900 the police of England and Wales recorded under a hundred thousand crimes, less than three for every thousand people. In 1974 it was almost four for every hundred people. This is over thirteen times as many. And those are indictable offences, not minor infractions . . . In 1974 there were over three hundred thousand more crimes than in 1973—an addition more than three times as great as the total amount recorded for 1901.[4]

During the 1980s the number of serious offences recorded by the police was even greater and rose from about two and a half million offences, or five for every hundred people, in 1980, to nearly four million in 1989.[5]

Some of the increase in recorded crime is, of course, statistical rather than real and has occurred merely because victims have become more willing or eager to report crimes (e.g., because it is a condition of making an insurance claim) and the police have become more efficient at recording them. The figures from the British Crime Survey, which asks a sample of the population whether they have been victims, indicates that for the crimes covered in the survey, there was an increase in the number of offences committed of only 30 per cent between 1981 and 1987, whereas the numbers recorded by the police showed a 41 per cent increase.[6] However, the surveys show that even if the 'real' increase in crime has in *some* cases been less than indicated by police records, it is nonetheless very substantial.[7] Attempts by the bureaucrats and by some criminologists to explain away rising crime as a mere statistical artifact are a piece of inane and sometimes self-interested chicanery. Things have got worse, and for those who live in 'bad' inner city areas or council estates (housing built and owned by municipalities), they have often become intolerable.[8]

4

The new disorder not the result of poverty or social conditions which were far worse in the late 19th century

To blame the British slide into lawlessness on social conditions such as bad housing, poverty or unemployment, however, makes little sense, for there was far more of all three in the earlier part of the 20th century, but very little crime. Explanations in terms of urbanisation, industrialisation, or increased affluence, or the more widespread ownership of stealable property, are equally absurd for the citizens of England and Wales experienced all these social changes, if anything in a more drastic form, in Victorian times when crime rates fell. Indeed, one may derive a certain amusement from the fact that the same social and economic variables have been used to explain the earlier fall *and* the contemporary rise in crime. It likewise makes no sense to invoke social and economic inequality as a cause of crime, for crime rates were at their lowest in plutocratic Edwardian England.

British rates of recorded crime fell as markedly in the latter part of the 19th century as they have risen since. The overall incidence of serious offences recorded by the police in the 1890s was only about 60 per cent of what it had been in the 1850s[9] and, given that the efficiency of the reporting and recording of crime was improving at the time, the *real* fall in the crime rate was probably far greater than that indicated by official statistics.[10] Thus in 1900 Britain was not only a less violent and dishonest country than today, but also less violent and dishonest than it had been in the earlier part of the 19th century. It is worth noting in passing that 'progressive' opinion in the 19th century was unwilling to accept that crime rates were falling in capitalist free market Britain, just as their successors of today have tried to deny that crime has risen inexorably since the introduction of state welfare and other forms of socialistic or 'liberal' social engineering. However, the U-curve model of deviance that I first postulated in 1983[11] has been amply confirmed by the subsequent independent work of the British social historian Stephen Davies,[12] and the Swedish criminologist Jerzy Sarnecki has shown that the Swedish crime statistics conform to essentially the same pattern.[13] Furthermore, as noted earlier, the U-curve pattern applies to illegitimacy, drug and alcohol addiction[14] and football crowd disorders[15] as well as crime, though with some differences in the turning points, depending on which form of deviant behaviour is being explained.

Similarly there is little evidence to support the thesis that all talk of moral deterioration is based on a false view of some past mythical golden age.[16] On the contrary, during the low phase of the U-curve of deviance, social observers as diverse as George Orwell and Geoffrey Gorer were amazed at the way in which British society had been transformed from a rowdy, dangerous place to a state of remarkable orderliness. In 1944, for instance, Orwell wrote that:

> [An] imaginary foreign observer would certainly be struck by our gentleness; by the orderly behaviour of English crowds, the lack of pushing and quarrelling . . . And except for certain well-defined areas in half a dozen big towns, there is very little crime or violence . . . The prevailing gentleness of manners is a recent thing, however. Well within living memory it was impossible for a smartly dressed person to walk down Ratcliff Highway without being assaulted, and an eminent jurist, asked to name a typically English crime, could answer: 'Kicking your wife to death . . .'[17] It is not much more than a hundred years since the distinguishing mark of English life was its brutality. The common people, to judge by the prints, spent their time in an almost unending round of fighting, whoring, drunkenness and bull-baiting . . . What had these people in common with the gentle-mannered, undemonstrative, law-abiding English of today?[18]

Likewise, Geoffrey Gorer, in his study *Exploring English Character*, commented:

> . . . in public life today, the English are certainly among the most peaceful, gentle, courteous and orderly populations that the civilized world has ever seen. But from the psychological point of view this is still the same problem; the control of aggression which has gone to such remarkable lengths that you hardly ever see a fight in a bar (a not uncommon spectacle in most of the rest of Europe or the USA), when football crowds are as orderly as church meetings . . . this orderliness and gentleness, this absence of overt aggression calls for an explanation . . .[19]

What made this situation even more puzzling for Gorer was that he knew it had not been like that in England's rowdy past and that he, therefore, also had to account for the *decline* in aggressive and anti-social behaviour: 'What [he asked] has happened to all this aggression, this violence, this combativeness, and mockery?' Why had 'one of the most lawless populations in the world' become 'one of the most law abiding?'[20] Nor can it be simplistically blamed on corrupting welfare. Explanations of Britain's curious pattern of moralization followed by demoralization, including my own earlier account, have tended to stress material factors such as the shift from the welfare institutions of the 19th century, which were local, voluntary and kept a strict watch on the moral behaviour of claimants on behalf of their fellow contributors, to large impersonal welfare bureaucracies that do not concern themselves with the moral status of their clients.[21] The analogy here with present-day Switzerland, which has a set of locally-based and watchful welfare institutions and is a relatively crime-free and illegitimacy-free, though by no means drug-free, society is an obvious one.[22] Likewise Bryan Wilson has suggested that the changing nature of work, from being an activity demanding a high degree of personal self-control to a process that is externally regulated by bureaucratic rules or even mechanical checks, has undermined the market value of a good moral character exhibiting such qualities as diligence, reliability, punctuality and honesty.[23]

The authors whom I have cited above have taken care to locate these factors within a more general framework of moral change, but among American policy-mongers recent parallel arguments to these have sometimes degenerated into a crude rational choice model in which people are moral or immoral depending on which pattern of behaviour has the higher material payoff. At first sight this mode of explaining for deviance appears to make individuals morally accountable, but it is really just one more way of avoiding the language of guilt and innocence, and of refraining from heaping blame and shame on those whose shallow egotism leads them to choose an anti-social way of life merely because they know that an ill-designed welfare system will protect them from the worst consequences. To argue that there is not something wrong with the behaviour of that minority of people who respond to welfarism in this fashion, is to adopt a lower standard of morality than that held by the vast majority of people in straightened circumstances who do not exploit the system like this. It is also very close to the sentimental view that all people are essentially good, but are corrupted by institutions. For the Left the villain is capitalism and for the Right it is welfare; both are ways of avoiding the conclusion that wicked and irresponsible choices are made by wicked and irresponsible individuals.

What has happened is a rise in the number of aggressive, impulsive and destructive people

Paradoxically, it is actually easier to see how personal moral responsibility was first established and later eroded historically in Britain by starting from the apparently deterministic contrast between extrovert and introvert personalities used by psychologists to explain why some individuals are more likely to commit deviant acts than others. It must be stressed from the start, however, that I am assuming that the overall balance between introversion and extroversion exhibited by the aggregate of individuals in a society is not an immutable, unchanging physiological fact by a social variable that differs between societies and is an aspect of the culture of any one society that can and does change over time.

Psychologists have made great use of the contrast between extroverts and introverts for a number of purposes. The extrovert 'craves excitement, takes chances, acts on the spur of the moment, and is generally an impulsive individual . . . prefers to keep moving and doing things, tends to be aggressive and loses his temper quickly; his feelings are not kept under tight control and he is not always a reliable person'.[24] By contrast 'the typical introvert is a quite retiring sort of person . . . [who] tends to plan ahead, "looks before he leaps" and distrusts the impulse of the moment. He does not like excitement, takes matters of everyday life with proper seriousness and likes a well-ordered mode of life. He keeps his feelings under close control, seldom behaves in an aggressive manner, and does not lose his temper easily'.[25]

This dichotomy has been employed by psychologists to contrast the temperaments of different individuals which are said to be a reflection of more fundamental differences in the nature of their nervous system. If this is the case, it helps to explain why some individuals are more attracted to risk and excitement and others to the competing values of reliability, diligence, caution and sobriety. Also psychologists have argued that when these personality types are combined with a high degree of emotional instability, this can result in strongly contrasting forms of deviant or, in some sense, destructive or self-destructive behaviour. Extroverts, for example, would be more likely to commit crimes (particularly those involving violence or vandalism) while introverts would be more likely to suffer some kind of mental breakdown or to become obsessed with a sexual fixation or fetish.[26] These are, of course, merely overall statistical differences and do not undermine the basic assumption that individuals are responsible for their actions. You cannot plead extroversion to a charge of bank robbery.

One of the chief limitations of this model for explaining human behaviour in aggregate is that it is essentially static in nature. It posits that individuals vary (in a more or less normal distribution) continuously from the very extrovert to the very introvert with the bulk of the population somewhere in the middle. It explains why some types of individuals rather than others are more likely to behave in anti-social ways, but it would seem to have no relevance to the study of social change. However, when the studies that psychologists have made of introversion-extroversion during the period 1935-1979 were compared by Richard Lynn and S. L. Hampson, they found that the average extroversion scores (far from remaining constant over time as the theory suggests) tended to rise steadily after 1950[27] for most industrial countries including Britain, whereas previously they had often been steady or falling, and that they differed markedly from one society to another, with particularly high extroversion scores being found in those countries with the highest crime rates.

If we assume that the *distribution* of extroversion scores remains roughly constant (and presumably normally distributed) then even a moderate shift towards the extrovert end of the spectrum in the average scores as described above would mean a very large rise in the numbers of people at the extreme extrovert end of the introvert-extrovert scale who have a very marked appetite for sensation, excitement, risk-taking and, indeed, impulsive and aggressive behaviour. This is, of course, entirely consistent with the marked rise in crime, drink and drug abuse, illegitimacy and hooliganism that has taken place in Britain as well as in many other societies.

The differences in extroversion scores between countries pose difficulties of interpretation, but the rise in extroversion scores within a single, fairly homogeneous country such as Britain can only be explained in terms of a change in the entire culture and morality of the society and particularly in the way children are brought up. It is difficult to take seriously alternative explanations based on a major and unexplained volcanic shake-up of the central nervous systems of the individuals who comprise the British people, such that they become less easy to condition.

There has been a change in national character—a reduction in conscience and self-control

What the rising extroversion scores confirm is that, during the second leg of the U-curve, there has been not simply a series of isolated shifts in the way British people behave, but a change in the very character of the people. We are now seeing a *reversal* of the shift towards more civilised and restrained patterns of behaviour that Gorer regarded as crucial to an understanding of the first leg of the U-curve when he wrote 'During the 19th and the first half of the 20th centuries, the strict conscience and self-control which had been a feature of a relatively small part of the population became general throughout nearly the whole of the society as the present study has indicated'.[28]

In other words, an earlier generation of Britons succeeded in changing the character of their people and producing a diminution in the many forms of deviance that have reappeared and flourished in our own time, because they saw them as constituting not a social but a *moral* problem whose solution lay in the reform of personal conduct. One key agency in spreading and transmitting Gorer's 'strict conscience and self-control' from being 'a feature of a relatively small part of the population' to becoming 'general throughout nearly the whole of society' was the Sunday school whose enrollments rose as the incidence of deviant behaviour fell in the late 19th century. Significantly, the numbers enrolled in and the influence of this institution then fell in the years prior to the reversal of the U-curve of deviance which has produced Britain's present high level of moral problems. There seems to be a clear inverse relationship between the rise and fall of the Sunday school, as indicated in **Table 1**,[29] and the fall and rise of deviant behaviour.

By 1888 about three out of every four children in England and Wales attended Sunday school, 'a remarkable proportion when it is remembered that parents of the higher social groups did not particularly favour attendance'.[30] In 1957, 76 per cent of those over 30 years of age had attended Sunday school at some time in their lives, but for those under 30 the corresponding figure was only 61 per cent.[31]

The postulate that there was a link of some kind between the rise of the Sunday school and the original decline of deviance is reinforced by the geographical evidence as well as the aggregate changes over time. Wales, which historically had been one of the more violent and lawless parts of Britain, became in the later 19th century an especially peaceable and law-abiding place, characterised by temperance and a strict moral code.[32] But it was precisely in Wales that the Sunday schools organised by the Protestant Nonconformist chapels were at their strongest, and they also had the distinctive feature of being attended by children,

Year	Numbers Enrolled	Percentage of British Population Enrolled
1851	2,614,274	13
1881	5,762,638	19
1901	5,952,431	16
1906	6,178,827	16
1911	6,129,496	15
1916	5,572,194	13
1921	5,256,052	12
1931	4,823,666	11
1941	3,565,786	8
1951	3,047,794	6
1961	2,547,026	5

TABLE 1

adolescents and adults at one and the same time, thus bringing and holding the generations together.

The consensus on what constituted moral behaviour has been undermined—a culture of moral confusion and moral excuses created

It is pointless to ask whether children became moral and respectable as a result of the teaching they received in Sunday school, or whether the key factor was the pre-existing aspirations of their parents who sent them there. What is important is that these reinforced one another and that any potential delinquents were confronted on all sides and from all sources with the consistent moral view that forms of anti-social behaviour with clear and direct harmful consequences such as violence, theft, illegitimacy and drunkenness were quite simply wrong. Contrariwise, honesty, self-control and a helpful concern and respect for those with whom one came into contact were virtues to be fostered regardless of one's class, sex or social position. Success and high status might be limited to a few but self-respect, respectability and a reputation for decency and probity were fit and proper aspirations for everyone. However much the members of the various social classes might differ on other issues, on these basic and straightforward moral questions, they could agree.

Today by contrast, there is a babble of confusion on moral issues among the members of the middle classes, and they can no longer offer the kind of moral leadership they successfully provided in the past. A vociferous middle-class minority has made the straightforward and immediate moral issues discussed above appear complicated by treating them as social rather than moral questions. Yet, at the same time, the members of this minority have responded with simple-minded moral hysteria to distant and complex problems such as acid rain, the culling of seals, or the owning of tobacco shares by charitable organisations. Where their ancestors saw the just as being those who gave others their due according to their moral deserts and who, because they always took into account the immediate consequences of their actions for those around them, chose civility over brutality, the members of today's middle-class moral minority have instead elevated the nebulous concept of social justice.

Social justice is the stuff of which self-righteous and inconsiderate gesture politics is made, and provides little guidance to the ordinary person on how to lead a moral existence. 'Social justice' has the kind of tenuous link with justice that social worker has with worker. To rob a word of its meaning, all that is needed is to add 'social' to it. These progressives have created a culture, not merely of moral confusion, but of moral excuses. For the puzzled would-be deviant, there is always available some kind of middle-class provided or reinforced account of his or her behaviour which not merely explains, but excuses it. Theft, violence, addiction, illegitimacy, are mere expressions of a general entitlement to excitement and self-importance and no one, except the members of a small, powerful and thus culpable elite, is really to blame for any deviant or anti-social behaviour they commit. In this way the workable moral order and moral consensus constructed by previous generations has been dismantled and the British are now paying for their folly. There is a lesson here not just for the British, however, but for those in other countries who can recognise similar trends and patterns in their own history and culture.

CHAPTER 2

Manliness and Civility:

Lost Sources of Self-Restraint and Social Cohesion

Simon Green

Civic virtue and manly courage

In 1900, when he was just 18 years old, Sam Rayburn, a future and legendary Speaker of the House of Representatives, told his father that he wanted to go to college. Politely, but curtly, his father told him that he had no money to send him to one. But Sam insisted that he did not want any money, just permission to go. His father promptly gave him it. On the day of his departure, his clothes rolled up and tied because he owned no suitcase, Rayburn's father drove him in the family buggy to the railroad station. Waiting for the train to arrive the two men were silent. Then as it pulled into the remote country station, and Sam made to board the train, his father reached into his pocket, pulled out 25 dollars and handed them to his son. Rayburn never forgot that gesture. He talked about it for the rest of his life. He could not imagine how his father had managed to save the money, 'we never had any extra money', he recalled, and he could not forget that his father had chosen, at that moment, to give it all—what little extra he in fact had—to him. Nor did he forget the words his father said to him as he boarded the train. Indeed, according to Robert Caro, he was to tell friends that he had remembered them at every subsequent crisis in his life. For as he bid farewell to his son, his father said, 'Sam, be a man'.

Nearly 40 years later, writing about the principles of *Civilisation*, Winston Churchill made a particular point of reminding his readers that the regime of 'civilian' government, where 'violence, the rule of warriors and despotic chiefs, the condition of camps and warfare, of riot and tyranny', had given place 'to parliaments where laws are made, our independent courts of justice in which over long periods of time those laws are maintained' and—still more—the life of 'freedom, comfort and culture' that went with that regime, required not merely a general adherence to law and principle. They required also a will to enforce law and principle. For 'it is vain to imagine', he concluded, that 'the mere perception of right principles, whether in one country or in many countries will be of any value unless . . . a very large majority of mankind unite together to defend them and show themselves possessed of a constabulary power before which barbaric and atavistic forces will stand in awe'. Unless, in fact 'right principles' were defended by 'civic virtue' and civic virtue were supported by 'manly courage'.

What did Sam Rayburn's father mean by those simple parting words? And why did Winston Churchill so particularly associate manly courage with civic virtue in his impassioned defence of European civilisation at the moment of its extreme agony? Finally, was there and is there a connection between apparently so simple a quality as manliness and so complex a virtue as civility? At a time when prevailing concepts of manliness are so uncertain and, still more perhaps, contemporary understanding of the true and proper content of civility so obscure, these are far from trivial questions. And, unfortunately, our capacity to address them generally falls far short not merely of Churchill's rich historical imagination but even of Rayburn senior's primitive folk decency. In part this is a problem of neglect. As Joseph Epstein recently put it, scarcely anyone uses the term 'manly' any more. So it cannot be very surprising that no one really knows what it means, or once meant. The contemporary fate of the idea of 'civility' is little better. Few use the term. Fewer still appeal to its merits. Just think, which was the last active politician to invoke this virtue either for himself or for his opponents? Henry Cabot Lodge perhaps?

Manliness—most derided among Victorian virtues

This is not just a question of the loss of collective memory. For, amongst the educated classes at least, it would be difficult to imagine a more derided Victorian virtue than the 19th century ideal of 'manliness'. This is because the pursuit of the physical which it apparently implies, the image of the aggressive which it usually invokes, and, indeed, the mere recognition of sexual difference which it necessarily embodies, all grate upon the modern, supposedly reflective sensibility. To modern cultivated souls, the idea of 'manliness' smells (though they rarely express it so) of proletarian boorishness. To committed feminist minds (usually less inhibited) it reeks of masculine assertiveness. To both it appears unambiguously to encapsulate malignant notions not merely of illegitimate power but also of unrestrained force. That is, it is bad, and it is uncontrollably bad. As such it is condemned as an affront—perhaps *the* modern affront—to civilisation, decency, fairness and (of course) equality. Hence to find it extolled amongst the Victorians as a positive virtue is to appreciate just how benighted they truly were; how, despite (or perhaps because of) their Christianity, their liberalism, and their inquisitiveness, they succeeded only in warping humanity's better self, and in elevating the violent masculine over the caring feminine, all to the detriment not merely of oppressed womanhood but to the whole of mankind, a mankind thereby condemned to imperialistic conquest, world war and finally genocide.

Civility also derided as hypocritical and bourgeois

Albeit for (apparently) very different reasons, the Victorian virtue of 'civility' fares little better. This is because whilst it is, strictly speaking, neither an aggressive nor even a masculine virtue, it most certainly is a repressive ideal. For, whatever else it is, civility is a product of educated restraint, an attitude defined by intelligent calculation, and a form of life possible only amongst the sophisticated, even perhaps the dissembling. Why? Because it is the social conscience of the self-interested agent. It demands deference towards the needs of the whole, but only insofar as that body promises fulfilment for the preferences of the individual. As such, it excludes the very notion of heroic self-sacrifice; still more the possibility of ascetic other-worldliness. It induces respect for the rights of others, but only in anticipation of their respect for one's own rights. In other words, it treats others as means, not ends. It demands that form of politeness—hypocrisy—in personal relations which seeks peace only because it expects profit in social relations. In sum, it is the quintessential bourgeois virtue. And in its artificiality, its cunning, its formality and its necessary incompleteness, it offends every modern notion of post-bourgeois spontaneity, authenticity and fulfilment.

Civility and manliness as joint oppressors

But what of the connection between the two? Manly aggressiveness and bourgeois formalism seem, on the surface of things, to have little more in common with each other than their general undesirability

19

to the fully emancipated sensibility. However, educated opinion and the emancipated sensibility are unimpressed by the mere surface of things. In this way, the psychoanalytic perspective links the two. Then radical social theory—cultural Marxism, feminism, post-modernism—tightens the link into a common cause. Violence *and* repression are traced to what has been called patriarchal possessiveness: the peculiarly masculine, rational, ruthless and narrow-minded urge first to control and then to manipulate the world, to possess it, remould it, and even (*in extremis*) to do away with it, an urge which has, so the argument goes, malignantly distorted and cruelly repressed our true human nature, and the real possibilities of human freedom, solidarity and creativity.

There is no need to rehearse all these arguments in detail. They are all very well known. And their persuasiveness, especially amongst the educated classes, is well attested. What is necessary is to challenge them: to point out their logical flaws, their historical inaccuracy, their profound sociological weaknesses. This is not merely to argue that the link between masculine aggression and civil politeness is unclear. It is, of course, unclear and it always has been. Rather, it is to suggest something bolder: that there *is* a link between manliness and civility; that the link is important, and that this link is almost wholly forgotten and thereby largely misunderstood. Moreover, our misunderstandings begin with the very notion of manliness itself.

Manliness not the opposite of femininity but of animalism

Modern notions of manliness are defined almost entirely by modern conceptions of the 'masculine'. And as this conflation of categories suggests, they are defined almost entirely *against* the feminine. So they posit strength against weakness, decisiveness against vacillation, and reason against emotion; conversely they also compare boorishness with sensitivity, abruptness with patience, and calculation with intuition. But both this conflation and that polarisation were alien to the Victorian concept of manliness. For it was a virtue which was defined expansively, its core meaning found in a cluster of qualities, themselves not presumed to be the exclusive property of any one sect or group. These included, by 19th century dictionary definition: courage, independence of spirit, honesty, uprightness. Their opposites were identified as childishness, effeminacy and sentimentality. Furthermore, in an interesting, and important, inversion of 18th century values, sentimentality—indulgence in superficial emotion—was considered perhaps the most 'unmanly' vice of all. But an aversion to sentimentality did not imply a rejection of emotion. On the contrary; it was the Victorians who invented the virtue of 'shedding a manly tear'. Nor was it even a rejection of meekness; one of their bravest sons, Thomas Hughes, was happy to publish a book entitled *The Manliness of Christ*. This was possible because the Victorian concept of manliness was not synonymous with the Victorian—still less with our own—stereotypes of masculinity. True, it included masculinity: it comprehended brute force, physical athleticism, endurance, aggression and competitiveness, but it was not limited by those qualities. It admired strength, but noted with Hughes that '[t]rue manliness is as likely to be found in a weak as in a strong body'. It praised men who stood up for themselves, but it understood that 'manliness' could express itself by turning the other cheek as much as by joining in the fight. Christ himself had said so.

Most important of all, it was precisely because it did not exhaust itself in the qualities of masculinity that the Victorian ideal of manliness rarely defined itself solely, or even primarily, in terms of an opposition to femininity. True, it disparaged the effeminate and especially the sentimentally effeminate. Charles Kingsley's tirades against 'fastidious, maundering, die-away effeminacy' made that clear enough. Even the rather more self-consciously sophisticated Leslie Stephen admitted a visceral 'hatred [of] the namby-pamby'. But real Victorian men cried in public. Sir Robert Peel, in England, was famous for it, so to, in America, was Henry Clay. In so doing, they displayed a manliness that was contrasted much less with the 'feminine' and much more with the 'bestial', that is the non-human or, as it was sometimes, revealingly, known, 'boy nature'. By implication it was also a quality of man which was contrasted with the child-like or the immature, or indeed, with those individuals who were all too capable of expending energy, but incapable of showing that degree of self-restraint and other considerations characteristic of mid-Victorian 'Christian manliness'.

Manliness the epitome of selflessness

For Christian manliness the highest ideal in life was 'self-forget-fulness', an ideal posited against self-absorption, self-importance or simply selfishness. 'Men' were those who thought about the needs of others, reflectively, ethically, but unsentimentally. They were 'good' men. But they were not holy men. Their reason, their maturity and their consideration stood in contrast to saintliness. This aspect of Victorian manliness has perhaps been the least understood of its many qualities. Much has been made, usually by unsympathetic critics, of the overtly religious aspects of Victorian manliness. So much so that the very idea of 'Muscular Christianity' is now a popular joke amongst the thinking classes. Less, however, has been appreciated about how the undoubted spiritual dimensions of Victorian manliness—important though they were—invariably shunned, or at least marginalised, the most ethereal pretensions of the priesthood. Here, we need think only of the most famous 'muscular Christian', Charles Kingsley, and of *his* attitude to the effeminate priestliness of John Henry Newman. But we might also consider some of the more far-reaching arguments of contemporary nonconformists. For them, the desirability of manliness in a minister was more than a question of averting the perils of creeping effeminacy amongst priests. It was, in their eyes, a state of being incompatible with the claims of the priesthood itself because manliness claimed no peculiar spiritual state of being for itself. It was, on the contrary, an *ordinary* state of spiritual being. Naturally it presumed worthiness, even excellence, in this field but only in an ordinary way. For a nonconformist minister in late Victorian England, and still more for his congregation, being 'a man' was necessary *and* sufficient in order to lead one's fellow men in a life of Godliness; whereas, in the words of one contemporary, the Reverend Edward Pringle of Devonshire Street Congregational Church, Keighley, being 'a starchy ecclesiastic,' was not.

The ordinariness of manliness

In other words, it was precisely in its ethical ordinariness that the Victorian ideal of manliness effectively encompassed much of what was quite genuinely ordinary, that is, natural, in man. Hence its willingness to celebrate man's powers of reason or his capacity for morality was no pretext to deny his animal virility. So much so that Leslie Stephen was inclined to 'measure a man's moral excellence by his love of walking'. In another way, to value the restraint of adulthood was no reason to suppress the high spirits of young boys. So much so that Frederick Temple, sometime headmaster of Rugby, gave a lenient eye to boys caught fighting, provided their 'combat' was conducted in a spirit 'without malice'. Finally, to demand of men that they be good did not require self-destructive saintliness. 'Cheat no more than you have to', Benjamin Jowett advised an Oxford trader who had complained to him that it was no longer possible for an honest man to make a living in his chosen line of business.

Victorian manliness, in other words, was a virtue which acknowledged what was innate, what was latent and what was common to man, and yet which also sought out the very best in all of these aspects of his being, seeking the best out of what actually existed, what might reasonably be hoped to develop, and what could be expected to be shared from the common sum of human attributes. It did not despair at the paucity of human genius. Rather, it simply spared itself the search for prodigies. It did not denounce men for their self-love. Rather, it required of human beings that they be as worthy as they could this side of saintliness. Finally, it demanded of no one that he be a hero. For as it rejected the Christian ascetic ideal, so too it aimed somewhere far lower than the pagan pursuit of glory. Manliness demanded courage but not (in the literal sense) self-sacrifice. It admired fighting qualities, but did not praise belligerence. It presumed 'the duty of patriotism', but it never envisaged that every man should be willing to fight for his country every day of the week at the slightest hint of impugned national honour.

Nevertheless, in rejecting both material abnegation and physical recklessness as the essential models for human endeavour, the Victorian ideal of manliness did not simply endorse whatever men were, or whatever they chose to do. True, it recognised what they were and did not try to make them something wholly else, but it did not thereby acknowledge—far from it—that no improvement could be made. It appreciated that men had free will, and that they would not always choose selflessly, but it understood that, even or perhaps especially in a free society, individual choices could be influenced for the common good. So it attempted to make men (and women) 'manly' by cultivating, improving, refining and polishing the best parts of their ordinary nature. It made this attempt by working from what was common to what was ideal through a process of restraint and remission which, both in theory and in practice, rejected no person's claim to manliness *a priori* (not even, indeed, a woman's claim), but which, on the contrary, dedicated itself to the improvement of all in every aspect of their beings. Manliness, in other words, was a highly various social ideal to which anyone in Victorian society could reasonably aspire. Everyone either knew, or could reasonably be expected to find out, what it was, however complex it may seem in retrospect. And everyone knew that he (or she) might legitimately be expected to try to achieve it. Thus it was that Sam Rayburn's father could tell his parting son so simply to 'be a man'. And, just as importantly, so it was that young Sam knew exactly what he meant.

Manliness—rational, reasonable and *civil*

It is, accordingly, not merely facile but actually false to presume that 'being a man' in East Texas in 1900 meant little more than brawling, drinking and fornicating. It did not. If nothing else, Sam Rayburn's life proves it did not. It is, however, perhaps less easy to see what the real point of 'being a man' then was. That is, what good things resulted for society by everyone behaving in a 'manly' way, either in rural America or urban Britain. At the very least, we can say that being a man, whether in East Texas or in East Grinstead, meant being strong, decisive and rational. It also meant being reasonable (in the *other* sense of the word rational), restrained and considerate. Another way of saying that, as true for rural East Texas as for suburban England in 1900, was that it meant being 'civil' or, more accurately, it meant possessing the necessary resources of personal character—of manliness especially—in order to be civil. And that was important, for if manliness was the quintessential 'Victorian' value, then civility is, as Clifford Orwin has forcefully argued, the defining virtue of liberal democracy, or the cardinal social quality of the characteristic political regime of Victorian and post-Victorian Britain and America.

Civility—being a liberal citizen

'Civility' here means not simply politeness or obedience to the law. It means being a liberal citizen. And the liberal citizen, as Orwin notes, is a curious beast. For his is something less than an ancient citizen. He does not dedicate his life to the public sphere. Though he pays his taxes, and even if necessary performs his military service, his concerns are essentially private. Still less does he subordinate his every loyalty to the dictates of a confessional church. Though he may be a believer, and may indeed be a practising member of a denomination, he expects his and any other church to recognise, through the state, the limitations of its claims both upon him and upon his fellows generally. Yet, though his essential concerns are, in these senses, private and personal, his relations with his fellow men are not 'guided by . . . mere egoism varnished by deceitful politeness'. On the contrary, they are 'informed by a genuine respect for the rights and dignity of his fellows which he conceives as equal to his own', within a 'community of beings each of whom goes his own way while recognising the right of each of the others to do the same and sharing a common interest in maintaining that right'. How?

A liberal citizen, let us be clear, is bourgeois man. But he is not bourgeois man in the sense that Rousseau first defined and denounced him. He is not a pure calculator. He is not wholly selfish. Above all, he is not simply rapacious. True, he lives in society yet he is not 'a part of a greater whole'. He is dependent upon society for the fulfilment of his basic needs, and upon his fellow man—especially his fellow bourgeois —for his psychic and emotional purposes, but he is not devoted to society, and he remains in detached competition even from those fellow bourgeois. He is their neighbour, but like the proverbial good neighbour, he is divided from his fellows by a steady metaphorical (and sometimes literal) fence. The significant form of that division is the legal force of personal rights; of rights against others, whether other institutions such as churches, or even against the state. But the 'spirit' of the division, Orwin suggests, a spirit which is at once divisive in the obstacles which it raises to the occasions on which the state, those intermediate institutions and even other individuals may intrude into the life of a person, and yet which is also solidifying, even unifying, is the spirit of civility. This spirit, civility, is the sense of reasonableness, restraint and consideration that informs the life of a liberal citizen; a spirit which at once persuades him to respect the rights of others as much as his own and convinces him that whilst '[c]ivility requires respect for rights . . . not ever assertion of rights is compatible with civility'.

Civility, in other words, is the sense of community that bourgeois man, in a liberal democracy, reasonably acknowledges. This is not to say that it is the *only* sense of community which he acknowledges, reasonably or otherwise. Civil men (and women) may be moved by Christian charity, or even by pagan nobility, at least at the margins of their existence. Tocqueville, for one, believed that it was probably just as well for the future health of liberal democracies that they were, for there were, he believed, 'a great many sacrifices which can only be rewarded in the next . . . world' and, it necessarily followed, such sacrifices would only be undertaken by men who actually believed in it. That was why Tocqueville insisted that the legendary notion of self-interest, rightly understood in early 19th century America was, in fact, less of a 'hidden hand' and actually something closer to a 'calculating principle' based upon an 'uncalculating hope'. In another way, Kipling, writing about late 19th century Britain, hoped the inculcation of a new 'imperial' ethic might take the place of an altering public spiritedness in an increasingly democratic Britain. That, so he believed, was what the 'white man's burden' was really about.

Yet, even insofar as such hopes were realised in the lifetime of these two thinkers, they represented then, and so much more clearly they represent now, non-renewable cultural resources in the ethical life of liberal democracy. They were bound to diminish. They might even be said to have finally departed, if not in America, then certainly in Britain. The Victorian idealists of manliness predicted and feared that this would be so. They did not hold out much hope, in England, for the survival of Christian charity. And some, like Leslie Stephen, could not in all honesty bring themselves wholly to lament that fact. They held out even less belief that the imperial ethic might truly supplant the ancient citizen's sense of public spiritedness in an affluent, and democratic, liberal society. And many, from Richard Cobden to J. A. Hobson, were happy to see that particular spirit die. So they put their trust in what was, paradoxically, a peculiarly modern, even indeed, a peculiarly democratic ideal, the ideal of manliness as the best means to sustain the moral capital of liberal democracies. It was this ideal which they hoped would instruct a modern, limited, even post-Christian, citizenry into its rights *and* its duties of civility.

The precariousness of civility

In so doing, they judged—rightly enough as it turned out—that civility was, and is, a public virtue that cannot easily be sustained by and of itself. For civility, though not a particularly demanding moral taskmaster (at least by Western, historical standards) is a curiously unsubstantiated and complex virtue. At one level it depends for its fulfilment as much upon anachronistic, traditional virtues, whether Christian charity or pagan heroism, as upon its modern, and rational, demands. At another level it evokes longings and desires within the framework of those, earlier and more encompassing virtues, which it cannot possibly fulfil. Hence its bad favour amongst many of the most idealistic sections in society. For in its limitations, in its tempered egotism and calculating consideration it is easily misjudged as hypocrisy and small-mindedness, still more as cold-heartedness. Hence it is often denounced as bourgeois formalism, as the mere gesture the bourgeoisie makes towards concern for others, concealing in its stilted manners an essential indifference to the lot of the rest of humanity.

Civility—the control of capitalist economies

But it is no such thing. The Victorians understood this much better than we do. They recognised that the old virtues would not survive in modern, liberal society. Christian charity could not sustain a commercial, capitalist economy. Pagan valour could not live long amongst a peaceable and prosperous people. But nor, unsupported by traditional religious imperatives or political duties, would many other virtues—civility ironically included. For if a commercial, capitalist economy demands that men deploy their resources rationally, it also tempts them to grasp everything for themselves. And if it requires restraint in the conduct of business, it also encourages recklessness in the pursuit of profit. Finally, if it implies consideration for the needs of others in production and exchange, it also condones dishonesty in the calculation of public well-being. We all know this. There is no need to be a crude Marxist to acknowledge these simple, unavoidable facts of life in a liberal, commercial society. The real point, as the Victorians poorly understood, is to *control* them, and to direct them in a way that will maximise the benefit that all might reap in a community in which reason, restraint and consideration triumph over rapaciousness, recklessness and calculation, for the benefit of the one and of the whole.

Through manliness to civility

Civility is just another description of that state of social being. Manliness was the means by which the Victorians hoped to achieve it in and through the lives of each of their subjects and citizens. For civility, though an unremarkable virtue requiring neither peculiar physical courage nor moral purity, was, and is, nevertheless a stern and even a forbidding taskmaster in rousing expectations that it cannot wholly fulfil. As such it can be practised only by those individuals who possess the *character* to demand less of their society than, strictly of right, is theirs to take. The pursuit of manliness was motivated by the search for such a character. In that way it was, quite consciously, an ideal defined *against* ancient ideals of virtue. It was not an ideal devoted to the cultivation of martial skills relentlessly applied to the public service. Similarly it was, equally consciously, an ideal conceived in opposition to the Christian goal of saintly charity. It was not about ascetic habits dedicated to the good of others, but it was an ideal concerned with strength, power, decisiveness and clarity, and it was about decency, about other-regardingness, law-abidingness, a sense of common ends. Above all it was about the cultivation of that sense of reasoned and responsible restraint that is defined in a civil nature. Consequently it could never be understood solely as a set of rules. The rules were never enough. Civility would not survive if everyone merely understood the rules. Each man had to have the character to abide by them even when, at least in the short term, he (or she) did not seem to derive from them the fulfilment of immediate personal gratification. In short, every man (and woman) had to be 'manly' in order to be civil.

The decline of civility

It is common today to speak of the decline of civility. Many have traced its course, in the poverty of contemporary manners, in the willingness of individuals (even respectable individuals) either to break the law themselves or to condone others who do so, finally in the increasing disregard for the (competing) rights of others that characterises so many of our typical modern campaigns for moral and political reform. Many have tried to identify the causes of this phenomenon and possible explanations abound: the decline of the patriciate; the unleashing of the business ethic; the rise of the adversary culture; even (curiously combining all three) the secularisation of modern society. None convince. For the 'polite patriciate' is a modern invention, almost a modern bastardization; the European nobility was, in essence, a warrior class. The passing of polite gentlemen is more a sign of the demise of its moribund, than of its virile form. By contrast, the 'business ethic' was born in a commercial society which positively extolled the virtues of civility. So, if it has now become rapacious then it has degraded, not fulfilled itself. Finally, the 'adversary culture' was nurtured amongst the most educated classes for whom the quality of civility was once presumed to be a defining characteristic. In other words, if civility has really declined, then these are symptoms, not causes.

Manliness jettisoned

Is the real cause of the decline of civility the demise of manliness? This may seem a far-fetched theory, yet in his contempt for formality, coupled with his suspicion of manliness, modern man (and woman) has effectively jettisoned one of the most important sources of self-government which his Victorian forbears placed in his (and her) arsenal: the capacity for strenuous responsibility. By equating the 'manly' solely with the masculine, and by defining the manly and the feminine as opposites, modern man has forsaken one of the most important resources of personal character, which his Victorian forbears held dear.

The football hooligan, almost the prototype modern in his false understanding of manliness and his ignorant contempt for civility, only stands out in this respect. His essential form can be discovered also in the modern intellectual, even in the modern female intellectual. The former can perhaps be excused his limitations, if not their consequences. The latter much less so. For in his (and her) presumption that a liberal society can function other than through the continuous sustenance of the good character of its citizens—in and through their civility—this thinking ignoramus has forgotten (even rejected) the moral and emotional basis of its future success, even one might say, of its viability. They have educated a generation against manliness. So effectively so, indeed, that the last practitioners of it amongst us have become those—of whom the football hooligan is only the most extreme example—who understand it least, and who champion it more as a form of rebellion against the social order than as its bulwark. This is not only profoundly ironic, it is also deeply socially disruptive, even degenerative, for it is indicative of a society not merely subject to isolated bouts of loutishne s (all hitherto existing societies have been so inclined), but also one which has positively turned its back upon the cultural resources, the very means, of its own affirmation and rejuvenation.

CHAPTER 3

Toleration:

And the Currently Offensive Implication of Judgement

John Gray

Toleration unfashionable because it stresses human imperfectibility . . .

Toleration has lately fallen on hard times. It is a virtue that has fallen from fashion because it goes against much in the spirit of the age. Old-fashioned toleration—the toleration defended by Milton, and by the older liberals, such as Locke—sprang from an acceptance of the imperfectibility of human beings, and from a belief in the importance of freedom in the constitution of the good life. Since we cannot be perfect, and since virtue cannot be forced on people but is rather a habit of life they must themselves strive to acquire, we were enjoined to tolerate the shortcomings of others, even as we struggled with our own. On this older view, toleration is a precondition of any stable *modus vivendi* among incorrigibly imperfect beings.

If toleration has become unfashionable in our time, the reason is in part to be found in the resistance of a post-Christian age to the thought that we are flawed creatures whose lives will always contain evils. This is a thought subversive of the shallow optimistic creeds of our age, humanist or Pelagian, for which human evils are problems to be solved rather than sorrows to be coped with or endured. Such pseudo-faiths are perhaps inevitable in those who have abandoned traditional faiths but have not relinquished the need for consolation that traditional theodicy existed to satisfy. The result, however, is a world-view according to which only stupidity and ill-will stand between us and universal happiness. Grounded as it is on accepting the imperfectibility of the human lot, toleration is bound to be uncongenial to the ruling illusions of the epoch, all of which cherish the project of instituting a *political providence* in human affairs whereby tragedy and mystery would be banished from them.

. . . And because it is inherently judgemental and therefore objectionable to relativists

Toleration is unfashionable for another, more topical reason. It is unavoidably and inherently judgemental. The objects of toleration are what we judge to be evils. When we tolerate a practice, a belief or a character trait, we let something be that we judge to be undesirable, false or at least inferior; our toleration expresses the conviction that, *despite* its badness, the object of toleration should be left alone. This is in truth the very idea of toleration, as it is practiced in things great and small. So it is that in friendship, as we understand it, our tolerance of our friends' vices makes them no less vices in our eyes: rather, our tolerance of them *presupposes* that they are vices. As the Oxford analytical philosophers of yesteryear might have put it, it is the *logic* of toleration that it can be practiced in respect of evils. So, on a grander scale, we tolerate *ersatz* religions, such as Scientology, not because we think they may after all contain a grain of truth, but because the great good of freedom of belief necessarily encompasses the freedom to believe absurdities. Toleration is not, then, an expression of scepticism, of doubt about our ability to tell the good from the bad; it is evidence of our confidence that we have that ability.

The idea of toleration goes against the grain of the age because the practice of toleration is grounded in strong moral convictions. Such judgements are alien to the dominant conventional wisdom according to which standards of belief and conduct are entirely subjective or relative in character, and one view of things is as good as any other. A tolerant man, or a tolerant society, does not doubt that it knows something about the good and the true; its tolerance expresses that knowledge. Indeed, when a society is tolerant, its tolerance expresses the conception of the good life that it has in common. Insofar as a society comes to lack any such common conception—as is at least partly the case in the U.S.A. and Britain today—it ceases to be capable of toleration as it was traditionally understood. The appropriate response to a situation of moral pluralism, in which our society harbours a diversity of possibly incommensurable conceptions of the good life, and the bearing of such a circumstance on the traditional understanding of toleration, are questions to which I shall return.

Neutrality not toleration the new political ideal

Toleration as a political ideal is offensive to the new liberalism—the liberalism of Rawls, Dworkin, Ackerman and suchlike—because it is decidedly non-neutral in respect of the good. For the new liberals, justice—the shibboleth of revisionist liberalism—demands that government, in its institutions and policies, practice *neutrality* not toleration, in regard to rival conceptions of the good life. Although in the end this idea of neutrality may not prove to be fully coherent, its rough sense seems to be that it is wrong for government to discriminate in favour of, or against, any form of life animated by a definite conception of the good.

It is wrong for government so to do, according to the new liberals, because such policy violates an ideal of *equality* demanding equal respect by government for divergent conceptions of the good and the ways of life that embody them. To privilege any form of life in any way over others, or to disfavour in any way any form of life, is unacceptably discriminatory. This is radical stuff, since—unlike the old-fashioned ideal of toleration—it does not simply rule out the coercive imposition of a conception of the good and its associated way of life by legal prohibition of its rivals. It also rules out as wrong or unjust government encouraging or supporting ways of life—by education, subsidy, welfare provision, taxation or legal entrenchment, say—at the expense of others deemed by it, or by the moral commonsense of society, to be undesirable or inferior. It rules out, in other words, precisely a policy of toleration—a policy of not attaching a legal prohibition to, or otherwise persecuting, forms of life or conduct that are judged bad but which government tries by a variety of means to discourage. What the neutrality of radical equality mandates is nothing less than the *legal disestablishment of morality*. As a result, morality becomes in theory a private habit of behaviour rather than a common way of life.

The incoherencies of neutrality—reverse discrimination

In practice things are rather different. The idea of the moral neutrality of the state with respect to different ways of life, considered as a political ideal, faces the problem of what is to count as a *bona fide* way of life. Since there is nothing in the idea of neutrality that addresses this problem, its adherents fall back on the deliverances of the *bien-pensant* opinion of the day. If it has any clear sense at all, the idea of neutrality among different ways of life or conceptions of the good tells us that the way of life of the smoker, the drinking man, or the man devoted to pleasure even at the expense of health should not by any government policy be disprivileged, disfavoured or otherwise discriminated against; but these categories of people have been afforded no protection from the New Puritanism—the Puritanism that is inspired, not only by ideas of right and wrong, but by a weakness for prudence that expresses itself in an obsession with health and longevity. The smoker of unfiltered Turkish cigarettes or the would-be absinthe drinker will get short shrift if he argues that these pleasures are elements in a way of life animated by a definite conception of the good that deserves equal protection along with those of the jogger and the non-smoker. At the level of theory the problem of identifying genuine ways of life is insoluble, since it requires an evaluation of human lives that will inevitably be non-neutral among some ideals of the good. The life of the drinking man may be stigmatised as alcoholism, which is not a way of life but an illness; or the life of a housewife may be characterised as a form of oppression—not an embodiment of any coherent conception of the good. In practice, favoured minorities will obtain legal privileges for themselves while unfashionable minorities will be subject to policies of paternalism and moralistic intervention in their chosen styles of life that earlier generations of liberals—including John Stuart Mill—would at once have rejected as intolerable invasions of personal liberty.

The practical legal and political result of these newer liberal ideas is found in policies of reverse or positive discrimination and in the creation of group or collective rights. For those who have constituted themselves members of a cultural minority group, to be the object of a policy of toleration is to be subject to a form of disrespect, even of contempt or persecution, since they are thereby denied equal standing with mainstream society. More, what is needed to remedy this discrimination, in their view, is not merely parity of treatment, but a form of differential treatment in which their group is accorded privileges over the majority, or over other minority groups. So it is that in the United States—where these practices, predictably, are at their most extreme—there are quotas in universities in favour of some minority groups, and, if rumour is to be believed, there have been quotas against disfavoured groups such as Asians. Some who may not hitherto have considered themselves members of a cultural minority—such as many homosexuals—are encouraged by such practices to constitute themselves as one, thereby transforming a sexual preference into a culture or a way of life that demands protection or privilege along with those of selected ethnic minorities. In all these cases, as with quotas created for women in American universities, it is group membership that now confers rights. Indeed, the rights of groups may well now often trump those of individuals when they come into conflict with each other.

Neutrality breeds intolerance—the case of homosexuality

These departures from the old-fashioned ideal of toleration are all too likely to breed more old-fashioned intolerance. The case for toleration appeals in part to the fact that our society contains a diversity of strong and incompatible moral views. Consider the case of homosexuality. There are those, such as some traditional Christian, Jewish and Muslim believers, who hold that homosexuality is immoral in itself; others, such as myself, regard it merely as a preference that by itself raises no moral issue of any kind; and yet others who regard it as a form of cultural identity, with its own lifestyle and literature. These are deep differences among us, since they reflect not only divergent judgements on moral questions but also different views as to what is the subject matter and character of morality itself. An attempt to give legal force to any one of these views, in circumstances of deep pluralism of the sort we have now, is likely to further fragment us, and to evoke more intolerance among us. A policy of toleration, in which homosexuals have the same personal and civil liberties as heterosexuals and in which neither bears burdens the other does not, seems the policy most likely to issue in a peaceful *modus vivendi*. (I take for granted here, what is plainly true, that a policy of toleration with regard to homosexuality is incompatible with its criminalisation.) Such a policy might involve remedying anomalies and abuses to which homosexuals are still subject. It is at least arguable that the difference in the age of consent for homosexual acts is anomalous; the pretence that homosexual activity does not occur in prisons is both absurd and—in a time when prophylaxis against AIDS is vitally important—harmful; and discrimination by insurance companies against homosexuals (and others) who have responsibly had themselves tested for the HIV virus and proved negative is plainly unjustifiable and should be the subject of legislation. These, and similar reforms might well be part and parcel of a policy of toleration.

What a policy of toleration would *not* mandate is the wholesale reconstruction of institutional arrangements in the U.S.A. and Britain such that homosexuals acquire collective rights or in every context treated precisely as heterosexuals. As matters stand, there is a single form of marriage entrenched in law in Britain. Complete neutrality between heterosexuality and homosexuality would entail legal recognition of polygamous marriage. If we go this route, we are not far from the radical libertarian *reductio ad absurdum*—the abolition of marriage itself and its replacement by whatever contracts people choose to enter into. This last prospect is one we have good reason to avoid, given the value that the legal entrenchment of a single form of marriage possesses in conferring social recognition on the relationships of those who enter into it. (It is often overlooked that marriage has this value even for those who elect simply to live together, since it constitutes a public standard for their relationship they have chosen not to endorse.) This is not to say that the current law of marriage is fixed for all time, any more than the rest of family law, such as the law on adoption, is so fixed. Nor is it to say that future changes in family law, reflecting changes in society at large, may not in time extend recognition to homosexuals within family law. It is to say that any such changes should be part of a policy of toleration rather than applications of a doctrine of radical equality. Further, it is to say that such extension of legal recognition would not be to homosexuals as a group but to individuals regardless of their sexual orientation.

Toleration versus the equal rights of collectivities—abortion, prostitution and pornography

The creation of group or collective rights is probably the worst form of the legalism that has supplanted the traditional ideal of toleration, and I shall have occasion to return to it in the context of multiculturalism. Founding policy in areas where our society harbours radically divergent conceptions of the good on a legalist model of rights may be injurious to society even when the rights are ascribed to individuals. To make a political issue that is deeply morally contested a matter of basic rights is to make it non-negotiable, since rights—at least as they are understood in the dominant contemporary schools of Anglo-American jurisprudence—are unconditional entitlements, not susceptible to moderation. Because they are peremptory in this way, rights do not allow divisive issues to be settled by a legislative compromise: they permit only unconditional victory or surrender. The abortion issue in America, where it is treated as an issue of constitutional rights rather than of legislation, is the clearest example of a divisive issue rendered yet more dangerous to civil peace by being elevated to an issue in constitutional law and the theory of rights. For such a status precludes stable settlements being reached on the issue of various sorts, at the level of the state legislatures, many of which would no doubt involve compromises—on the term in pregnancy when abortion was no longer permitted, say—which might reflect the views on no one party to the controversy, and yet constitute a settlement most could live with. On the issue of abortion, my own views are those of a liberal, even an ultra-liberal, in that no moral issue arises in my view, at least early in pregnancy, and the entire controversy is likely to be defused, except in Ireland, Poland and the United States, by the French abortifacient pill. I would not, however, try to impose this opinion of mine on others by representing it as a truth about their basic rights; rather I would attempt to persuade others of its cogency, and in the meantime reconcile myself with whatever settlement achieves a provisional stability.

Analogous reasonings apply to the issues of prostitution and pornography. A policy of toleration would not criminalise them but would contain them by a variety of legal devices—such as the licensing of sex shops, and perhaps zoning for them—that would itself vary from time to time and place to place, according to changing circumstances. Such flexibility in policy is not possible if, as in some rights theorists such as Dworkin, thought about them is done on a legalist and universalist model. Here we have a signal advantage of toleration—that it allows for local variations in policy, according to local circumstances and standards, rather than imposing a Procrustean system of supposed basic rights on all.

Toleration better at handling multiculturalism than group rights

It is in the area of multiculturalism that a policy of toleration is most needed, and ideas of radical equality and positive discrimination most unfortunate. We have already noted one disadvantage of policies of affirmative action—that they are applied on the basis of group membership and so entail the collectivisation of (at least some) rights. When the groups in question are ethnic groups, policies of affirmative action that include quotas come up against one of the most characteristic facts of pluralism and modernity—the fact that, with many of us, our ethnic inheritance is complex. Policies which result in the creation of group rights are inevitably infected with arbitrariness and consequent inequity, since the groups selected for privileging are arbitrary, as is the determination of who belongs to which group. The nemesis of such policies—not far off in the United States—is a sort of reverse *apartheid*, in which people's opportunities and entitlements are decided by the morally arbitrary fact of ethnic origin rather than by their deserts or needs.

The necessity of a common basic culture

There is a deeper objection to policies of multiculturalism that issue in the creation of group rights. This is that a stable liberal civil society cannot be radically multicultural but depends for its successful renewal across the generations on an undergirding culture that is held in common. This common culture need not encompass a shared religion and it certainly need not presuppose ethnic homogeneity, but it does demand widespread acceptance of certain norms and conventions of behaviour and, in our times, it typically expresses a shared sense of nationality. In the British case, vague but powerful notions of fair play and give and take, of the necessity of compromise and of not imposing private convictions on others, are elements of what is left of the common culture, and they are essential if a liberal civil society is to survive. Where multiculturalism and toleration diverge is in the recognition within the ideal toleration that stable liberty requires more than subscription to legal or constitutional rules—it requires commonality in moral outlook, across a decent range of issues, as well. We can live together in deep disagreement about abortion, but not if we also disagree about the propriety of using force on our opponents.

The example of the United States, which at least in recent years has been founded on the belief that a common culture is not a necessary precondition of a liberal civil society, shows that the view that civil peace can be secured solely by adherence to abstract rules is merely an illusion. Insofar as policy has been animated by it, the result has been further social division, including what amounts to low-intensity civil war between the races. As things stand, the likelihood in the United States is of a slow slide into ungovernability, as the remaining patrimony of a common cultural inheritance is frittered away by the fragmenting forces of multiculturalism.

The Rushdie affair

In Britain things have not yet come to such a pass, but the Rushdie affair suggests that the web of the common culture that undergirds liberal civil society in Britain is far from seamless. This is not to say that all Muslim demands for opportunities of self-expression in Britain are a threat or a danger to civil society. A strong case can be made, indeed, in favour of extending to Islamic schools the state aid that goes to Roman Catholic and some Jewish schools: some such policy may even be required by the ideal of toleration. Such state aid should be extended, however, only if Islamic schools, like other schools, conform to the National Curriculum—which includes the requirement that both girls and boys be instructed in basic skills of numeracy and literacy in English. Schools which treat girls and boys differently with regard to these basic skills, or which do not teach literacy in English, the language we hold in common, should not receive state support. Conformity with the National Curriculum in these basic respects is a sign of willingness to adopt the British way of life—a way of life that many British Muslims find in no way incompatible with their faith.

The evidence of the Rushdie affair is that a minority of fundamentalist Muslims are unwilling to accept the norms that govern civil society in Britain. Here a policy of toleration must be willing to be repressive—to arrest and charge those who have made death threats against the writer or those associated with him. Toleration does not mandate turning a blind eye on those who flout the practices of freedom of expression that are among the central defining elements of liberal society in Britain: it mandates their suppression. We may judge that Rushdie's work is worthless, or even pernicious; but that judgement does not deprive the writer of the freedom he rightly enjoys as a subject of the Queen and a citizen of a liberal society. There is, to be sure, an argument that Rushdie's work is a blasphemy on Islam, which does not receive the protection afforded by the blasphemy law to Anglican Christianity; but the blasphemy law looks increasingly anomalous, with abolition rather than its extension being the most reasonable reform. The key point, however, is that even if Rushdie's work had been in breach of an extended blasphemy law—a law that would be objectionable because of its cumbrous indeterminacy and its incursions on free expression—that could in no way sanction the challenge to the rule of law in Britain mounted by the death threats against him. This key point may be put another way. A great deal of cultural diversity can be contained within the curtilage of a common way of life. Differences of religious belief and of irreligion, of conceptions of the good and of ethnic inheritance may be many and significant, and yet the inhabitants of a country may yet be recognisably practitioners of a shared form of life. The kind of diversity that is incompatible with civil society in Britain is that which rejects the constitutive practices that give it its identity. Central among these are freedom of expression and its precondition, the rule of law. Cultural traditions that repudiate these practices cannot be objects of toleration for liberal civil society in Britain or anywhere else.

Multi-racial peace depends on common culture

Consideration of the Rushdie case brings us back to the vexed question of multiculturalism. An upshot of the forgoing reflections is that a society that is multiracial is likely to enjoy civil peace only if it is *not* at the same time radically multicultural. By contrast, the multiculturalist demand that minority cultures—however these are defined—be afforded rights and privileges denied the mainstream culture in effect delegitimates the very idea of a common culture. It thereby reinforces the rationalist illusion of radical liberalism—an illusion embodied in much current American practice and inherited from some at least of the early theorists of the American experiment, such as Thomas Paine (but not the authors of the *Federalist Papers*)—that a common allegiance can be sustained by subscription to abstract principles, without the support of a common culture. Indeed, the very idea of a common culture comes to be seen as an emblem of oppression. Accordingly, the largely healthy pressures on minority cultures to integrate themselves into the mainstream culture are represented as inevitably the expression of prejudice, racial or otherwise, and so condemnable. (Pressure for the integration of ethnic minorities into the mainstream culture may be unhealthy when, as perhaps in Britain today, the cultural traditions of some ethnic groups embody traditional virtues better than the larger society does.)

We reach a crux now in the idea and practice of toleration—its bearing on the idea and fact of *prejudice*. The idea of prejudice is, perhaps, not as simple as it looks, but the essence of prejudice as a practice seems to be the discriminatory treatment of people on grounds of their belonging to a group of some sort, where this is not relevant to the matter at issue. Prejudicial law enforcement, or prejudicial hiring policies, would then be practices in which the treatment of people correlated not with relevant facts about them as individuals, but merely with their belonging to a certain group. Now there can be no doubt that prejudice of this sort can be a great evil—witness the long history of Christian antisemitism and the different treatment accorded to members of diverse racial groups by police and judicial institutions under the *apartheid* system in South Africa—and that is an evil against which there can, and ought to be, legal remedies. It is worth noting again, however, that policies of positive discrimination or affirmative action involving quotas are also condemned by any ideal that condemns prejudice. A consistent rejection of policies based on prejudice would be one that was blind to race, gender and sexual orientation, rather than one that merely reversed earlier or pre-existing prejudicial policies.

Toleration cannot support the modern project of the abolition of prejudice

There is a deeper question for the ideal of toleration posed by the reality of prejudice. As it is commonly understood, prejudice connotes not only discriminatory practices, but also, and more generally, conduct and perception based on stereotype or emotion rather than a dispassionate grasp of the facts. Radical liberals have seen in prejudice of this fundamental sort an evil that must be attacked by legislation—by laws against sexist or racist stereotypes in advertising or children's books, for example. For these liberals, prejudice is an evil that issues, in part at least, from a distortion of the cognitive faculties, which is to be remedied by a destruction of the offending stereotypes. What, then, does the supporter of the old ideal of toleration say of prejudice of this sort? He will not deny that it is often an evil. No one, I take it, who has been pigeon-holed or marginalised on the basis of offensive group stereotypes can pretend to have enjoyed the experience. There nevertheless remains a question about the radical liberal project of abolishing prejudice.

Is the abolition of prejudice desirable, or even possible? A school of conservative thought, taking its cue from Edmund Burke and Michael Polanyi, finds positive value in prejudice, conceiving it as a repository for tacit or practical knowledge—knowledge embodied in habits and dispositions rather than in theories—we would not otherwise have at our disposal. This view makes an important point in noting that much of our knowledge is possessed and used by us without ever being articulated. It is not entirely convincing as a defence of prejudice, if only because our fund of tacit beliefs contains tacit error as well as tacit knowledge. It was part of the fund of tacit belief of many Russians and Germans, in the last century, and in our own, that Jews poison wells and perform ritual sacrifices; and this falsehood made antisemitic policies more popular in those countries. As this example shows, tacit error can have serious and sometimes harmful consequences.

It does not follow, however, that the project of banishing prejudice from the world is a sensible one. Prejudice does serve a cognitive function that is ineliminable in expressing beliefs that have been acquired unconsciously and that are held unreflectively and unarticulated. The idea that we can do without such beliefs, whatever their dangers, is merely another rationalist illusion. The life of the mind can never be that of pure reason, since it always depends on much that has not been subject to critical scrutiny by our reason. The project of abolishing prejudice is hubristic in that it supposes that the human mind can become transparent in itself. In truth, such self-transparency is a possibility neither for the mind nor for society. As Hayek observed in *The Constitution of Liberty*:

> The appropriateness of our understanding is one way of making our conduct appropriate, but it is only one way. A sterilized world of beliefs, purged of all elements whose value could not be positively demonstrated, would probably be not less lethal than would be an equivalent state in the biological sphere.

The project of abolishing prejudice is, in fact, closely akin to the Marxian project of rendering social life transparent by transcending alienation. Perhaps they are but versions of the same project of reconstructing social life on a (supposedly) rational model. At any rate, they both involve attempting an epistemological impossibility.

A humbler, and more sensible approach—one suggested by the old-fashioned ideal of toleration, with its insight into the imperfectibility of the human mind—would be one that accepts the inevitability of prejudice and acknowledges that it has uses and benefits, while at the same time being prepared to curb its expression when this has demonstrably harmful effects. In general, however, we should guard against the harmful effects of prejudice, not by engaging in the futile attempt to eradicate it, but by trying to ensure that everyone has the same civil and personal liberties. A policy of toleration, in other words, will even be one that tolerates the many false beliefs we have about each other—providing these do not result in the deprivation of important liberties and opportunities. When prejudice does have such an effect, it is usually the liberties and opportunities it threatens that we should aim to protect, rather than the prejudice we should seek to eradicate.

A further problem—what is prejudice?

The argument so far, then, is that we will do better if we seek to rub along together, tolerating each other's prejudices, rather than attempting the impossible task of ironing them out from social life. A policy of toleration with regard to all but the most harmful prejudices makes sense for another reason: there is not much agreement among us as to what counts as a prejudice. For some, the idea that heterosexuality is the norm from which homosexuality is a departure is quite unproblematic; for others it embodies unacceptable prejudice. This deep difference of view amongst us exemplifies a pluralism in our society that is perhaps deeper than ever before in our history. Our society harbours conceptions of the good life and views of the world that, though they may overlap, are sometimes so different as to be incommensurable: we lack common standards whereby they could be assessed. Consider the traditional Christian and the person for whom religion has no importance. The difference between these two may be far greater than that between the traditional Christian and the traditional atheist, such as Bradlaugh, say. For the latter pair had a conception of deity in common and differed only as to its existence, while the genuinely post-Christian unbeliever may find the very idea of deity incoherent or flatly unintelligible. With respect to the religious beliefs of others, the latter sort of unbeliever is in a very different position from the believer in any universalist religion, such as Christianity, Islam or Buddhism. Such universalist faiths can practice toleration with regard to others' beliefs but their universal claims commit them to a policy of proselytising and conversion. For the post-Christian unbeliever, as for the adherent of particularist faiths such as Judaism, Hinduism, Shinto and, perhaps, Taoism, which make no claim to possess a unique truth authoritative and binding for all men, old-fashioned toleration is irrelevant in respect of the religious beliefs of others. Theirs is a more radical tolerance—that of indifference.

The radical tolerance of indifference not adequate— old-fashioned toleration still necessary

An analogous situation holds in moral life. As has already been observed, among us there is disagreement not only about answers to moral questions but also about the subject matter of morality itself. For some, sexual conduct is at the very heart of morality; for others, it is a matter of taste or preference and acquires a moral dimension only when important human interests—such as those of children—are affected. For those who hold the latter view, such as myself, the appropriate approach to homosexuality, say, is not toleration but the radical tolerance of indifference: I have no more reason to concern myself about the sexual habits of others than I do about their tastes in ethnic cuisine. It is this tolerance that homosexual activists should be aiming at, rather than the divisive project of group or cultural rights, if they remain dissatisfied with old-fashioned toleration.

The radical tolerance of indifference has application wherever there are conceptions of the good that are incommensurable. If there is an ultimate diversity of forms of life, not compatible with one another and not rankable on any scale of value, in which human beings may flourish—an idea defended in our time by Isaiah Berlin—then the adoption of one among them is appropriately a matter of choice or preference. It seems plain that our own society contains such incommensurable conceptions and that the tolerance of indifference is for that reason relevant to us. Nevertheless, several important caveats are worth making. First, the claim that there may be, and are present among us, conceptions of the good that are rationally incommensurable is *not* one that supports any of the fashionable varieties of relativism and subjectivism, since it allows, and indeed presupposes, that some conceptions of the good are defective, and some forms of life simply bad. One may assert that the conceptions of the good expressed in the lives of Mother Teresa and Oscar Wilde are incommensurable, and yet confidently assert that the life of a crack addict is a poor one. Secondly, the radical tolerance of indifference is virtually the opposite of old-fashioned toleration in that its objects are not judged to be evils and may indeed be incommensurable goods. Very different as they undoubtedly are, these two forms of toleration seem no less necessary and appropriate in a pluralistic society such as contemporary Britain or the U.S. But thirdly, and most importantly, recognition of the value of the radical tolerance of indifference does not mean that we can do without a common stock of norms and conventions or the older virtue of toleration. A common culture—even if one defined thinly in terms of the practices and virtues that make up a liberal civil society—is essential if we are not to drift into chaos; and even such an attenuated common culture will be renewed across the generations only if it is animated by a shared sense of history and nationality. For these reasons, the tolerance of indifference can never be the dominant form of tolerance in a free society; it must always be a variation on the very different, and inescapably judgemental, tolerance I have called old-fashioned toleration.

Being left alone in peace

We return to the thought with which we began. Toleration is a virtue appropriate to people who acknowledge their imperfectibility. Such people will not demand that their preferences be accorded special rights or privileges, or expect that their style of life will receive universal respect. They will be satisfied if they are left alone. Rather than pursuing a delusive utopia in which all ways of life are given equal (and possibly unmerited) respect, they are content if we can manage to rub along together. In this they are recognising a profound truth, suppressed in the Panglossian liberalisms that dominate political thought today—that freedom presupposes peace. As George Santayana, a neglected political thinker of our time, expressed it in *Dominations and Powers*:

> In order to be truly and happily free you must be safe. Liberty requires peace. War would impose the most terrible slavery, and you would never be free if you were always compelled to fight for your freedom. This circumstance is ominous: by it the whole sky of liberty is clouded over. We are drawn away from irresponsible play to a painful study of facts and to the endless labour of coping with probable enemies.

We are most likely to enjoy an enduring liberty if we moderate our demands on each other and learn to put up with our differences. We will then compromise when we cannot agree, and reach a settlement—always provisional, never final—rather than stand on our (in any case imaginary) rights. Oddly enough, we will find that it is by tolerating our differences that we come to discover how much we have in common. It is in the give and take of politics, rather than the adjudications of the courts, that toleration is practiced and the common life renewed.

The virtue of toleration is of universal value because of the universality of human imperfection. It is, nevertheless, of special value for us. With us, the skein of common life is often strained where it is not already broken, and our danger is that of ceasing to recognise one another as members of a common form of life. We will achieve a form of common life that is tolerable and stable, most reliably, if we abandon the inordinacy of radical neutrality and cultural rights and return to the pursuit of a *modus vivendi*, shifting and fragile as it may be, in the practice of toleration.

CHAPTER 4

Domestic Economy:

Improvidence and Irresponsibility in the Low-Income Home[1]

Digby Anderson

Two explanations of poverty

1. Income support levels (social security) are now responsible for determining the living standards of one person in seven in the UK.[2]
2. When Jack was first unemployed [he and his wife, Mary] were fairly regularly overspending. They say they did not really bother about budgeting . . . [Later] . . . 'we sort of pulled ourselves together' . . . Mary and Jack had no debt or arrears at all during [the year of unemployment which followed]. This was largely a result of their philosophy that you organise yourself around the amount of money you have to spend.[3]

What initially pushes families into poverty? Why do some remain in poverty and others escape? The scholars differ. Currently the main dispute is between two camps.

Poverty the result of inadequate incomes, something outside the poor family's control

The larger camp might be described as the poverty establishment. It comprises most of the poverty lobby, the professional campaigners and many social policy and left-wing or progressive intellectuals and politicians. They argue that poverty is, generally, the result of low incomes: whether wages which are inadequate; or insufficient government subsidies. Poverty, according to this view, is imposed on poor families by forces outside their control. As Bradshaw and Holmes put it, the income, fixed by factors outside the poor family's control, *determines* its standard of living; 'Income Support levels are now responsible for *deter-*

mining the living standards of one person in seven in the UK'. The problem, for such commentators, lies with employers or government or the economy in general. Many such scholars go on to argue that if the government raised taxes and benefits, if employers raised or were made by government to raise wages or if the economy were changed to a controlled or regulated one which ensured, for instance, that there would be no unemployment, poverty would be largely eradicated.

In the two studies mentioned above, household incomes were respectively just below £80 and anything from £53 to £149, housing costs set aside as rebated or paid direct. Bluntly, the Determinist view is that such levels are inadequate and this is the nub of the problem; nothing else needs much consideration.

Poverty the result, in part, of the way the poor act

A very different view is that much modern family poverty is the result of the families being badly formed or unstable or managing incompetently. Associated with conservatives, especially in the United States, these analysts point particularly to the connection between single parenthood and poverty, notably the rise in 'never married' young mothers and poverty and welfare dependency. More than a quarter of American children and nearly two-thirds (63.5 per cent) of blacks[4] are now born out of wedlock. The British overall rate is over 20 per cent and over two-thirds for young mothers. 15 million American children, a quarter of the total, are brought up without fathers. The figure for inner cities in Britain has been estimated as one in three. Many of them have also to do without the income those fathers might have brought and their contribution to child-rearing. This sort of single parenthood is associated with low educational performance and high delinquency rates among the children and, of course, poverty and dependency on governmental subsidies. Douglas Besharov of the American Enterprise Institute has estimated that between 70 and 90 per cent of children born out of wedlock later become dependent on welfare. The cost of welfare payments to single parents in Britain is some £4,000 million a year. In the U.S., commentators claim that even progressive poverty scholars are alarmed and are calling for more financial support for the two-parent family and reform of the divorce law. Elaine Kamarck of the Progressive Policy Institute is quoted, 'There is plenty of evidence now that even excluding the economic effects, divorce is bad for children. A one-parent family is not an alternative lifestyle'. In a recent review of British research for a conference of poverty scholars from all viewpoints, Norman Dennis of Newcastle University concluded that 'all the serious statistical studies we have examined [show that children who have lacked their natural father] do worse'.[5]

If the behaviour of the poor causes poverty, then subsidies alone are no solution—behaviour has to change

The aspect of this second view, which has received most publicity, is that which shows how the actions of the poor themselves or those close to them, for instance, having children without the continuing presence of the, or a, father, lead to poverty. But the more general insight is the emphasis on poverty as in part a behavioural or cultural phenomenon. People are poor in part because of the things they, or those close to them, choose to do.

Less attention has been paid to another aspect of behaviour which is the behaviour of people already in poverty, especially how they budget, manage and run their households. But it emerges, as in the second quotation at the beginning of this chapter: some do better than others with the same amount of income. Indeed, in the particular example, the same family learns to do better with the same amount as time goes on: 'They said they did not really bother about budgeting . . . [Later] . . . "We sort of pulled ourselves together"'. The remedy for poverty involves behavioural change, whether that behaviour be the factor which causes the poverty or whether it be that which exacerbates it, and cannot be restricted simply to giving money. The remedy might even be through reducing subsidies—if they are acting as incentives to the behaviour, for example, encouraging early single parenthood. It might be by making funds conditional on change of behaviour—as is now done in *Workfare.*

So the behaviour related to poverty is not just unstable families, it can also be deficient household management

This chapter draws attention to this lesser noticed aspect of the second view, the emphasis on household management. It has been somewhat lost in the noisy battle over single parenthood and other behaviour involving highly charged personal matters. It is, at least at first sight, about skills in shopping, cooking, mending, budgeting and saving.

As with the sexual behaviour which promotes poverty, those who draw attention to it are accused of 'blaming the poor' and bringing morals in where only needs should count. This is only part of the truth. Certainly it is conceivable that some poor people may be responsible for producing their own poverty or failing to overcome it or exacerbating it. But some of the behaviour may be less blameworthy or carry no blame at all. Novak and others point to the poor's isolation as a key factor. They do not have stable contacts to lean on to learn to handle their problems. Budgeting problems can be due to never having been taught such skills at home or in school. Groups working with the extremely poor, such as ATD Fourth World, have pointed out the need for basic education among those with whom they work and their lack of self-confidence. Certainly a lack of confidence is a behavioural factor, possibly a moral one, but it is not something for which one would blame the extremely poor. To identify behaviour as a cause of poverty does open the possibility of blaming the poor (and it is arguable that to consider them beyond responsibility, and hence beyond praise or blame, is far more degrading than blaming them), but it does not necessarily involve the attribution of blame. It is also possible, as we shall see, that some of those with low incomes may be responsible for others being in poverty, e.g., husbands denying their wives their 'share' of a low income.

The lack of research into household management

But if explanations in terms of incompetent household management are potentially moralistic, the morals involved look, at first sight, comparatively dull. What is potentially blameworthy is, apparently, failing to acquire or practise skills—household mismanagement—not even a grave or interesting fault in today's moral lexicon. It is one thing to blame the poor for sexual irresponsibility, quite another to carp at them for not keeping their accounts straight.

And because it is such a dull explanation, little research has been devoted to it. The Determinists can muster batteries of effects of unemployment on poor families. The Family-Failure school can produce terrifying figures about trends in illegitimacy and divorce and welfare dependency. But next to no one has done detailed studies of how poor people manage—detailed studies and studies where the data is published in full and not used to illustrate some hobby-horse of the researcher. As will become apparent, because of its minor place in the curriculum, domestic science cannot even give us a reliable picture of how competent or incompetent school leavers are in household management—or in anything else, since there are not, and never have been,

any universal leaving examinations. There are exceptions. In poverty research, Ritchie's 1990 study of 30 unemployed families is one.[6] But even
this is not detailed enough to show, say, whether money on food is
being spent efficiently, how shopping is done in detail.

So the researcher who wants to study management and poverty
is dependent for the most part on rooting among the research waste left
behind by those more interested in grander explanations, the facts
whose implications for management they are not bothered with. This
tangential evidence is, as we shall see, all the stronger for being unintended.

But before we review some, we ought to give this management
explanation of poverty its proper name which connects it with a tradition and suggests that it is about much more than a few unlearned skills:
domestic economy. For one of the first uses of 'economics' in the *Econom-
ica*, attributed to Aristotle, was not about the running of the nation but
of the household—the etymology of economics being 'managing the
household'.

'Managing' and 'non-managing' families

The Ritchie study is important in that it is one of only a few
which explicitly acknowledges the issue. She herself divides her unemployed into 'managing families', 'marginally managing families', 'marginally non-managing families' and 'non-managing families'. It is also
explicit that those who manage successfully do not necessarily have
higher incomes than those who do not. Nor do they necessarily have
higher replacement ratios (income in unemployment minus housing
costs over income in employment minus housing costs). 'There are just
as many managers amongst those whose income [unemployment] had
reduced by 50 per cent or more as among those whose income ratio was
higher'.[7]

Managing well is rather simply defined in the study as avoiding
debt and balancing income and expenditure. But the comments and
case histories of the interviewees, both those who managed and those
who didn't, show some of the tactics, skills and commitments involved.

Ritchie summarises the common features as:

> organising themselves around the amount of money they had, cuts in ex-
> penditure . . . controlling their money so that big or unexpected bills did
> not mount up . . . meters for gas and electricity . . . money set aside for

clothes . . . catalogues or clubs to pay for clothing by small amounts each week . . . shop[ping] around . . .'always buying the cheapest brand' or 'going to cheaper supermarkets'.[8]

But there is something else. It emerges in the advice the families would give to others in their situation, 'never borrow, struggle all you can, go without but never borrow'.[9] This is what Ritchie calls a *terror* ('terrified') of debt, a 'deep-rooted dislike' of 'not paying your way'. This is not the language of skills at all. Terror is not a skill but a *moral* reaction. And she makes clear that while managing is about skills and precision, it is also about courage and ruthlessness, perseverance, determination and commitment. Other studies speak of courage and fidelity. Indeed, there is a tradition in the study of low income families, a paradoxical tradition in those which argue that there is nothing the family can do about poverty, of portraying the families as heroic. Thus, especially feminist studies tend to paint a picture of the wife as passive and oppressed victim yet courageous and competent manager.

Gender studies which show damage families do to themselves

There are sources of evidence on household management which are less explicit than Ritchie. I have said that the majority of social policy professionals tend to explain poverty as the result of forces outside the family over which it has no control. The tendency is under a novel challenge. Recently gender analysts have been studying economic patterns in the British family. Several, notably Jan Pahl,[10] have drawn attention not to what external forces do *to* the family, but what it does *with* itself. They concentrate on its internal workings, particularly the way money is allocated in the family as between husbands and wives:

> It was clear that some of the husbands had substantial incomes but had kept so much for their own use that their wives and children lived in grim poverty.[11]

Arguing for more attention to what families do with their income, she cites Michael Young, 'We do not know except in the sketchiest fashion how income is distributed between people within families'.[12] Pahl does much to answer such questions though she is overwhelmingly concerned with who has how much, husband or wife, and who spends on what, housekeeping, luxuries, rather than on *how* money is spent.

Thus such studies need to be viewed with caution as a guide to the family's internal workings in general. They are directed at one matter of particular concern, the allocation of money between husbands and wives. Pahl does not, as it were, gather descriptive data about the internal family economy then see what it highlights.

Nevertheless, such studies are of extreme interest for several reasons. First, they draw attention to what happens within the family. They allocate a hefty chunk of responsibility and, in some cases, the reader might feel, blame to a member of the family rather than external forces—the man.

Second, they show a variation in the way families handle money. There are not only variations in technique, for example the different allocation systems (all money to wife and an allowance received back by the husband, an allowance to the wife, pooling of resources, two earners keeping their own earnings), but variations in competence and commitment. Some adults are rough and ready:

> We don't budget. The money comes and we pay what has to be paid that week. I . . . put aside money for food, then cigarettes for me and he has his money to go to the pub.

This couple saved nothing. He spent £5 to £10 a week, out of the £90 earnings, on tobacco, drink and gambling.[13] Or, as one husband said when asked how they decided how much to give to housekeeping, 'the girl at the checkout tells you what it comes to'.[14]

Others, especially the wives, are impressively careful. Some husbands keep their housekeeping allowances up to inflation. Others lag badly. Some, such as one unemployed man, make extraordinary efforts: 'I go fishing at night . . . I dig my own bait . . . I've got a freezer full of cod: it's a good meal, cod, full of protein'.[15] Let us be judgmental. Let us moralise. For this man *deserves* our praise. His wife is indeed fortunate, as are the husbands whose wives spend so carefully.

Ignorance and managing

The surveys on the proportion of income spent on housekeeping also suggest enormous variations though rarely do they show an interest in looking at the value for money got for each pound spent. Thus Gail Wilson[16] found that the level of housekeeping money among her families ranged from £20 to £100 a week in the low and middle income groups. When she took those cases where the wife was responsible for all collective domestic expenditure and where the housekeeping was her only source of income, within the lower income group, 'one had £31 a week, one had £52, two had £59, one had £68 and one had £170'.[17] Miss Wilson is understandably concerned at this variation. But it is also a matter of concern how the money was spent and what it bought in terms of value, that is, how skillfully and knowledgeably was it spent? In judgmental language, were some overspending?

She does, however, record instances of husbands' lack of knowledge of prices of different foods or food price inflation. These clearly make the wife's task more difficult:

> He wanted prawns and sardines and tuna, and in the end it [the money] was all gone . . . he won't come [shopping]. He'll be too busy doing something.[18]

Another husband did come shopping:

> What does he spend on? Oh, mangoes, papayas and things I've never eaten. And he buys, well, he's terrible, because no matter what, if he sees something he'll buy it for himself.[19]

She comments on this husband that it illustrates how husbands can indulge in expensive fads and hobbies while few women have the time or money to do so.

But she shows little curiosity about the wives' level of knowledge or shopping skills. Certainly they are presented as spending less and as self-denying in comparison to their husbands but what exactly they bought, how well they managed their extreme variations in income is not seriously considered. The prime topic, after all, is the men-women division rather than the competence or incompetence of both.

The data displayed in several gender studies can then be reinterpreted by those not interested in gender divisions rather differently. They show that what a family does with its income makes a substantial difference to its standard of living. A family's poverty can be reduced or aggravated by its own habits, skills and moral commitments. As Pahl herself makes clear, the gender discovery about the importance of how families organise their financial affairs has been documented before, most notable by Rowntree, who described it as 'secondary poverty', attributed it to the 'mismanagement' of money and dealt with it in 'a very cursory way'.[20]

Poverty studies which unwittingly show the importance of domestic economy

The gender studies offer at least a recognition that the actions of family members themselves affect the quality of life in the family. There are other studies which unwittingly show the same thing. Bradshaw and Holmes' analysis of the living standards of families on benefit in Tyne and Wear is accompanied by the dominant social policy line about poverty being inflicted on poor families from outside.[21] One solution advocated is greater government subsidies. Yet the evidence suggests the difficulties are caused or at least compounded by the poor's inability to manage. Poverty in part is cultural not just financial. And some policy implications are clear and quite different from those advocated by the authors. Above all the data raise the question of whether it is sensible to spend billions of pounds of public money without taking any interest in whether that money is finally efficiently spent.

It is the way Bradshaw and Holmes' families spend money, their *domestic economy*, which merits as much attention as the level of their income. Their *income* does not make them tragically poor. It does not, as the authors would have it, 'determine' the quality of life, though it does restrict it. Most of the families have their housing and rates in effect more or less free, plus some £80 a week in benefits and whatever they earn informally. They have the normal run of household goods though sometimes in below average condition. Three-quarters have full central heating, nearly all fridges, televisions (75 per cent coloured), vacuum cleaners and washing machines, more than half have a video recorder and 70 per cent have a deep freeze.

Incompetence with food—the biggest single item in the budget

The biggest single item in their weekly expenditure is food which accounts for a third. However, there is little sign that most take much time and trouble to shop well or to cook well, though clearly they are not short of time. They buy expensive convenience foods designed for people who do not have time: tinned pies, tinned hamburgers, tinned carrots, packets of shepherds pie, ready prepared stuffing, soups and sauces, fish fingers, crumble mix. They do not buy breasts of lamb (75p each at the time of the study and yielding over 1lb. of lean meat) and bone, stuff and roll them or mince them. In the main they don't buy ox-liver or kidney (both under 50p a pound) and make stews and fillings for pies. They don't use inexpensive pulses, dried peas and lentils. Next to all their shopping seems to have been done at the nearest supermarket—there's no evidence of scouring the much cheaper markets—and although they obviously heat things up, there is little sign of cooking in the true sense, certainly no weekly kitchen management and not the slightest hint of traditional northern food. Very few appear to bake their own bread, cakes and pies or make their own jams and preserves. Yet they complain of boredom and these adults spend half the week—more in the case of the men—either asleep or watching television. The men, despite years of unemployment, do not help with such little shopping and cooking as their wives do.

In psychological language they are unmotivated, in moral language, possibly demoralised or lazy, certainly incompetent in the management of the kitchen's food, and this has enormous impact as a third of the budget. There is also some evidence that they fail to educate their children whom they highly indulge with sweets and several of whom refuse to eat what were then free school meals 'preferring to take money to spend in snack bars or on fish and chips'.[22] The parents are not much interested in health aspects of diet or, we must presume, the consequences of their dietary management on their children's health. The authors of the study feel that the household diets are indeed deficient in calcium, iron and fibre and inadequate in quantity.

Incompetence with money

It is not clear from the study how far this incompetence extends to other parts of the domestic economy though it seems maintenance and mending of clothes is haphazard. Though much local public transport is free or reduced for many family members, 'very few actually planned their journeys within the times set for special fare reductions',[23] e.g., 91 per cent do not use the cheapest mechanical form of transport, a bicycle. One or more adults smokes in 81 per cent of the households and the other members do not appear to resent the 7 per cent of the budget spent on tobacco. Most obviously, incompetence clearly often extends to overall financial management. Many families are in debt, paying an average of 11.5 per cent of their net income in repayments. But 'most families seemed unaware what terms they had agreed for interest or the period of time for repayment accepted when they first took out the loans'.[24] Many of these families with time on their hands choose to shop from their albeit less than average condition armchairs by comparatively expensive mail order. Two-thirds of the families owe money to the mail order companies.

The authors of the report show little interest in these questions of management. Conspicuous by absence is any notice of these rather dramatic behavioural aspects of poverty; namely, that the families' problems are caused or at least compounded by the way the families themselves spend money and run the home. For them the problem is lack of income inflicted on the families by the government's meanness or some other outsider's behaviour. The smoking is explained as the 'only pleasure left' or caused by low self-esteem resulting from the families' poor condition. The incompetent shopping and cooking are unconvincingly explained as the only ones possible without spending more.

This reluctance on the part of the researchers to see, what is to this author, so obvious in their own evidence—that the behaviour of those on low incomes is at least contributing to their problems—requires explanation. Is it that they are so eager to demonstrate what they see as the need for higher public subsidies that any other message is seen as a distraction? Or is it that they are determined not to 'blame the poor'?

If the latter, one must insist again that to focus on the behaviour is not necessarily to blame. Being 'unaware' of the interest rate when taking out a loan may be put down to something blameworthy, lack of effort, or it may be due to incompetence with figures, lack of confidence or a preoccupation with present needs, none of which is necessarily blameworthy. But whichever it is, it needs attention, not playing down.

And if the reason is the first, namely, a desire not to distract from the call for higher subsidies to these families, then it is misguided. For there is no point in increasing their incomes unless something is done to help them use them efficiently. And that 'something' requires considerable thought because the study also reveals that the families mostly ignore the advice centres already available to them.

Is incompetent household management a general problem?

Evidence from a quite different source suggests, as Ritchie notes, that variations in home management are not the monopoly of the poor. If we know how competent British families in general are at their domestic economy, this will be some more, albeit indirect, evidence of how competent low income families might be. How good is the average British family—including the poor—at shopping and cooking? The food scares of recent years have led to much public attention on farms, food companies, shops and other producers of food, but there is considerable evidence that much of the trouble can be put down to food behaviour on the part of the consumer which is not just inefficient but dangerous. While less that 11 per cent of those responding to a Ministry of Agriculture, Fisheries and Food survey in 1988, just before the food scares, recognised the home as a source of food poisoning, an estimated 50 per cent of cases start there. The survey reveals incompetence in food purchase and storage—a tendency to put food anywhere in the fridge 'as long as it fits' and alongside anything else—cooked and uncooked meats alongside. Two-thirds of consumers were unaware that keeping such food at room temperature was likely to cause infection. Roughly the same percentage never adjusted the temperature control dials on their fridges. Many customers did not check sell-by dates. In short what little evidence we have about home management of food, and indeed fatal domestic accidents in general, 5,100 in 1989, just below the 5,373 road deaths and way above the 650 deaths caused by industrial accidents, suggests that there are substantial numbers of homes run incompetently or without adequate commitment.

This has several implications. It is further evidence that the low income families may indeed have poor managers among them because many families do. But it also suggests that, outside issues of danger in food, many more affluent families may be able to afford what in a poor family would be damagingly inefficient budgeting. As we have noticed, with a third of income going on food, incompetent food buying or preparation can do considerable economic harm. Correspondingly, efficient domestic economy is particularly helpful the lower the income.

Further evidence about the expenditure of low income families on food is contained in a Health Education Authority report cited under the *Daily Telegraph* headline, 'Burger and fish finger diet of poor'. The families are reported as cooking from raw only once or twice a week, relying heavily on relatively expensive take-aways, snacks and convenience foods, shopping at nearer more expensive shops and eating food with a lower nutritional value than that eaten by better-off families.

Earlier unfashionable sources

The view that deprivation and suffering in the home can indeed be alleviated by competent and committed domestic economy was not always unfashionable. And earlier sources, unlike some more modern ones, *explicitly* claimed that domestic economy was a moral as well as a skills enterprise. It is fashionable to smile at such undisguised morality.

But is it really so different from the more oblique references to Ritchie's 'determined' poor or Pahl's courageous wives? In almost any foreword to a study on poverty involving interviews, you will find praise for the fortitude of the poor. Some imply that such qualities are to do with bearing the inescapable with strength. But with most there is the implication that indeed some of the poor manage their circumstances and that morals as well as skills play a part in this. However, when the claim is made explicitly as in the Chief Rabbi's paper *From Doom to Hope*,[25] which suggested that values indeed help minority communities to rise out of poverty, the claim is denounced by progressive opinion as moralising.

Smiles wrote:

> The lesson of self-denial—the sacrificing of a present gratification for a future good—is one of the last that is learnt.
>
> To secure independence, the practice of simple economy is all that is necessary . . . [Economy means] the spirit of order applied in the administration of domestic affairs: it means management, regularity, prudence and the avoidance of waste. The very effort . . . is itself an education; stimulating a man's sense of self-respect, bringing out his practical qualities, and disciplining him in the exercise of patience, perseverance and such like virtues.[26]

Today, debt problems, for example, are presented as the fault of low wages, unemployment, and above all 'irresponsible' lenders who 'make' reluctant borrowers borrow against their will. The solution is more government control of lenders, more government spending on education budgets, in schools and on campaigns, and more government money for debt counselling agencies such as the Citizens' Advice Bureau.

It's a far cry from the introduction to an 1820's manual on domestic economy for the 'mistress of the family' in which appears no reference to the government at all let alone the lender and which identifies the problem fairly and squarely as moral and puts the onus and indeed the blame on the borrower. She is warned that 'to make tradesmen wait for their money injures them greatly and, besides that, a higher price must be paid'. She is instructed to keep an account of all her transactions, even the smallest, in a standard form—'*March's Family Book-keeper* . . . saves much trouble' and warned that for carelessness and waste the Almighty will 'hereafter call her to strict account'.

The much later *Sins and Their Remedies*[27] is even more to the point, 'non-payment of debt is sinful'. 'A wife may not dissipate money needed for the maintenance of the home and a husband must only spend out of his income what is necessary for his station in life'. A more detailed moral theology of the same date (1935) makes it clear that the sin has to do with contract and is a grave one involving infidelity and injustice.

The old moral line urged extreme wariness: one should count the cost before borrowing and envisage unfortunate changes of circumstances. Reinforced by the knowledge that there was no one to bale out the debtor and reinforced by the shame and stigma of unpaid debt, it protected many a family from imprudent borrowing. Especially over the last 20 years affluence, property owning and easier credit have resulted in much more borrowing, most of which brings substantial benefits. Were it any other field, forward looking opinion would welcome easier credit as providing increased 'access'. Most of these loans are repaid punctually and without harm. The old ethic is by no means dead. But there are problems, especially for those with lower incomes, and many are caused by the erosion of the old ethic. Government is to blame though not at all in the way the progressives suggest. Government-countenanced inflation diminished the benefits of responsible saving and taught that previously imprudent borrowing was sensible. State welfare has consistently taught the lesson that government will bale out those who get into debt. Lax governmental monetary policy has promoted excessive borrowing.

The progressives call for government campaigns to explain what are the true interest rates. But it is plain from their own data that some consumers are not much interested in the rates but just the level of repayments. Others, after spending 15,000 hours in government schools are now leaving at age 16 unable to divide and multiply and work out that the annual rates of some store credit cards can be over 30 per cent. Yet the *Modern Encyclopaedia for Children* of 1952 thought it appropriate that nine year olds should know the calculation for compound interest—after reading about Insurance and before Intermezzo.[28]

The point is not that an efficient domestic economy is the sole answer to family problems, but that it is a necessary part of the answer.

The content of a revived domestic economy: information and morality

What should a revived domestic economy consist of and how

can it be revived? One view is that it consists of knowledge or skills and attitudes. Thus a study looks at 'the knowledge/information needs of the disadvantaged'.[29] It is a review of 725 studies which present evidence about the knowledge poor people lack. It cites several researches which suggest their diets are low in 'green and yellow vegetables, citric fruits and dairy products', which aver that they are more ignorant of food and nutrition than the general population, which show them more susceptible to food myths and which argue that they lack the motivation to use what information they do have. The research reveals the disadvantaged person as unaware of his need for help in improving housekeeping and as being a 'poor planner and budgeter'.

As a shopper he gives less attention to product quality than the average adult. He has gaps in what he knows when compared to the average consumer. He appears to be gullible. He does not understand the game of comparison shopping and unit pricing. He cannot interpret the information on product labels and is especially poor at long term planning.

This ignorance is exacerbated by attitudes and habits, problems in deferring gratification, incompetence in bargaining and a general lack of motivation. Thus the solution, for instance, to ignorance about the home may indeed be information education of some kind, 'how to manage money, plan meals, prepare food, mend and alter clothes, clean the house, repair the house, keep the house safe, adopt a new attitude to sanitation, understand the importance of planning tasty meals', but 'rarely is information seen (by the researchers) as a cure . . . invariably the solution to home and family problems is . . . an attitude that needs to be learned, or a habit that needs to be reformed'.

If this is anywhere near correct, money alone, more income will not solve this sort of poverty. What is needed instead, or as well, is information, skills, motivations. For what the studies describe is, in substantial part, secondary poverty, deficient domestic economy.

Solutions: education in domestic economy

One obvious candidate solution is education in domestic economy. The nearest thing to it used to be called domestic science in Britain and is now called home economics. It covers nutritional education, consumer education and social and personal skills. Somewhat of a Cinderella subject it has tried and succeeded in improving its status since its change of name but it is not in the core National Curriculum. The most important fact about it from the point of view of this chapter is that because it is often not taught as an officially delineated subject, but is subsumed in technology, biology or whatever, and because any examination in it is for most pupils piecemeal, information about its character is missing. We simply do not know how competent today's school-leavers are to start to run a home, feed a family, buy goods and budget, nor whether they are more or less competent than leavers ten years ago. We do not even know how many pupils study the different component parts of home economics or how many teachers are teaching it. However, an informal consultation with senior members of the National Association of Teachers of Home Economics suggests that there are few grounds for complacency. School-leavers' competence was variously rated as 'poor', 'not as good as it used to be' and 'barely adequate'. A minority which thought that it was satisfactory also feared that it would worsen over the coming years.

And one should be cautious about the potential of home economics. In a bid to compete with other subjects, home economics has recently been stressing the career potential for those who follow it in depth and if anything the emphasis has understandably reduced a little on home-making skills. Further, current teaching fashions hardly emphasise the role of traditional virtues in home management. And even if it were restored and some competence taught to all pupils and examined, this would not answer the more difficult questions about whether success in running a real home was much helped by learning information and skills or whether motivation, parental example and habit are more important. School home economics may have a part to play in promoting stable, well-run homes and helping low-income and other families to make the best of their resources, but there is no guarantee that it is the whole answer.

What is clear from the discussion in this chapter is that domestic economy is not just a set of skills which can be taught. It is also a set of habits to be practised and, most of all a *moral* commitment. Dated as the language of *Sins and Their Remedies* may sound, the notion of precise and weighty moral obligations it contains is the key.

Lest this view be thought exclusively 'conservative', it is worth reminding the reader that progressive analysts, as we saw above, also imply the importance of morality and a few acknowledge it explicitly. Thus Jeremy Seabrook has pursued a related theme:

The old respectable working class . . . grew up proud of how much they could do with very little money; whereas their counterparts today are ashamed of how little they can do with a lot . . . What were regarded by a majority as improvidence, irresponsibility, selfishness, living in the present, an absence of moral values, have all been transformed, if not into virtues, at least into general norms; whereas the older prevailing way of life—with its endurance and frugality, self-denial and deferring of joys and pleasures until they disappear—became a deterrent, the worst thing that can happen to you, a sign of failure.[30]

And if the occasional progressive can recognise the importance of homely virtues and skills, then opposition to that recognition can also come from more 'conservative' quarters. The recent lobbying for state subsidies to nursery provision is an odd alliance. For to those feminists who think that paid employment is woman's true place have been added the voices of employers worried that demographic changes might cause labour shortages and seeking to entice more women from their homes as a cure. Neither shows much respect for the importance of well-run homes.

And that, at least is one contribution to a solution, the recognition throughout tax and welfare and education policy that well-run homes, homes receiving skills and commitment, are important. Such a home is not, for instance, something women can be costlessly detached from to fill some current shortage in the work force. It can be aided by labour-saving devices but not reduced to them.

It is not that contemporary society ignores the home: far from it. But it is portrayed, especially in certain women's magazines and advertisements as what Janice Winship calls a centre of 'the delights of consumption'[31] rather than a web of work and responsibilities. My own research into cooking standards, or, rather, women's magazines' expectations of them, shows a similar thing, the all-importance of values of novelty, making an impression, or displaying wealth and the absence of emphases on skill, hard work or commitment.[32] There is plenty of interest in the home but, once again, it is not based on those moral virtues which are part of an efficient domestic economy.

More candidate solutions

Such problems—problems of morals, attitude, behaviour—are not susceptible to a quick fix by social policy. The general policy implication is that since poverty results from income and behavioural factors, attending to only one of these is not the answer. If incompetent shopping is the problem, larger handouts will not cure it. Higher subsidies will not reform bad budgeting. Whatever the behavioural cause—be it isolation, lack of parental example in domestic economy, illiteracy, poor motivation, depression, self-indulgent or incompetent expenditure by husbands, those husbands selfishly not handing over enough to their wives, a failure to look beyond today—simply increasing social security will not solve it.

Lest this be thought a criticism of care for the poor, it is worth being very clear; what is being said is that handout-care cannot solve behavioural problems. The families which have such problems need quite other sorts of care in addition to, sometimes instead of, mere transfers of money. Isolated people need to be brought back into the mainstream of society. The illiterate need education, the incompetent instruction, the lazy motivation, through incentive. Those who manage carefully and courageously on low incomes need rewarding with public esteem, those who do not, rebuking with public disapproval. In other words, the obligation on better-off citizens is one of re-involving themselves with poorer families by their understanding, advice, example, by learning about them and how much they differ from each other and why. Care for the poor is a moral obligation which cannot be sloughed off and delegated to government functionaries through purely monetary assistance.

The high government handouts demanded by the poverty lobby are not too much but too little. The sort of community care needed is much more demanding. It demands personal involvement on the part of the better off, not just tax-benefit transfers.

CHAPTER 5

Duty and Self-Sacrifice for Country:

The New Disparagement of Public Ideals

Jon Davies

The contemporary disdain for obligations

When I entered the word 'DUTY' into the University's on-line catalogue the screen responded with the phrase 'DUTY FREE'. This is perhaps as accurate a comment on contemporary attitudes to the notion of duty as we are likely to find. We have gone beyond ethical pluralism— i.e., the premise that one ideal is as good as any other ideal or that what is binding on or good for you isn't necessarily binding on or good for me—to the more radically laconic view that the very idea of ideals is in itself oppressive, or old-fashioned, or inconvenient, or *boring*. There is no clash of ideals in our culture: there is simply no interest in ideals at all.

There is little other response other than ribaldry or amused dis-belief to even the utilitarian version (I would not dare to mention the transcendental version) of the proposition that membership of society entails the formulation and recognition of objective supra-individual vir-tues in terms of which individual behaviour can and should be both measured and constrained. There is even less support for the proposi-tion that such virtues must be clearly maintained as moral examples no matter how far below those virtues actual behaviour may fall. In the post-pluralist world, 'human' failings are held to require neither stric-ture nor sanction nor correction, but rather the abolition of the stan-dard (the virtue) in terms of which those failings are measured. The of-fence lies in the existence of the standard, not in the behaviour which transgresses it. Examples of bad behaviour can be turned into at least socially neutral behaviour, if not into positive virtues, by abolishing the standards of good behaviour.

In such a world discussions about morality are not so much about the nature of public obligation or public duty as about the nature and availability of private gratifications and pleasures. In this private sphere, 'morality' in the traditional sense is pursued only to limit it to as narrow a range of human activities as possible.

Dead White European Males and public duty

In the residual public sphere, debates about notions such as duty or obligation consist almost entirely of 'credential parades' proclaiming 'authenticity' of the group membership or allegiance of the participants in the parade. 'Authentic' statements are those emanating from newly 'empowered' groups (in the 1950s the proletarians; in the 1960s people with black skins from the third world; in the 1970s women), while the historically 'empowered' groups are either invited or pressured to abandon any faith in their own rationality, to publicly forswear their own history, and guiltily to confess the ideological nature of all (their) public moralities. One of the main historically empowered groups is totally anathematised in the U.S.A., under the name of 'DWEMS'—Dead White European Males.

In this intemperate world, in which *ad hominem* argument is the norm, special contempt is reserved for those members (who are actually the majority!) of the disempowered 'minorities' who fail to profess the authentic voice of the minority to which they are allocated. Such dissidents destroy the amiable symmetry of the dogma of authenticity—and re-invoke the possibility not only that there is a need for some form of general, public morality but also that such a morality can exist and be discussed independently of the question of its origins in individual or group pathology. The existence of such dissidents also re-invigorates the idea that moral identity is perhaps more a question of hard-won and never-ending individual accomplishment than of chance membership of some 'authentic' social group.

It is in this context that I discuss the question of Duty as exemplified in the behaviour of a group of people (white, working class and middle-class—even upper-class!—Western men), in whose military activities and Remembrance is to be found (or so I will argue) the fundamental paradigm of public or civic duty in the Western democracies. The concept of duty of these DWEMS (Dead White European Males) will be illustrated by their war memorials and war cemeteries—the lapidary witnesses of the self-sacrifice of millions of Western men. In the Great War alone, 60 million men were mobilised: 21 million were wounded; and eight million were killed. The lapidary witness of war memorials and war remembrance clearly involved, directly or indirectly, the majority of Europe's people—men, women and children: no one could be ignorant of the fact that these eight million died, whatever philosophical or theological interpretation one chose to put on those deaths.

The supreme sacrifice

The issue of public duty and of the death of young men in war is a constant theme of Western culture—the Great War being only one, but perhaps the most powerful occasion of its articulation. In 1899 Rudyard Kipling wrote *The White Man's Burden* in which he warned the American people of the grim and serious business of the duty of Empire (the Americans were about to liberate and create a Protectorate in and of the Philippines). The poem is a list of terrible dangers in store (the 'savage wars of peace' surely include Vietnam), but presented throughout as a duty to be faced up to, not as reasons to avoid involvement. 'Go bind your sons to exile', says Kipling, 'To serve your captives' needs'; and the fourth verse describes

> The ports you shall not enter, The roads you shall not tread, Go make them with your living, And mark them with your dead!

Thirty-six years earlier, on 19 November 1863, Edward Everett, the 'official orator' at the dedication of the cemetery at Gettysburg, began his (two-hour) oration with the words of Pericles:

> The Whole Earth is the Sepulchre of Illustrious Men.

President Lincoln's (three minute) reply in part re-emphasised Pericles' view that the deeds of the dead were their own memorial:

> We cannot dedicate, we cannot consecrate, we cannot hallow this ground. The brave men, living and dead, who struggled here have consecrated it far above our poor power to add or detract. The world will little note, nor long remember what we say here; but it can never forget what they did here.

Pericles' words appear in full on the Royal Scots Fusiliers Memorial in the Scottish National War Memorial in Edinburgh:

> The Whole Earth is the Tomb of Heroic Men, and Their Story is not

Graven in Stone Over Their Clay, but Abides Everywhere Without Visible Symbol, Woven into the Stuff of Other Men's Lives.

On the American War Memorial at Epinal in France are the words:

Citizens of Every Calling Bred in the Principles of the American Democracy.

On the pedestal of the small memorial to the Burma war dedicated in 1991 in Newcastle upon Tyne are the words also to be found on the Memorial at Kohima, Nagaland:

When you go home, tell them of us and say: for your tomorrow we gave our today.

This new memorial in Newcastle stands near the Boer War Memorial (*Dulce et decorum est pro Patria mori*) and near the 1914 Memorial, entitled 'The Response' in commemoration of the voluntary nature of British enlistment until 1916. This memorial also carries the words *Non Sibi Sed Patriae*. The war memorial in the small town of Luche-Pringe, in the Sarthe Department of France, is dedicated to '*Les Enfants de Luche-Pringe Morts Pour La France*'. The men of Luche-Pringe died in a series of wars starting in 1870 and ending (if ending it be) with the war in Algeria.

The death of young men in war is everywhere regarded as the paradigm of public virtue; these deaths are the Supreme Sacrifice, the *ne plus ultra* of Duty, the gauge by which all other duties and obligations are measured: they are the very latitude and longitude of our moral journey. In the light of self-sacrifice, all lesser but no less socially necessary forms of self-restraint become proper and fitting obligations and duties, the small and large chivalries of our day-to-day lives. By the death of these young men the very existence of the community is guaranteed; without them, or more accurately without the general acceptance of the duty to hazard one's own life and to put other people first, the existence—physical and moral—of the community is endangered. The ubiquitous war memorials of Europe—there are probably between 40,000 and 100,000 in the UK alone—are the most visible form of public statuary: and of all monuments probably the ones most commonly understood: who does not know the meaning of 1914-1918? War memorials tend, given the nature of war, to express concepts of male duty: and in a generally Christian culture, they tend also to mobilise peculiarly Christian concepts of duty and self-sacrifice: 'Greater Love Hath No Man

Than This, That He Lay Down His Life For His Friends'.

There are, obviously, national and regional differences in the iconography and epigraphy of Western war memorials—Joan of Arc does not appear on British war memorials! Patriotism is a common theme, though the prolonged experience of war which is most of this century's experience for Europeans tends to result in grim Duty rather than glad Chivalry being the most communicated feeling—Americans perhaps moved in this direction after Vietnam—and there are of course powerful emotional nuances relating to the discrete experiences of national victory or national defeat.

In general, though, the boundaries of Western history, the cultural and spatial markers of the ebb and flow of its life, the story of the formulation of its (Christian) concepts of Duty, and all its related virtues and contrary vices, are symbolised by and in and on our war memorials and war cemeteries—where, as Kipling puts it, they are marked out with our dead. These memorials, more surely than the Treaty of Rome or the Atlantic Charter, are our real articles of association.

Dutiful self-sacrifice a male responsibility

What, then, is the nature of duty which can be read on and from these memorials? What are we being asked to remember when we are asked to remember these men?

The memorials already mentioned cover a mere hundred years of war, from the War between the States to the war between France and Algeria. Several dominant themes can be found on these stones. The themes are both specific to the particular war they commemorate but they are at the same time deeply grounded in the archeology of Western moral attitudes towards war and the duties the exigencies of war imposed upon its citizens.

The iconography endlessly states that dutiful self-sacrifice is a particularly *male* responsibility. The bronze relief on the 1914 memorial at Newcastle upon Tyne depicts a group of men kissing their wives and children goodbye and abandoning their spanners and wrenches to pick up rifles and to follow the angel-led drummer-boy summoning them to war: *arma virumque cano.*

Sceptics may well hint that this vacating of the domestic scene is just another way of avoiding the washing-up; and cynics may insist that it reflects a powerful and pathological male dislike for female company—or at least the company of females as mothers or females as wives, while females as sex are more likely to be found in the 'over there' to which these men are now heading.

Equally, these scenes of war as journey, as a move away from the security of family and familiar trades and into the dangers of the unknown in the company of other men is a major Western theme, a central part of the male role in the great saga of Western expansion, whether with Homer and Malory into the perilous wastes of Europe itself or with James Fenimore Cooper and Stephen Crane into the great lands of the Americas. There are war memorials which either name or depict women and their death and self-sacrifice in war time—the statue of Edith Cavell is an example; and women often appear on the more complex monuments as Angels—of Peace, or Mercy, or Victory. Essentially though, the war memorials of the West, the great cemeteries such as those at Arlington or Verdun or Jerusalem, or the thousands of smaller memorials and cemeteries all over the world, celebrate the full commitment to military duty of men. Our Glorious Dead are men—The Men of this Parish. War is the business of men—of soldiers, young men, in uniform.

> Here dead we lie because we did not choose To live and shame the land from which we sprung. Life, to be sure, is nothing much to lose; But young men think it is, and we were young.   *–A. E. Housman*

War memorials are in part funerary monuments: many of the dead of the Great War simply disappeared in the mud of battle; and the British decision not to repatriate the bodies of dead soldiers that were found meant that for many people the war memorial was (and is) the 'grave' of their son, or husband, or brother, or father, even though the 'grave' is a cenotaph—an empty tomb. The several forms of 'Tomb of the Unknown Soldier' are a collective attempt to create a 'real' grave; and there were considerable (and occasionally, as in France, quite vigorous) arguments about appropriate iconography, epigraphy, liturgy and location: the Republican soul of France wanted the Unknown Soldier to be interred at the Pantheon, the Catholic soul at Notre Dame, the compromise being the Arc de Triomphe. In America, the Tomb of the Unknown Soldier for the Vietnam War remained empty until 1984, awaiting the recovery of unaccounted-for Americans, 'the highest national priority', said President Reagan.

Death for country, mankind and comrades

At whatever level, whether in the nation's capital or in the smallest village, it was clear to those involved in the commissioning and creation of the war memorials that they were commemorating the death of men who had died so that the community might survive: *Les enfants de Vaas Morts Pour La France.* There are, obviously, a variety of symbolic ways in which the war memorials define the nature of the collectivity for whose safety the soldiers gave their lives—from 'King and Country', to just 'Country' to 'Comrades' to 'Mankind': but there is no mistaking the fact that in building their war memorials the war survivors were both identifying and reorganising the boundaries of the social entity in dutiful loyalty to which their young men had died.

There was, and is, a degree of controversy about that social entity. The British placed their Unknown Soldier in Westminster Abbey; this is a Christian building, being neither synagogue, nor mosque, nor Hindu temple, nor Sikh gurdwara: indeed, it is an Anglican building; the King for whom so many British Catholics died is not allowed to adopt the faith of those who died for him. The Cenotaph, however, where the nation publicly remembers its dead, is dedicated simply to Our Glorious Dead. It is a symbol very deliberately recognising that the boundaries of the social unit to which one owes duty change to encompass larger measures of humanity. The architect of the Cenotaph (Lutyens) and the main source of war memorial epigraphy (Kipling) know that Hindus, Sikhs, Muslims and Jews were among those who gave their lives: and that the war memorial must therefore widen the definition of the more traditional focus of civic and public duty.

In June 1980 the American Veterans Administration planned to remove 627 bodies of unknown Civil War soldiers to a new mass grave bearing the inscription 'Now We Are One'. The plan did not quite work out—but the concept of unity behind it is one exemplified in many war memorials. The process of actually planning and constructing war memorials can transcend old enmities and create new alliances and friendships. In 1991 Soviet Rear Admiral Sergei Alexeyev, deputy commander of the Black Sea Fleet, on a visit with British military personnel to the battlefields of the Crimean War, discussed plans for a proper memorial for the 23,000 British dead. The Admiral said that 'Only a people which respects its history has the right to dream of a better future'. British Marines then played the last post . . .

Duty a voluntary act

Duty to what? Duty to whom? Duty of whom? Hitler grotesquely narrowed the German community by stripping German Jewish ex-servicemen of their right to wear their Great War medals. Most war memorials extend the concept and incidence of duty. War memorials may seem parochial; but as didactic moral statements their very ubiquity and their essential sameness can (not always!) provoke a discussion about and contemplation of 'Duty' which transcends (without in any way abandoning) the historical or inherited social referent. In this way ancient and redundant enmities can be re-evaluated without jettisoning the basic premise of the necessity of duty, seen indeed as being the very attribute making possible social change and adjustment.

This, I would argue, is particularly true of the explicitly Christian content of war memorials: and I hope I can present this case without falling into the trap of Christian triumphalism. DWEMs are, tacitly at any rate, Christian if not Christians.

Many war memorials carry Christian symbols. They are often shaped like a cross, or carry the cross on them; or they are located in, at or near a church; they carry Biblical or Christian statements; and they are regularly the central focus of Christian liturgical practices, often specifically written for 'Remembrance Day'. They are therefore sacred objects. They are almost never vengeful, indeed they rarely even refer to 'the enemy'. The single word most commonly employed on them is the word 'GAVE'. The single message most insistently propagated is of the entirely voluntary nature of the sacrifice they celebrate. The single warning they most adamantly proclaim is of the trouble which will befall those people or communities who betray the dead by failing to remember, in word and deed, the cause, occasion and passion of the Dead.

The dead, the monuments say, will not have died in vain as long as the living remember them: and the community of the living will retain its moral standards as long as the living carry in their consciences the example of the dead.

The sacrificial theology of war memorials

At the Parish Church of St. Augustine, Kensington, is a memorial which states that 'This Calvary was erected by their friends'. The central figure of the Christian religion is a young celibate male whose self-sacrifice at Calvary is re-enacted at every celebration of Mass or Communion. His story has three themes: betrayal, sacrifice, salvation via both sacrifice and remembrance. In one liturgical form or another, Christians know that God

> Didst give thine only Son Jesus Christ to suffer death upon the Cross for our redemption; who made there (by his one oblation of Himself once offered) a full, perfect and sufficient sacrifice, oblation and satisfaction for the sins of the whole world . . . and did institute . . . a perpetual memory of that precious death . . .

And the people (including young men taking Communion just before going over the top) respond:

> By the merits and death of Thy Son Jesus Christ, and through faith in his blood . . . we here offer and present unto Thee, O Lord, ourselves, our souls and bodies, to be a reasonable, holy and lively sacrifice unto Thee.

This 'story' underpins the theology of war memorials. It may be bad theology: it may even be heresy: but nearly two thousand years of Christian missionary activity in the West has set the example of the crucified Christ firmly in our constructions of public duty. The following inscriptions reproduce, sentiment for sentiment, the Passion story.

> These gave their lives that you who live may reap a richer harvest ere you fall asleep   *–the memorial at Shrewsbury*
>
> They died that we might live   *–the memorial at Kilmartin, Argyllshire*
>
> Through the Grave and Gate of Death we pass to our Joyful Resurrection
> *–the memorial at Sandridge, Herts*
>
> Greater love hath no man than this, that a man lay down his life for his friends   *–ubiquitous*

This Christian, or perhaps *Christianised* view of duty, of the duty to lay down one's life in war, or to be prepared to, seems to me to steer a path between both pacifism and facile jingoism or nationalism. Pacifism, of course, was and is a serious option: the war memorials are fiction in that they proclaim the giving not the taking of life: no one, friend or foe, either kills or dies 'like cattle' on war memorials. Pacifist 'war poets' can and do lay claim to the Christ story in support of their concept of civic duty: and a rigorous concept of duty it very often is, offering the imperative of self-sacrifice without the option (the easier option?) of taking life. The war memorial version, however, in putting death in war (which everyone knows involved also the business of killing) alongside the Passion story, also lays claim to a serious and sombre duty, the duty to die or to risk one's life for serious and sombre purposes: war is neither to be entered into lightly nor to be seen as savage self-indulgence for narrow nationalistic purposes—and it must always, of course, be seen as entailing self-sacrifice, not self-aggrandisement or self-indulgence, neither collective aggression nor collective vengeance. It is for these kinds of reasons, for example, that hostage-taking is regarded with such repugnance in the West—there is no endangering of self in capturing middle-aged clerics, and such activities are for that, as well as other reasons, quite properly to be regarded as 'terrorism'.

Dying for country or for freedom

The 1914-1919 war memorial at Heriot's School in Edinburgh bears the '*Dulce et decorum est . . .*' epitaph of Horace: that is to say it stresses the duty of *patriotism*. The 1939-1945 extension or addition to the memorial states of the schoolboys-become-soldiers that 'They saw their duty plain, their lives they gave for Freedom, Truth and Right'. The concept of duty is here moved along from 'patriotism' (always a difficult concept for Christians—and others) to more *abstract and universal* virtues. In 1863 President Lincoln at Gettysburg also located the moral nature of the deaths on that battlefield in the context of a sacrifice for the abstract virtues of equality and freedom:

> From these honored dead we take increased devotion to that cause for which they gave the last full measure of devotion, that we here highly resolve that these dead shall not have died in vain, that this nation, under God, shall have a new birth of freedom.

Lincoln got no thanks for transcending the immediate and partisan controversies of the battle—he referred not to the *Union* dead but to 'these brave men, living and dead, who struggled here'. Every struggle, of course, is a struggle with the past in order to construct and re-construct the future: and in this task, as Lincoln knew full well, the death of men in war has to be fittingly memorialised if those deaths are not to be in vain; and they would indeed be in vain if remembrance was merely a re-statement of antique enmities and an invitation to remain frozen in them. Duty is a virtue which has to be worked on, because the circumstances of its invocation change—as was seen in the recent war in the Gulf. No doubt oil was and is an issue; no doubt the rulers of Kuwait were and are a pretty shoddy lot; but it is also the case that in and for that war, Duty called in the name of the relatively abstract virtues adhered to by President Lincoln and listed on the memorial at Heriot's School, Edinburgh.

War memorials preserve and broadcast the response to duty of men engaged in conflicts which themselves may no longer trouble the world; the memorials and remembrance practices maintain and relocate the exigencies of dutiful behaviour in the new and larger conflicts of the modern world, 'the unfinished work', said Lincoln, 'which they who fought here have thus far so nobly advanced'. War memorials, properly understood as being objects proclaiming moral as well as historical lessons, and properly understood in their theological complexity, provide clear views of the nature of contemporary duty. They have, obviously, particular historical referents: they also, however, place those referents in perspective: and on the basis of this moral pedigree contribute to the formulation of a contemporary set of public virtues. The memorials, the war cemeteries, the acts of remembrance provide the firm foundation for the elaboration of a proper sense of civic duty. 'Sleep well, our Heroes', said Boris Yeltsin as the people of Moscow buried the three young men who died resisting the putsch of August 1991: 'Sleep well—let the whole earth be your soft pillow'.

Postscript

The war memorials of the Loire Valley in France, between the towns of Chateau sur le Loire and la Fleche, all refer to '*Les enfants de* [name of parish or commune] *morts pour la France*'. The men who die in war are usually young men: and no doubt that is what the French use of '*enfants*' in part means. I argued at the beginning of this chapter that we live in a post-pluralist culture in which 'Ideals' in themselves are regarded as non-relevant, and that this is one reason why a discussion of public or civic moral duty is so difficult. We also live in a culture which has no formal maturation system, primarily because adult roles in such a culture have been infantilised: there is no point in organising the transformation of young men into adults when the culture has no particular respect for or need of adult behaviour. It is hard to believe that in 20 or 30 years time, when most of the old soldiers and veterans are dead, that it will still be possible to describe war memorials as the most easily understood of all forms of public statuary; or that they will be comprehended as part (a grim but necessary part) of adult membership of our society: but it is entirely possible to believe that in 20 or 30 years

81

time British tourists in France will genuinely be able to think that the French are (or were) a nation which sent its babies off to war.

Author's note

War memorials can be read everywhere. Two 'surveys' are to be found in Colin McIntyre, *Monuments of War*, Hale, 1990; and Derek Boorman, *At the Going Down of the Sun*, The Ebor Press, 1988.

CHAPTER 6

Service and National Service:

The Obligations of Citizenship

Christopher Dandeker

Citizenship: obligations as well as rights

At least in the Anglo-American context, recent discussions of citizenship have tended to focus on the question of *rights* rather than *duties* or obligations, thus obscuring the proper relationships between, and responsibilities of, both citizens and states. For example, it should be stressed that, in continental Europe, the generation of citizenship rights over the past two centuries was closely associated with the military *duties* of citizens as in the *levee en masse* of the French Revolutionary period and, more effectively, in the conscript armies that spread throughout Europe after Prussia had revealed the military effectiveness of its version in the Franco-Prussian War. More generally, none of the rights of citizenship can be properly understood except in the context of the more or less reciprocal exchange of rights and duties including, besides military service, payment of taxes, jury service and so on.

Turning to more recent political debates on the nature of citizenship, as Charles Moskos has argued in the American context:

> [p]olitically, the radical egalitarianism of Rawls and the conservative libertarianism of Nozick could not be more at odds. Yet both de-emphasise the role of citizen duties in favour of a highly individualist rights-based ethic. Whether political theorists favour an activist state handing out benefits, as liberals do, or a state that needs to be curbed, as conservatives do, the view of citizenship remains the same: individuals exist apart from one another bound by no meaningful obligations.[1]

What Moskos is getting at is that Marxism obliterates the person as a responsible individual with rights and obligations by subsuming the willing agent into collectivist structures. In contrast, 'conservative' proponents of the political and economic virtues of free markets focus on individual actors as self-seeking egos without moral responsibilities to society as a whole—in the well-known phrase, there is no such thing as society. To refer to Turner's analysis of citizenship, in the former, the totalitarian public displaces the private; in the latter, the private displaces the public—citizens become consumers or customers.[2]

Moskos goes on to argue that, in recent years, there has been something of a '[r]ecovery of the civic in public philosophy' as, for instance in the work of Sandel. He has expressed the 'emerging disenchantment with the idea of a social world made up of civically unencumbered individuals'. Rather, Sandel defends the

> classical republican tradition, in which private interests are subordinated to the public good and in which community life takes precedence over individual pursuits.[3]

The role of civic duties—social cohesion

Why should an imbalance between private and public—rights and duties—be redressed? More specifically, what part do civic duties in general and national service in particular play in the proper functioning of a liberal market society? From the point of view of benefits to society, there are four key arguments for a robust public sphere. The best starting point is the idea of *social cohesion*. Interestingly, some of the limitations of 'conservative' free market philosophies of citizenship were identified by Durkheim in his critique of Herbert Spencer's analysis of the transition from Militant to Industrial society and thus a world of contractual relations amongst individuals. As Anthony Giddens has indicated, Durkheim argued that

> rights and liberties are not inherent in man as such . . . society has consecrated the individual and made him pre-eminently worthy of respect. His progressive emancipation does not imply a weakening but a transformation of social bonds.[4]

As Giddens himself has argued, Durkheim viewed the modern cult of the individual 'as based not upon egoism, but upon the extension of quite contrary sentiments of sympathy for human suffering and the desire for social justice'.[5] Thus individualism should not be confused with egoism: it is not a case of absence of restraints, rather one of accepting (and celebrating) those legal and ethical restraints on others and ourselves that provide the social and moral basis of personal autonomy. As Durkheim argued,

> [E]ven where society relies most completely upon the division of labour, it does not become a jumble of juxtaposed atoms, between which it can establish only external transient contacts. Rather the members are united by ties which extend deeper and far beyond the short moments during which the exchange is made . . . [6]

In rejecting Spencer's claim that common social order ends with the passing of Militant society, Durkheim argues that

> [A]ltruism is not destined to become, as Spencer desires, a sort of agreeable ornament to social life but it will forever be its fundamental basis. How can we ever really dispense with it? Men cannot live together without acknowledging and, consequently, making mutual sacrifices, without tying themselves to one another with strong, durable bonds. Every society is a moral society.[7]

Without civic duties—abuse of government power, and corruption of the morality of individualism

A second argument in favour of a robust public sphere is that a healthy democratic society depends upon civic virtues because the absence of an informed and active citizenry can lead to the abuse of power by governments. Thirdly, without a citizenry active in the public sphere, the moral framework of individualism atrophies—lack of respect for the rule of law, selfishness, lack of compassion—and becomes an empty shell in which egoism or civic privatism flourishes. That is to say there is a retreat into competitive success at work, the family and domestic sphere, leisure and concerns for 'personal development'. Finally, the public sphere and the civic virtues attached to it are crucial factors in the moral development of the self through the realisation that the good of self and other are interdependent.

National service and civic duty

How can national service contribute to the development of a citizenry engaged in the public sphere and thus to the moral individualism upon which a successful liberal market society depends? Would not such a scheme lead inevitably to the expansion of the bureaucratic state and thus to the emergence of a new set of dependent relations between the administrators of national service and the client citizens involved? The significance of Charles Moskos' recent book *A Call to Civic Service* is that it addresses both these questions directly.

He argues that national service entails activities which are high in civic content because they embrace

> . . . some concept of serving societal needs outside the market-place, upon some sense of participation in a public life with other citizens.[8]

Moskos stresses that national service schemes should only encompass activities that are societally needed but which 'the government cannot afford and in which the private sector finds no profit'.[9] He is careful to argue that those proposing national service schemes should ask themselves the following question:

> Are the means employed more likely to achieve the purpose and at less cost than some other means? If the answer is no then the activity is not suitable for national service. If it is yes then national service is the practical means to meet societal needs that would otherwise go unmet.[10]

It is noteworthy that Moskos argues that in order to avoid a drift to statism and bureaucratic centralism in the implementation of national service arrangements, a good deal of these can be organised through relying on existing voluntary organisations and charities in the form of effectively monitored grants awarded as contracts. Such a mixed public/private provision with effective performance monitoring and cost controls would make economic and political sense.

Areas for service—the family, crime, the environment

Four strategic areas of activity suited to national service have been identified by Moskos: social support in the form of creche and related services for families with both parents working; assistance in the maintenance of correctional institutions especially at what Cohen has called the 'soft end' of the criminal spectrum;[11] care for the environment; and finally care for the aged—an increasingly significant sector of the population, the financial demands of which are already stretching personal and state finances to the limit as has been reflected in the recent media reports on 'granny dumping'.

Why not military service? A change in the type of force needed from mass to 'force in being'

Another area is that of military service which, as I pointed out earlier, for many countries has been the main focus for national service. However, military service could not play a pivotal role in any effective national service scheme today. Why?

For military, political and social reasons the equation between citizenship and military service has been eroded and today those countries in the Western world still equipped with conscription have diluted its requirements and are debating the merits of moving more closely to the all-volunteer force models of the Anglo-American type. These developments have been broadly conceptualised in terms of a decline of the mass armed force model that was established in the period 1870-1945.

In Western nation states since 1945 a substantial restructuring of military power has occurred—what military sociologists in the 1970s such as Janowitz and Van Doorn referred to as the decline of mass armed forces and the emergence of a force in being. As James Burk has argued, these two types of military organisation can be contrasted in terms of three dimensions: missions, force structure and citizenship service.[12]

The primary goal of the mass armed force is to achieve military victory wherever it is deployed. The mission of the force in being is not so straightforward. Of course no armed force deliberately seeks to fail in achieving its objectives. However, in this case the main goal is to deter the outbreak of international conflict in the first place and to limit its scope should conflict occur. Indecisive outcomes are acceptable if that is the price to be paid for a political settlement.

In terms of force structure, the mission of war winning leads mass armed forces to build numerically large forces in wartime as the relatively simple division of labour dependent on rifle infantrymen—paralleling the mass production work force in the civilian economy—allows for a reliance on non-professionals conscripted in time of war and demobilised in time of peace. A relatively small professional cadre remains on active duty for war preparation and to train conscripts.

In contrast, for the force in being, the mission of peace-keeping requires it to be permanently mobilised while its dependence on technologically sophisticated weapons of mass destruction means that the military division of labour is much more complex. Consequently, greater emphasis is placed on longer service professionals instead of short term conscripts. Even if the formal system of conscription is retained it is diluted in the interests of professionalism (thus, in Europe over the 25 years 1961-1986 the average number of months which conscripts have to serve decreased from a minimum of 18 months to a minimum of 12). The size of the force in being is moderate, and while larger than the mass armed force in time of peace it is smaller than the mass armed force at war. By being permanently mobilised there are relatively small fluctuations in the force in being over time.[13]

There have been three main causes of this broad shift in the social structure of military power: first, modern weapons technology requires skill levels which limit the usefulness of short term conscripts. Furthermore, in the nuclear age, the destructive power of modern arsenals, in addition to their expense, means that it is difficult to retain war winning as the defining mission of armed forces. Deterrence places constraints upon the goals of military organisations.

Secondly, since 1945 shifts in international relations, and particularly the collapse of the colonial empires of the UK, France and Belgium, altered the military requirements of these states' armed forces. The growth of Third World nationalism and the establishment of numerous new nation-states limited the utility of force in serving the political aims of ex-colonial powers, while the Cold War focused military efforts on the development of a force in being to face the Soviet threat.

The third cause of the decline of mass armed force is socio-cultural change: specifically post-Second World War affluence and a reluctance to forego the benefits of consumerism for military service; a more individualistic climate and changing attitudes towards authority; and a reluctance to express a commitment to the national state through military service.

The end of the Cold War

The end of the Cold War, a main foundation of the force in being, heralds further changes in the social organisation of military power, but the point to emphasise is that popular perceptions about the decline of military threats to the West and the significance of military preparedness are likely to reinforce trends towards a further dilution of conscription systems in Europe, as is evident in debates about AVF systems in Italy, France and Germany.

For example, in France, as Bernard Boene has argued recently, despite the fact that the legitimacy of conscription is fairly robust (partly because of the exemptions granted to those most likely to oppose a more egalitarian spread of military obligations) that system is likely to change.[14] In the 1970s, with a more individualistic social climate and a more competitive, less deferential social structure, it became clear that the relationship between citizenship and military service had changed: citizenship rights were being disconnected from military service, as for example with the enfranchisement of women who were nonetheless exempted from military service, and of 18 year-old males too early for them to have served in the forces. More significantly, the schooling of the nation, and, more broadly, the function of social cohesion were being performed by the mass media, education and other institutions, thus marginalising the traditionally central role of military institutions in these matters.

In response to this new social climate, in which the status of military service declined, leadership styles and authority relations within the armed forces were reformed, pay was increased, more exemptions were offered, and the armed forces spent greater efforts in providing non-military services to the community in order to buttress their legitimacy. In all this the forces were largely successful.

However, with the end of the Cold War, further change seems inevitable. With the prospect of out-of-area operations ill-suited to conscripts, there will be a greater demand for volunteers and a decline in that for conscripts. Once the number of conscripts becomes a minority in an age cohort, the legitimacy of the draft will be undermined. The option of reducing the length of service is ruled out because it is already at the limit (10 months) beyond which the military effectiveness of such troops is very questionable.

Boene argues that instead of what might seem to be a natural drift to an AVF, the most likely outcome will be the continuation of a minority draft buttressed with arrangements for different types and lengths of service with better pay or compensation, e.g., in terms of credits for educational or other benefits. In short this would involve what Boene calls a relative 'professionalisation of draftees'. The other option, which Boene considers unlikely, at least in the French context, is to convert the conscription system into a general national service for all in which military and civilian service become alternatives depending upon the preferences of individual citizens required to serve.

A civilian rather than a military draft

Boene, echoing Moskos, argues that a conversion of a military draft to a civilian one is not likely because of the individualist social climate prevailing today. This is why Moskos' idea for national service with military and civilian service as options is advocated as a voluntary not a mandatory scheme. Interestingly, this same line of argument has been deployed amongst those seeking to reform the draft in Germany.[15] But is it impossible to overcome the obstacles to compulsory national service? Indeed, is not voluntary national service, at least from the point of view of the rights and obligations of citizenship, a contradiction in terms if only a minority of citizens is involved?

National service and education

Given that the significance of national service lies in redressing the balance between public and private in modern liberal democracies, does it not make sense to integrate national service schemes into the education system and, more broadly, into the rites of passage whereby a young person becomes an adult and thus entitled to the full rights of citizenship? In the U.S. context, Moskos has observed that '[a]n emerging idea is to treat national service as an extension of compulsory education'.[16] In some cases schools are already making community service a condition of graduation with similar developments occurring in some colleges. In terms of timing, a national service commitment could be made part of each phase in the compulsory and optional, i.e., post-16 education and training programmes. Indeed, as Moskos argues, school-leaving certificates and college qualifications should be awarded only on satisfactory completion of a national service commitment and no grants should be provided for an individual's education and training unless the contractual obligation to perform such services is recognised. In short, there are ways of making national service compulsory and legitimate in today's individualistic society although this would, of course, entail a robust challenge to egoism!

The benefits of national service for civic culture and the public sphere—emphasises the moral character of free society

How could national service help to redress the balance between public and private and thus to encourage the development of individualism rather than egotistical conduct, that is conduct 'determined by sentiments and representations which are exclusively personal'?[17] At this point, let us focus on the specific advantages in terms of the development of the individual person.

First of all, national service is a means of focusing on the fact that individual freedom presupposes a recognition that one is morally obliged to comply with certain normative standards of behaviour. As Giddens has argued in relation to Durkheim's view of individualism,

> It is only through acceptance of the moral regulation which makes social life possible that man is able to reap the benefits which society offers him.[18]

that is to say, by participating in the market and making the choices offered by liberal capitalism.

By being involved in national service schemes based on the assumption that these are meeting significant social needs which the market cannot satisfy and the government cannot afford, participants would be reminded that *social life is more than a process of market exchange crucial though that process is to the maintenance of both liberty and prosperity*. An effective market rests on a moral basis: 'everything in the contract is not contractual'.[19] Durkheim argued,

> [t]he greater part of our relations with others is of a contractual nature.
>
> If, then, it were necessary each time to begin the struggles anew, to again go through the conferences necessary to establish firmly all the conditions of agreement for the present and the future, we would be put to rout. For all these reasons, if we were linked only by the terms of our contracts, as they are agreed upon, only a precarious solidarity would result.
>
> But contract-law is that which determines the practical consequences of our acts that we have not determined . . . Of course, the initial act is always contractual, but there are consequences, sometimes immediate, which run over the limits of the contract. We cooperate because we wish to, but our voluntary cooperation creates duties for us that we did not desire.[20]

Rather than viewing the law of contracts as 'simply a useful complement of individual conventions', Durkheim views it as 'their fundamental norm'.[21]

Integrates a diverse citizenry

A further benefit of national service would be the social integration of the citizenry, diverse in terms of ethnicity, class and region. This social mixing and integration was one of the traditional benefits of military conscription. A revised scheme of national service would allow this still important role to be performed.

A key element of national service would be a focus on those members of society whose needs cannot be met either by the market or the state. This would involve the provision of services to those aged persons, for example, who cannot afford to pay for what they need. These services would be performed by those working in national service schemes as part of their normal citizenship obligations *and* by those who, at later stages of their lives, have not acquired sufficient resources to meet their needs through normal participation in the market. Thus receipt of benefits would be conditional upon participation in national service schemes which would not only be designed to provide needed services but also valuable re-training for those on such schemes in order to allow their more effective re-entry into the market.

National service should encompass participation from all young adults, including those most likely to attain positions of leadership as well as those with less favoured circumstances and qualities. Here it is important to note that leadership is, for the most part, gaining the hearts and minds of people in order to attain a common purpose, and in this an important lesson to be learned is to have some experience of *serving others*. For example, as has often been pointed out by commentators on the British army, a good officer does not look to his own meal unless and until he is sure that his own men have been adequately provided for.

Conclusion

I argued earlier that national service should be a universal and compulsory system although, by including a well-considered range of options, from military, social and environmental service, the tastes of all sectors of the population should be catered to. The weakness in the arguments of those who propose national service schemes today is the emphasis on voluntarism and the contention that compulsion would not be possible in today's individualistic social climate.

The disadvantages of voluntaristic schemes have been clearly recognised by Moskos who argues,

> . . . there is no voluntary scheme that can insure [sic] the participation of
> the very rich in national service . . . Regarding those who choose not to
> serve because they are both rich enough to dismiss student aid and unaf-
> fected by civic considerations, one feels regret for them and their coun-
> try.[22]

Universal compulsory service—enforced through the laws as with those
relating to jury service and the payment of taxes—would clearly indicate
that despite the inevitable socio-economic inequalities in liberal market
societies, there is a basic equality of citizenship; that there are certain
civic responsibilities that *all* citizens should perform even if they do not
need the material benefits provided by the state in return for the effective performance of these services. Without universality and compulsion,
those who, as a matter of economic necessity, would have more frequent
recourse to national service schemes later on in their lives could justifi-
ably feel aggrieved about those citizens who have never participated in
them. The response of the latter: 'I have paid my taxes and that is
enough' will not do.

CHAPTER 7

Fidelity in the Family:

Once Absolute, now Another 'Choice'

Patricia Morgan

Fidelity—at the heart of society

Fidelity, faithfulness and loyalty necessarily refer to something which lies at the root and at the beginning of human society. David Hume spoke of '. . . the observance of promises [which have] become obligatory, and acquire[d] an authority over mankind'. Fidelity is at the opposite pole to transactions or relationships based on principles of contract or exchange—even if the current tendency is to see it in partnerships which can be renegotiated or reasonably wound up if the expected profits fail to materialise.

Given the appearance of the uniquely human capacity to make and observe rules, anthropologist Meyer Fortes relates how it was with the transformation of procreation from biological processes into morally and legally validated institutions of kinship and marriage, that social organisation emerged in our evolutionary history.[1] Human beings need an elaborate process of education to equip each generation with the skills and possessions essential for the survival of both individuals and society. To meet the task, fatherhood emerged and motherhood itself became a relationship of personal *commitment*. Institutionalised fatherhood is not even established on the basis of undeniable biological events, but as purely the creation of society, exemplifying the rule-making and rule-following without which no culture is possible.[2]

If the mating and parenting of human beings came to express the 'sovereignty of the rule' then, in Genesis, is the realisation that:

All of nature shares with God the property of being creative, of bringing

99

new life into being, but only humanity shares with God the moral choice of bringing new life into the world. Only for Adam and Eve is the phrase 'be fruitful and multiply' experienced not just as a blessing but as a command. Bringing children into the world thus presupposes moral responsibility, for one might have chosen otherwise. That responsibility for those one has brought into existence extends to caring from them in their dependency, and to ensuring that they will have a world to inherit.[3]

For, as Jonathan Sacks continues:

In the family three great ethical concerns arise: welfare, or the care of dependents; education, or the handing on of accumulated wisdom to a new generation; and ecology, or concern with the fate of the world after our own lifetime.[4]

Through the agency of the human family the self-sacrifice and care shown in parental behaviour are converted into moral imperatives involving binding mutual interdependence and willingness to forego selfish gratification for the sake of others. Fortes speaks of 'prescriptive altruism' to refer to patterns of sentiment, value and action that are generated in family and kinship relations and are distinctive of this domain —but nevertheless, work to maintain the mutual trust underlying all social relationships.[5]

In the nurturing attachment of mother and child 'mothers ideally give life, love and nurture freely, offspring take freely'.[6] If it is 'in this relationship of pure gift and unconditional mutuality' that altruism is originally experienced by the individual, so the model is provided for what emerges as a moral principle.[7] This is seen in operation where fathers are bound to take a responsible part in the upbringing of their children. As Malinowski insisted, 'the necessity for imposing the bond of marriage is . . . practically and theoretically due to the fact that a father has to be made to look after his children'.[8]

The impulse to care needs bolstering by law, morality and custom

The way in which marriage brings commitment to the father role is well illustrated by comparison of natal fathers, stepfathers and mothers' boyfriends in relation to child abuse—which is likely to come from a man who has neither blood, *nor a legal tie* to children in the household.[9] In turn, fathers whose children are born outside of marriage are less involved with their children in every way and, when relationships break up, are less likely to pay support or maintain any contact. This has to be seen in relation to the general low level of involvement which divorced fathers themselves have with children from former marriages.[10] It has been assumed that, if a married man was a loving, sensitive and attentive father, then his relationship with his children must carry over after divorce. The 'stunning surprise' is that, without the marriage structure, men seem unable to 'maintain their perspective as fathers or to hold in view the needs of their children'. Many a father 'seems to have lost the sense that his children are part of his own generational continuity, his defence against mortality'.[11]

If we do have any impulse to care, then this is only raw material on which law, morality and custom go to work and organise the attitudes and activities through which our inclinations find appropriate application and consistent, enduring expression.[12] Altruistic obligation is, most importantly, 'morally binding in its own right, as regardless of feelings of affection, or of likes, or dislikes, or of familiarity, as of reward'.[13] It does not establish claims to equivalent returns and nor must it be seen as costing anything in terms of time or property that could better be spent elsewhere—it only being assumed that the beneficiaries will act in a similar way in similar contexts.

Family obligations not from consent or choice, but unrenounceable and unconditional

Thus perceived as non-optional, unrenounceable and unconditional, family obligations are owed simply in recognition of filial ties:

> This sense of obligation is not founded in justice—which is the sphere of free actions between beings who *create* their moral ties—but rather in respect, honour, or (as the Romans called it) piety . . . Impiety is the refusal to recognise as legitimate a demand that does not arise from consent or choice. And we see that the behaviour of children towards their parents cannot be understood unless we admit this ability to recognise a bond that is 'transcendent', that exists as it were 'objectively', outside the sphere of individual choice.[14]

A family that views itself 'solely as an association of common interests, a corporation for organising production or maximising wealth or pleasures, is setting itself up for bankruptcy and dissolution'.[15] Yet, filial obligation operates in ways which are consistent with and support political and legal institutions—providing the 'cornerstone of the social attitudes . . . described by solidarity' which underpin social control in all societies, to curb the aggressive, destructive and self-centred propensities that militate against their very existence.[16] There may be special duties to those with whom the individual most strongly identifies, but the almost universal custom is to identify altruism with brotherhood. The development of moral character is 'along the axis of the widening range of imaginative identifications'. In Jewish ethical tradition:

> By the book of Exodus the conventional family of Abraham and his children has become a nation. But obligations to other members of one's people are still often couched in terms of the word 'brother'. Duties are extended beyond the nation . . . together with the rider, 'You know the heart of the stranger, for you yourselves were strangers in the land of Egypt'.[17]

In contrast to systems sustained simply by force, leadership also has both recognised authority and responsibility for the exercise of power. It is here that the ability to recognise a transcendent bond

> . . . is transferred by the citizen from hearth and home to place, people and country. The bond of society . . . is just such a transcendent bond, and it is inevitable that the citizen will be disposed to recognise its legitimacy . . . to bestow authority upon the existing order.[18]

Thus the family is the primary moral domain and, in Durkheim's phrase, the 'key link of the social chain of being'—meditating between the individual and other institutions. Shakespeare's *Titus Andronicus* dwells upon the significance of the familial bond; for Titus, in destroying his own blood, wreaks through that action both the destruction of his clan and the ruin of the state.

Freedom from wider kin means heightened marital obligations

A particular view of marriage was established very early in northern Europe. Founded upon the mutual consent of the couple themselves,[19] its distinctive qualities were encouraged by Protestant emphasis upon the unique worth of the individual and of marriage as a divinely ordained state. Love purified sexuality within marriage, domestic virtues were praised, mutual trust and fidelity were extolled and marriage defined as a partnership based upon common labour and love.

However, the common reality in human societies has been that, at least, 'parties to a marriage must have sufficient trust in one another to be sure that the contract entered into will be fulfilled; and the partners must live together in sufficient amity to enable them to fulfil the tasks of parenthood adequately'.[20]

If this trust and amity are extensions of the altruistic commitments of kinship, so marriage brings what are initially non-kin relations—but ones vital to the creation and maintenance of further kin relationships—into their moral ambit.

The Western conjugal unit may have enjoyed considerable freedom compared with those societies where it is subordinated to wider kin or absorbed into extended families. But with this went a heightened emphasis on marital loyalty and the indissolubility of the marriage bond by the law and churches. Marriage vows constituted a covenant (rather than a contract), or a promise at large, to all witnesses, including God, that the vows (for better or for worse) would be kept until death.

Today one finds commentators speaking of easy separation in early times as precedents or models for modern mass divorce and illegitimacy—where 'sexual morality is returning to its origins', according to the religious correspondent in *The Times* of London (22 June, 1991). The tight regulation of marriage and the difficulties of dissolution in later centuries then appear as arbitrarily oppressive. Now, this often involves a misreading of disagreements in past times over how valid marriages were made as a blasé acceptance of their non-permanence. But there is also a failure to understand that in the societies which provide the vague references, kin or clan loomed large in people's lives. It may not be a coincidence that the greater responsibilities of the couple to each other developed with individualism.

A consequence of emphasising personal love and mutual respect as the basis of marriage between spouses was an improvement in the position of women within marriage. Men have had a certain leeway for sexual indulgence outside marriage in many times and places. This was denied to wives not just because they might palm off spurious progeny on husbands, *it was also overwhelmingly important to ensure that children had a complete set of kin relations, and could be properly placed in terms of their affiliations and social position.* This is not just advantageous for survival and success, it tells them, and everyone else, who they are. Moreover, a mother's continued pursuit of mates might put the welfare of the young at risk, or introduce into the home males bound by none of the responsibilities and incest prohibitions applying to legal fathers. But as marriage became a covenant of emotional commitment and mutual comfort, so *loyalty* now enjoined sexual faithfulness on the part of both parties and opposition to the double standard appeared.

The confirmation of the Western conjugal family as a 'sentimental reality', a zone of physical and moral intimacy, is also related to the emergence both of the household as a segregated locale for child-rearing and to a heightened sensibility, strongly linked to children and their education. If the conjugal family was explicitly recognised as the social and political bedrock, nonconformists brought this into sharp focus in 17th century England and America by arguing

> . . . passionately that the well-ordered family was the only institution capable of generating a saintly social order: 'if ever we would have the church of God to continue among us we must bring it into our households, and nourish it in our families. '. . . A sound marriage, based on a unique emotional bond William Baxter designated "Conjugal Love", was in the view of other Puritans "a business of greatest consequence, and that whereon the main comfort or discomfort of a man's life doth depend . . ." ' Conjugal love was the model and the guarantee of a stable, consensual society that these early evangelists hoped would replace the old order of privilege and birth.[21]

If Puritanism and then Evangelicalism defined the conjugal family as central to the 'positive moralisation' of society, they gave explanatory power and utility to older and wider ideational currents,[22] relating to the fundamental properties of family life. Simon Schema describes how this was the irreducible primary cell on which, ultimately, the whole fabric of the Dutch Republic was grounded:

> . . . the home was of supreme importance in determining the moral fate, both of individuals and of Dutch society as a whole . . . in the Netherlands it was the family household that was 'the fountain and source' of authority . . . 'The first community,' wrote Beverwijck, citing Cicero, 'is that of marriage itself; thereafter in a family household with children, in which all things are common. That is the first principle of a town and thus the seed of a common state'.[23]

In the family, the '. . . reciprocity of duties and obligations . . . had as their end a prospering of Christian peace and the procreation of more virtuous households'.[24]

Family values antithetical to competitive individualism

Family values are clearly antithetical to competitive individualism in subordinating self-interest to that of the group: enjoining the sharing of resources and denying merit or achievement as the basis of membership, approval or love.[25] But then, defenders of capitalism agree that the egocentricity, autonomy and acquisitiveness at its heart has 'threatened to shred social life altogether, leaving only egoistic nihilism in its wake'.[26] As Michael Novak observes:

> Those who hold that democratic capitalism will end, perhaps sooner than we imagine, by eviscerating itself do not usually locate its fatal flaw in the political system or in its economic system, both of which are superior to any known in history, but in its moral cultural system.[27]

From one point of view 'the institutions of democratic capitalism are designed to function with minimal dependence upon virtuous motives'. From another 'they cannot function at all without certain moral strengths, rooted in institutions like the family' which, if 'it is ignored or penalised, its weakening weakens the whole'.[28] The modern family provided motivation of immense importance by generating 'economically and socially constructive anxiety, ambition, and imagination, while keeping the baser human instincts and the individual ego under restraint'.[29] In turn, wealth served and sustained a secure and prosperous family life and improved child-rearing.

However, this depended upon the ways in which family values provided the impetus for compensatory measures which reduced the standard of living penalty and the opportunity costs of child-rearing. If economic imperatives dictate judgements about family life, this will seem a worthless and wasteful impediment to individual consumption and accumulation.[30] But, overwhelmingly important as the basis of protection as much else, the other area where continued vigilance was necessary if economic and social freedom was not to descend into anarchy— was the preservation of the marriage bond from self-interest.

It often seemed an unreasonable and oppressive anomaly that unrelated parties to a marriage contract, but no other, should be indissolubly bound. In the last analysis, such protest was invariably checked by consideration of the generative function. Mill complained that questions about divorce were usually discussed 'as if the interest of children was everything, and that of grown persons nothing'. But was it all pious humbug, to limit human freedom? Calling someone into existence puts you under an obligation. Your claim to personal liberty may be strong, but if children are to develop into free beings, they need a lot of help. If this is not forthcoming, it is '. . . a moral crime, both against the unfortunate offspring and against society'.[31]

Divorce law—the family seen as its individual members, not a social or sacred institution

Law and obligation have intertwined in all societies. Not least, laws, norms and rules that reflect the interests of society at large in maintaining cohesion and continuity have been brought to bear upon sexual and reproductive behaviour. Through literal and symbolic application, these must stress the altruistic component in kin relationships as against the potentiality of conflict and egoistic tendencies.[32] The report of the 1956 Royal Commission on Marriage and Divorce—appointed in Britain in response to attempts to extend the grounds for divorce beyond that of the matrimonial offence—insisted that 'people have good and bad impulses and we conceive it to be the function of the law to strengthen the good and control the bad'.[33] Bodies from the Catholic Union to the atheistic Ethical Union emphasised how the first function of the marriage law among Western nations was to uphold general standards, and protect the institution of the family as the assumed and approved foundation of society by confirming life-long monogamous union. If the right to divorce by consent or at will were ever conceded the number of divorces would increase enormously. Though doubtlessly reflecting the wishes of the parties concerned, it could not be defended on that ground for the evil of divorce was contagious.

Elsewhere this approach was castigated as hopelessly reactionary and unproductive.[34] To progressive social scientists the 'institutionalists' who held that the family and marriage '. . . had a value in their own right' sacrificed real people to meaningless abstractions.[35] If, in contrast, they boasted of their concern only for 'the earthly welfare of the persons concerned', so divorce was 'neither good nor bad, but should be judged in much the same way as one judges the decision to resign from a job'.[36] With the realm of belief and morality rejected as unreal and invalid, the law appeared burdened with the irrationality of historical tradition.[37] Tremendous certainty and rectitude combined with the failure to grasp that—even if there is no entity beyond individuals as the sources and subjects of moral rules—values do exist insofar as they are externalised in a common life. And, as social beings, people also make references or

create institutions to embody and carry on systems of meaning—which
are experienced as having some existence outside individual consciousness.[38]

In his history of Western marriage, John R. Gillis mentions how
people clearly separated the institution from the personal relationship.
Marriages often survived troubled times because of the

> . . . pronounced propensity to keep the matrimonial institution alive, de-
> spite unhappiness . . . People stuck with marriage as an institution even
> when they had lost all hope in their particular partners. Many were like
> Mary Foxon, who had wed at nineteen to the second man who courted
> her. He proved so shiftless that her mother advised her to leave him, but
> she endured the rocky first years, bore three children, and proved her
> mother wrong. 'I said, "I'd stick to my marriage vows" and she knew I
> would'. Surveys found that both husbands and wives responded to marital
> difficulties by blaming themselves and attempting to repair the damage.
> Women's first impulse was to improve their housekeeping and appear-
> ance, while men were in agreement with the worker who said he would
> first 'consider whether or not he is free from blame. Consider [well] if
> they have kiddies'.[39]

Those who believed that the absence of legal and moral regulation
would best make personal relations a thing of love and happiness, never
raised the question of how people might live together without interpersonal commitment and in the absence of everything that had shaped
and buttressed marital and family life. What in the end could the natu-
ralistic creed amount to other than the drive to 'assert the importance
of desires against all the world'.[40] As Allan Bloom observes in *The Closing of the American Mind*:

> This absoluteness of desire uninhibited by thoughts of virtue is what is
> found in the state of nature. It represents the turn in philosophy away
> from trying to tame or perfect desire by virtue, and toward finding out
> what one's desire is and living according to it. This is largely accomplished
> by criticising virtue, which covers and corrupts desire. Our desire becomes
> a kind of oracle we consult; it is now the last word, while in the past it was
> the questionable and dangerous part of us.[41]

Leaving decisions to nature: the concept of irretrievable breakdown

However, it was the old establishment which demolished the institutional constraints in the path of the 'revolution in morals'. Churchmen and lawyers who sponsored the transformation in divorce looked to nature for a way which both avoided value judgements and individual inconvenience, yet somehow left old virtues intact. They knew that to permit 'no-fault' divorce clearly destroyed 'the concept of marriage as a lifelong union', and substituted 'a private contract of partnership' terminable 'without any effective intervention by the community'.[42]

But the fancy was that reform might change nothing if marital dissolution could be based—not on wishes—but on a sort of scientific diagnosis.[43] On both sides of the Atlantic, this doctrine of 'irretrievable breakdown' promised to make divorce purely responsive and regulative: a tidying-up process, whose task was the 'decent burial' of 'dead' or 'hollow-shell' marriages. If the law simply declared defunct what had ended, then the sacrifice of principles for the benefit of those in uncomfortable circumstances need not be paid for with a deterioration in overall conduct. Since 'dead' marriages somehow arose spontaneously, and could be excised without repercussions for other unions or the future of marriage generally, a rise in the divorce rate would no more reflect than stimulate any change in marriage breakdowns. It would simply represent the dissolution of marriages which had existed only in legal theory or theology.[44]

The incentive effects of easier divorce

This curious juxtaposition of mutually incompatible voluntarist and determinist discourses was certainly 'sociological naivete of the most extraordinary sort',[45] which ignored the way in which 'divorce legislation itself provides incentives and disincentives to divorce', if only because it 'changes the nature of the marriage contract it terminates'. Neither rewarding good marital behaviour nor punishing violation of marital norms—it provides no moral brake which will make the parties consider the consequences of a course of action, before pursuing it. In the most socially significant of relationships, the law itself promotes the notion that it is indifferent to the morality of peoples' behaviour towards each other: 'letting it appear that it is of no public concern whether marriage partners adhere to their vows or not . . . it is seen to put a premium upon irresponsibility'.[46]

New norms of marital behaviour incorporated in liberalised divorce lead to marital instability precisely because all marriages become provisional. Minor disputes can readily develop into disruptive conflicts and they are open to the predatory activities of interlopers.[47] Marriages which can be ended by the unilateral decision of one party are vulnerable from the start, since vows 'of lifelong fidelity which can so readily be set aside . . . soon cease to be credible . . .'[48] Indeed, if marriage is no longer a status, but just a contract dissolvable at will, the possibility of separation is already the fact of separation:

> Imagination compels everyone to look forward to the day of separation in order to see how he will do. The energies people should use in the common enterprise are exhausted in preparation for independence. What would, in the case of union, be a building stone becomes a stumbling block on the path to secession. The goals of those who are together naturally and necessarily must become a common good; what one must live with can be accepted. But there is no common good for those who are to separate. The presence of choice already changes the character of relatedness. And the more separation there is, the more there will be.[49]

Between 1960 and 1985, divorces in America increased more than threefold, with one divorce now to two weddings. In Britain, as divorce became a simply administrative procedure, judged by speed and cheapness, the threefold increase happened in only 15 years, so that 40 per cent of marriages now end in divorce at an ever earlier phase in the marriage. Lawrence Stone, foremost family historian, observes how 'the metamorphosis of a largely non-separating and non-divorcing society, such as England from the Middle-Ages . . . into a separating and divorcing one in the late twentieth, is perhaps the most profound and far-reaching social change to have occurred in the last five hundred years'.[50] With de-institutionalisation of the British family complete, the Law Commission reported in 1988 how it saw no more need to 'buttress the stability of marriage' than other living arrangements.[51]

Children's pain at the betrayal involved in divorce

If it was parental duty which, if nothing else, had always predicated the binding commitment of spouses and overridden their discontents as grounds for dissolving a marriage, this went into reverse in the reform process. Parent-child ties passed under the aegis of free marital choice on the understanding that the parents' rights to pursue their interests was the course most conducive to the welfare of children.[52] By a lucky coincidence 'a marriage that is unhappy for the adults is unhappy for the children and, furthermore . . . a divorce that promotes the happiness of the adults will inevitably benefit the children as well'.[53] That death does not seem to have the adverse consequences associated with separation is attributed to the stigma and difficulty of divorce.

When actual investigations of children's experience of divorce got under way, Ann Mitchell in Scotland found that children respond with disbelief and very few are relieved that their parents part. Those who described argument did not believe this to be sufficient reason for breaking up the family.[54]

Similarly, in America, early researchers were surprised that the overwhelming majority of children whose parents divorced[55] did not necessarily equate conflict with an unhappy family life, and would have preferred to remain with an unbroken family, where there was at least the hope that parents would stop arguing. Such preliminary findings have been massively underlined by the detailed analysis of the long term effects of divorce by Judith S. Wallerstein and colleagues,[56] who found hardly a child pleased or relieved about divorce.

Children's need to make sense of what is happening to them is centred not only on dealing with the conflict but, often much more, comprehending the departure or disappearance of parents. The

> . . . children of divorce . . . taught us very early that to be separated from their father was intolerable. The poignancy of their reactions is astounding. They cry for their Daddies—be they good, bad or indifferent Daddies.

Children may blame themselves for this loss and be anxious that if one parent has gone, then so might the other, or they are frightened of being sent away themselves. Then they live with feelings of rejection, particularly from the same sex parent—with older boys feeling most rejected and wondering how their fathers could leave.

A pain long felt

For long afterwards, children also express wishes and entertain fantasies that the father will return, the mother will be happy, and the family they have always known and loved will be fully restored—even after one or both parents have remarried. At their five year follow-up period, Wallerstein and Kelly found that the majority of the children still hoped that their parents would be reconciled. The 10 to 20 per cent of children which studies show to be actually relieved that their parents part are those who have invariably got away from an abusive, rejecting or otherwise destructive parent. Here the parent-child tie is already absent, or has been abrogated. Only when the child voluntarily places a step-parent in the parental role does *substitution* occur as the active choice of a child who has usually been maltreated or repudiated by the original parent. For most children *their own parents are irreplaceable.*[58] They 'do not perceive divorce as a second chance . . . They feel that their childhood has been lost forever'.[59]

The impetus behind the parents is to escape a marriage which has become unacceptable to at least one party, and to build a new life. But the child compulsively clings to his disintegrating home. With divorce

> . . . children lose something that is fundamental to their development—the family structure. The family is a scaffolding upon which children mount successive developmental stages, from infancy into adolescence. It supports their psychological, physical and emotional ascent into maturity . . . Whatever its shortcomings, children perceive the family as the entity that provides the support and protection that they need.[60]

If infants are such helpless creatures and human young need their parents far longer than any other species, so 'children are tragically aware of the fact'. Accordingly, the reaction to divorce is terror:

> . . . they fear that their lifeline is in danger of being cut. Their sense of sadness and loss is profound. A five-year-old enters my office and talks about divorce with the comment 'I've come to talk about death'.[61]

But, unlike death, divorce as an act of will is experienced as:

> . . . an intentional rebuff to the demand for reciprocity of attachment which is the heart of these [family] relations. People can continue to live while related to the dead beloved, they cannot continue to be related to a living beloved who no longer loves or wishes to be loved.[62]

The pain felt as 'a great wrong'

The child feels not only bereft or forsaken—but judges what has happened as *a great wrong*. Anger and hostility also grow with age towards the parent or parents who the child believes gave priority to their own needs and initiated a separation for which they can see no justification.[63] There is implicit awareness of the moral commitment that provides the framework for cognitive and affective ties—and which must endure despite, and even independently of, the vicissitudes of emotion and fortune. Wallerstein and Blakeslee have 'yet to meet one man, woman or child who emotionally accepts "no-fault" divorce'. Adults almost inevitably blame each other, but rarely themselves. Children 'feel that their parents are to blame for having failed at one of life's major tasks, which is to maintain marriage and family for richer or for poorer, for better or for worse'.[64]

Abandonment or abuse from those who should be the ultimate sanctuary is the final outrage, or treason, because the basis of personal identity and self-worth is profoundly related to and affected by the sense of connection to the family of origin. The 'genesis of the self' proceeds in the context of intimate personal ties, where children are provided with concepts and values which shape self-identity and help root them in a particular language, culture and history. As the family betrays its elemental bonds, the child is victim to an exercise of arbitrary power.[65] The social world becomes unreliable and threatening, throwing doubt on the trustworthiness and legitimacy of the existing order. The separation of parents, with its 'capriciousness of wills, their lack of directness to the common good, and the fact that they could be otherwise but are not—these are the real source of the war of all against all'. Thus:

> Children learn a fear of enslavement to the wills of others, along with a need to dominate those wills, in the context of the family, the one place where they are supposed to learn the opposite. Of course, many families are unhappy. But that is irrelevant. The important lesson that the family taught was the existence of the only unbreakable bond, for better or worse, between human beings.[66]

The effects—depression, abuse, children unprotected and adults miserable

Divorce has not become a more 'normal', healthy and happy exercise as more go through it; the stigma has been removed and single mothers have, if anything, become deserving paragons—defended against any suggestion that one parent cannot provide as good, if not a better, home than the intact family. Instead, there are the reports of severer 'reactions in today's families . . . many more troubled, even suicidal children . . . acute depression in many adolescents . . . a rise in reports of child abuse and sexual molestation'. At the same time, 'all children in today's world feel less protected . . . even those raised in happy, intact families—worry that their families may come undone as well'.[67]

It has also turned out harder than originally believed for adults to sever their marital relationships. This is not surprising considering every individual needs to continually define his identity and place in the world[68] and Western culture has long defined the marriage partner as the most significant other in adult life. Spouses affirm and identify with each others' values and outlook as, over time, a superordinate identity forms, and it becomes difficult for them to see themselves outside the context of the marriage.

Hence, dissolution is personally devastating. Sadly, as well as the majority of children yearning for reconciliation, 50 per cent of divorced men—and up to a quarter of divorced women—wish they were still married,suggesting that divorce ends marriages which are by no means finished and invites marital break-up.[69] Many people do not know if their marriage has ended when they seek legal advice. If instead of receiving institutional affirmation for commitment, they are likely to be conveyed into divorce[70]—this 'inevitably marshals anger and sometimes intense rage—rage that people feel is justified'.[71] This helps to deny responsibility for the marriage's failure. But it is also a defence against feelings of worthlessness and abandonment, combined with a sense of 'having been exploited and humiliated to the core . . .' If, unlike in other life crises, that anger often erupts into violence, so people 'carry around angers that last and last'.[72] The aftermath is marked by high rates of suicide, parasuicide, psychiatric disorder and generally raised morbidity and mortality.[73] Ironically, 'by turning the family into a merely voluntary, optional relationship, we have . . . increased its capacity to make its members unhappy'.[74]

Conditional parenting?

Nonetheless, children's needs for their parents will always arise out of necessity. They have 'unconditional need for and receive unquestionable benefits from the parents: the same cannot be asserted about parents'. Where, therefore, is their motive to care for their children if they are no longer held to lifelong commitment?

Pathetically, there are the remnants of hopes that bounteous nature will oblige and provide the necessary instinctional determinants—

where mothers and even fathers 'bond' with their babies and maybe even couples will 'pair-bond' with each other, like the geese fixated or 'imprinted' on Conrad Lorenz's boots. But where 'rights and individual autonomy hold sway' the children may

> . . . say to the parents: 'You are strong, and we are weak. Use your strength to help us. You are rich and we are poor. Spend your money on us. You are wise, and we are ignorant. Teach us.' But why should mother and father want to do so much, involving so much sacrifice without any reward?[75]

What happens is that the parent-child relationship itself becomes conditional, in the way that modern marriage is conditional. 'Long live the New Family' cries a writer in *Cosmopolitan*.[76] This 'new family' is 'no longer primarily a social institution'. It might have once drawn upon 'duty and service' but now its bedrock is 'companionship and compatibility' and 'Family love . . . whether between partners or between parent and child—can no longer be taken for granted: it must be earned'. So if, for whatever reason, little Sarah or Johnny fails to satisfy—maybe they can join the increasing army of children abandoned by their fathers, and, now, even abandoned by their mothers.

Mothers deserting their children—the flaunting of adultery

The mother-child relationship may provide the primeval demonstration of unconditional love but, as delineated by Helen Franks, if women find that motherhood does not provide gratification, more now decide to pack it in and try something else, preferably with the status, autonomy and money that matter today and which parenthood does not supply.[77] Where this was once unspeakable, life-denying wickedness, we are now invited by the media to understand and empathise with mothers who desert their children. Their behaviour is another option for readers or viewers to consider—if even women with seemingly perfect husbands and children manage to walk out, why not you?

This follows in the footsteps of the way we have been beguiled with the possibilities of sexual infidelity—are you adventurous enough, do you want a change—why not try adultery? After all, we should be free to enjoy life to the limits of our capacity, to keep trying for real happiness. Is it not a sign of our higher personal expectations to keep shopping around for a better deal? And, indeed, more British and American husbands and (particularly) wives are committing adultery earlier, more readily and more often. They also flaunt it more, for is not ego-gratification essential to self-development and status? Yet, infidelity is the misdeed whose confession compounds the original fault, leaving the innocent party subject to the agonizing disappointment or self-hatred that inevitably follows in the wake of betrayal.[78]

De-institutionalisation has not only removed the confirmation essential to the uniqueness of family ties, but relationships are publicly recognised only in terms of temporary convenience. In a concerted drive to change people's perceptions, words like marriage, husband or wife, and parent, are expunged in favour of 'partner', 'relationship' and 'carer'. The presumption that children have two parents with a commitment to each other is mocked as a 'morality from the fairy tales which has to change', or for existing only as 'unreal expectations from a mythical past'.[79] Family defenders are indicted with 'setting up an ideal'—when 'the family' is precisely 'a morally loaded concept embodying an ideal image or model of relationships to be strived for and supported'.[80]

With insistence on the equal standing of all 'family forms' and 'sexualities', homosexuality is portrayed as a natural and normal, even desirable, 'alternative', where sexual release and 'style' are equal to parenthood as the most risky, costly and demanding endeavour of all.[81] Monogamy or promiscuity depend on whether your sex is focal or redistributive. Where 'everybody has their own definitions of family life' or there 'are as many definitions of the family as families', the individual alone chooses what is or is not a family, and anything the individual chooses is a family for her. As a matter of taste or personal inclination, it can always be redefined, reconstructed and discarded. Children 'are not significant in terms of the continuance of a group identity—national, cultural, or familial' but only 'in terms of the personalities of the parents'—like a rug or a Siamese cat.[82] In this triumph of positivism, the world is reduced to neutral facts, none of which is any more remarkable or preferable to the next.[83] The family as the clearest example of an institution based on a transcendent bond gives way to autonomous individuals with random living arrangements and sensory experiences, cut off from millennia of human experience. Without any vision, possible only through the family, of generations which stretch before and after us, much of the motivation for procreation is lost, and the child becomes 'an accident, an anxiety and a reminder of one's isolation'.[84] As such, the downfall of the family as the 'greatest tribute to, and the most brilliant invention of the human moral capacity,'[85] represents the greatest victory of the counterculture as the destroyer of all strictures, all absolutes, all verities—the very concept of verity itself.

The family as the 'Great Satan'

The animus towards the heterosexual married pair in the midst of the celebration of 'diversity' has been sharpened by the diffusion of the 'critical' approach to social analysis. This developed as the scholastic wing of the countercultural revolution, with its combination of self-absorbed hedonism, protest and rejection of every aspect of 'bourgeois' society. Marxist-inspired, it presents a picture of man's entrapment by an oppressive structure whose manifestations are all and everywhere evil. Explanation means revealing how a practice or institution like the family functions to the benefit of an alien and controlling class or power, like patriarchy.[86] All relations are exploitative, anything is an abuse and everything that happens is determined by power.

Thus, parental solicitude, female nurturing, male breadwinning, exist only to imprison men and women in gender identities. Paternal responsibility is no longer the incorporation of the altruistic constraint embodied in parental care into a cultural role, it is the apotheosis of egoistic tyranny and a licence for child abuse.[87] Filial obligations are outrageous for being absolute, and marital fidelity—no more the incorporation into the law of human life of what is implicit in creation—is a device for the enslavement of women. If, through kinship and marriage, men control women's sexuality and expropriate the products of their bodies, so infidelity is one challenge of 'brave' women who refuse to 'legitimate their sex lives'.

Familial commitment and membership, as the template for sympathetic identifications and loyalties which extend far beyond its confines, appear as the prop, as much as the product, of oppressive forces. In this discourse of paranoia, it is the poison of domination soaking through the social structure.[88]

State and individual: alternative bases of order in an alienated world

The answer to oppression invariably involves ridding us of the claims of childhood—as the *sine qua non* for the family. Apparently, it is possible to have a society without any responsibilities which are not optional, because the love 'locked up in the family' (but there corrupted by dependence, service and allegiance) can be redistributed like confetti, over everyone. In practice, the redistribution point is collective professionalised provision, and it is all a variation on the theme that society will spontaneously order itself when all 'need' is met. Here, everyone is 'free for everybody' without having to get involved, or doing anything they have not 'chosen' at that moment. The reality is unremitting alienation from the basis of human culture in which social relationships are grounded.

If this locates morality at the level of the state, then its predominant competitor of late suggests that it can only reside with the individual. Or rather, liberal capitalists propose a moral counterpart to the market economy—where there are no objective values to embody in public institutions. Public policy must be neutral between different conceptions of the good, or expressions of individual choice, in family life as elsewhere—limiting itself to the defence of persons and their property. Law is a technique for controlling behaviour, rather than a body of authoritative commandments: a matter of deterrence in a society which has no idea of the difference between right and wrong.

The misapplication of choice

But morality cannot simply repose in freedom of choice, without any regard for the quality of choices we make, and thus how they might be evaluated with regard to life's aims and values—independently of the person's wants. We make our ethical choices within a specific historical tradition, and within the context of a community in which that tradition is given living substance. It is also in such communities, of which the family is the most basic, that the moral enterprise gets under way as well as being at its most lucid. Freedom cannot arise by isolating man from 'history, from culture, from all those unchosen aspects of himself which are . . . the preconditions of the subsequent autonomy . . . ' With fatal conceit, market liberalism

> . . . tries to stretch the notion of choice to include every institution on which men have conferred legitimacy, without conceding that their sense of legitimacy stems precisely from their respect for themselves as beings formed, nurtured and amplified by these things . . .[89]

If marriage and procreation now appear like other market transactions, then it betokens the way in which, in the wake of the way that most common measures of right and wrong have been rejected by arbiters of culture, 'the liberal-capitalist revolution may have finally broken through the last social restraints placed upon the individual'. The autonomous ego 'untamed by received moral tradition and undisciplined by the responsibilities of family life—appears to be enjoying its afternoon in the sun' before the darkness closes in.[90]

In the absence of moral consensus, coercion is the only instrument for the maintenance of minimal social control. The demand for 'law and order' in a permissive society which, 'at first sight appears to attempt a restoration of moral standards, actually acknowledges and acquiesces in their collapse'.[91] The belief is that enforcement of regulations, not internal stability, is what keeps society from disorder. But if law is no longer regarded as the moral consensus of the community, but the way in which authorities enforce obedience, the subjects do not regard those authorities as benign, rather than hostile and restrictive. To the contrary. It is cynically taken for granted that power corrupts. The prospect of betrayal is omnipresent and, where there is no loyalty, no one will serve. If submission rests on intimidation, not loyalty, men submit 'not to authority, but to reality'.

Social disintegration

Endemic and mass violence already suggest that civilised restraints are much weakened, partly because of a deterioration in the care of the young. If, in the absence of shared moral values, a society must disintegrate, so by the same token 'There has to be a moral base, a sense of right and wrong upon which the stability of family life, the law and the cohesion of society depend'.[92] The de-institutionalisation of the family, its dissolution and social disorder are inextricably linked. If, in our households and in our families we are not bound to keep faith, what hope is left?

CHAPTER 8

Self-Control:
The Family as the
Source of 'Conscience'

Richard Lynn

Riots and self-control

The United States, Britain and many European countries are periodically plagued by riots—usually of youngish people. The reaction to such riots is typically to blame social conditions. Thus in September 1991 there was an outbreak of social disorder in the English city of Newcastle upon Tyne. A number of largely unemployed youths went on the rampage, looting shops and burning buildings. The Archbishop of Canterbury commented on this disorder by blaming 'social deprivation'. 'The events occurred', he told an audience of teachers, 'where people are socially deprived. Human wrong-doing is inextricably linked to social deprivation'. The Archbishop did not say that these young hooligans should be helped to exercise greater self-control over their lawless behaviour or that they should attempt to overcome the sins of violence and sloth. His reaction was typical of modern liberalism.

The traditional recognition of the part played by self-control in morality

Yet the necessity for self-control has played a prominent part in the moral systems of religions. In Christianity, several of the Ten Commandments prescribe self-control, notably the prohibitions on murder, adultery and covetousness. An elaborate medieval view of the sins of lack of self-control was given by Dante in his *Divine Comedy*. These sins were punished in the inferno and are divided into two categories. The less serious sins were punished in the first circles and consist of sins against the self. These are failures to control impulses which harm the self and include lust, gluttony, prodigality and avarice. Here Dante meets Mark Anthony, who was unable to control his passion for Cleopatra and whose weakness led to his own self-destruction. In the lower circles are found those whose sins were against society and which are regarded as more serious because they harm others as well as oneself. Here are found fraudsters, forgers of the currency, the violent and traitors who betray their countries or their leaders, such as Brutus and Judas Iscariot. All these succumbed to temptation of wrong-doing because they had inadequately developed self-control. Hence the importance of self-control has been recognised in Western culture for many centuries. In recent decades, however, this truth has been undermined and there has been an increasing tendency to attribute wrong-doing to social ills rather than to inadequate self-control.

Self-control also recognised in social science

Although it has become fashionable for liberal commentators to blame wrong-doing on social deprivation, among professionals in medicine and the social sciences the importance of developing self-control is well recognised. The principal advances over the last century have been in the description of the concept, analysis of the processes through which self-control is achieved, and theories of the development of mechanisms of self-control during childhood.

The psychopathic personality

Weakness of self-control was first described medically in 1835 by Prichard, a Bristol physician, who identified a condition he termed 'moral imbecility'. His description of the moral imbecile was excellent and could hardly be bettered today:

> The moral and active principles of mind are strongly perverted or depraved; the power of self-government is lost or greatly impaired and the individual is found to be incapable not of talking or reasoning upon any subject proposed to him, but of conducting himself with decency and propriety in the business of life.

The two points made by Prichard were that the impairment is one of what he called 'self-government', i.e., of self-control, and that the moral imbecile is of normal intelligence insofar as he can talk and reason well. The disability is not one of understanding but of moral control over self-destructive, anti-social behaviour.

The term 'moral imbecile' was in general use during the last century but in the present century the vocabulary has changed. The term 'imbecile' to describe a person of low intelligence has been replaced by subnormal or retarded; similarly, 'moral imbecile' has been replaced by the terms 'psychopath', 'sociopath' and 'anti-social personality'. The nature of the condition, however, remains as Prichard originally described it. Whatever it is called, there is a category of people who lack the capacity for self-control.

Two principal advances have been made in the description of the psychopathic personality. First, psychopaths can be classified into several types according to the kinds of anti-social behaviour which they fail to control. There are six main types: these are the aggressive, sexual, inadequate, fraudulent, drug abusing and creative psychopaths. The aggressive psychopath cannot control his anger and the sexual psychopath, his sexual urges. Inadequate psychopaths lack a sense of the moral obligation to work and make a contribution to society. Fraudulent psychopaths break the law in the world of financial dealing and are apparently not uncommon in Wall Street and Tokyo. Drug-abusing psychopaths have no sense of the moral obligation to maintain one's body in good physical condition. Finally, creative psychopaths are those who combine a high level of creative achievement with moral weakness in other spheres. Baudelaire, Augustus John and Bertrand Russell are examples of those who had some degree of this condition. The explanation for this syndrome is probably that high creativity involves an element of rule-breaking and rejection of the consensus way of viewing things, so that some insensitivity and non-conformity to socially accepted modes of thought and behaviour are an element in creative achievement.

A second advance has been in the description of psychopathic mental processes. The most conspicuous of these are an absence of guilt, conscience or anxiety about the future, lack of feelings of affection for others, impulsiveness and inability to control behaviour in the light of probable consequences, although these are known and understood.

A typical psychopath: Charles Manson

To convey an idea of the psychopathic condition it may be useful to sketch the life history of a well-known and typical psychopath. Charles Manson was born to a teenage prostitute. When he was five years old, his mother was jailed for robbery and he went to live with an aunt and uncle. At the age of 14 he left home and started on a career of petty theft. He was arrested and placed in a juvenile detention centre, but he ran away after three days and robbed a grocery store. He was then sent to a reformatory. During his late teens he was sent to 18 juvenile corrective institutions, from which he repeatedly escaped. In 1967 after release from jail at the age of 33, he moved to California, entered the world of flower children and hippies and gained a following known as the Manson family. In 1969 they broke into a house in Hollywood and killed five people, including the movie star Sharon Tate. The bodies were horribly mutilated. Before the gang left they wrote the word 'pig' in blood on the front door. The story is a typical one and has been told many times.

Freud's analysis of self-control

Freud made important contributions to the analysis of the psychological control mechanisms which psychopaths lack. He divided the mind into the id, the ego and the super-ego. The id consists of instinctive biological drives, notably those of sex and aggression. It operates on what Freud called 'the pleasure principle', that is to say the drives demand immediate gratification to obtain pleasure. However, society requires the control of these drives, and for this purpose the ego and the super-ego are developed.

The ego develops to mediate between the drives of the id and the prohibitions of social moves. It acts on the 'reality principle', according to which it recognises that a number of socially proscribed behaviours such as violence, inappropriate sexual behaviour, stealing, lying and the like, are met with punishment and disapproval. Most people dislike punishment and disapproval and control socially unacceptable behaviour likely to incur them through the operation of the ego.

The super-ego is concerned with ideals. It consists of two parts, the ego ideal and the conscience. The ego ideal sets ideal standards of behaviour, while the conscience is concerned with preventing morally objectionable behaviour and thoughts.

Both the ego and the super-ego develop gradually during the course of childhood. The ego develops as young children begin to control unacceptable behaviour because they come to understand that it is likely to be met with punishment and disapproval. The super-ego begins to develop later, typically by the age of five or six.

Children not naturally good

There are a number of elements in Freud's analysis which are widely accepted in contemporary medicine and psychology. First, he proposed that children are not born naturally good with an innate moral sense of socially acceptable behaviour. This sets Freud in opposition to the romantic tradition of Rousseau which holds that children are born good and are corrupted by society. According to the romantic view, it is the fault of society and especially of capitalist society, that people behave wickedly. This tradition remains strong among liberals and progressives, especially in sociology, but in medicine and psychology the contemporary consensus follows Freud.

Two mechanisms of self-control—
fear of consequences and conscience

A second important contribution of Freud was his identification of two separate mechanisms for the control of anti-social behaviour, operating through the ego and the super-ego. The ego checks us for our propensity to behave badly through fear of being found out, punished and disapproved of. The super-ego provides a further checking mechanism through feelings of guilt and conscience. Psychologists working in the field of personality have followed this dual mechanism model. R. B. Cattell uses Freud's terminology and postulates two traits of ego—strength and super-ego strength. These are envisaged as independent personality traits which vary in strength from one individual to another. H. J. Eysenck's personality trait of 'psychoticism' is essentially a super-ego strength trait and is labelled psychoticism because many psychotics as well as psychopaths are weak in the characteristic.

Psychopathic tendencies widespread

A third contribution of Freud lies in his conceptualisation of ego and super-ego strength as continually distributed among the population, in contrast to the opposing idea that psychopathic personality is a disease which marks the psychopath off as qualitatively different from normal people. The disease model would envisage psychopathy as a disease like cancer, which a few people have but most do not. The contemporary consensus follows Freud in adopting the personality model rather than the disease model of the psychopathic personality. According to this view there is a relatively small number of psychopaths in the population, probably amounting to about 2 per cent among males and one-half of 1 per cent among females. In addition there are also quite a lot of people with psychopathic tendencies. These are typically people who commit a few crimes as teenagers but mature into generally law-abiding citizens in their twenties. They may continue to cut corners a bit more than is strictly proper and remain prone to commit minor offences like exceeding speed limits, parking in prohibited areas and so on. In the middle of the continuum are the run of law-abiding citizens who obey the letter of the law although perhaps not always its spirit.

Finally there is a group with exceptionally strongly developed consciences. A good example is given by Robert Graves in his autobiography, *Goodbye to All That*. Graves describes how as a schoolboy he had to catch a train. He was late at the station and the train was just about to depart. There was no time to buy a ticket, so he rushed to board the train, intending to pay later. However, no ticket inspector appeared on the train and no railway official made any effort to collect his fare when he left the station at his destination. So he made his journey without paying. When Graves told his father about this, his father was deeply shocked. He upbraided Graves for his profoundly immoral behaviour. He then went to the original station of departure, purchased a single ticket to the destination, and tore it up. Here we see the operation of an unusually strong super-ego.

The development of self-control

The fourth of Freud's contributions to this issue was his theory of how self-control develops during childhood. He proposed that two processes are involved, namely anxiety and identification. When young children transgress moral rules, their parents typically disapprove of them, except in cases where the parents are themselves psychopathic. The parents' disapproval generates anxiety in the child, and through a process of learning this anxiety becomes associated with proscribed behaviours. Children come to anticipate that unacceptable behaviour is likely to have unpleasant consequences and this acts as a checking mechanism.

The second process involved in the formation of the super-ego is identification. This is the process by which children come to 'identify' with their parents, especially with the parent of the same sex as themselves. In this process the child typically adopts the behaviours, attitudes, beliefs, interests, opinions, and moral values of the parent of the same sex. In practice these are generally agreed family values, because people normally marry those with broadly the same attitudes and values as themselves.

Freud's theory of the operation of these two processes of anxiety and identification in the formation of the super-ego suggests that the psychopathic personality arises when something goes wrong with one or other (or both) of these two processes in childhood. Freud did not give much attention to this question because he was not greatly interested in the problem of the psychopathic personality, but this implication of his analysis has been taken up by a number of psychologists.

The development of moral reasoning and self-control in children

While Freud's theories of the processes and development of self-control are widely accepted as plausible by contemporary psychologists, the prevailing view is that they need to be tested by the normal scientific methods of observation and experiment. The leading work on the development of moral reasoning is that of Lawrence Kholberg.[1] He has devised a series of moral dilemma problems and given them to large numbers of children, adolescents and adults in an endeavour to discover how moral reasoning develops. Kohlberg's conclusion is that moral reasoning develops in three stages which he designates preconventional, conventional and post conventional. In the first, preconventional stage, young children evaluate the morality of behaviour in terms of whether or not it is likely to incur punishment. They believe that if you are punished for something, it must be wrong. This is typical of the moral reasoning of children up to the age of five to six. Children then mature into the second stage of conventional morality. Here it is recognised that society has laws and moral codes to ensure equitable and harmonious relationships and that individuals should obey these. In the third stage of post conventional morality, moral principles are evolved centring around recognition of the equality of human rights and respect for the dignity of all human beings, and the letter of the law has sometimes to be broken in the interests of higher moral principles.

One of the stories used by Kohlberg to study the development of moral reasoning concerns a man whose wife is dying of cancer. She might, however, be cured by an expensive drug. The man cannot afford to buy the drug, so he breaks into a pharmacy and steals a supply. The problem is whether this action was morally justified. In response to this problem a young child in the preconventional stage will say the theft is wrong because people who steal are punished. In Freud's terms, the ego is operating as a self-control mechanism to check socially proscribed behaviour because of an understanding that it incurs punishment. In the conventional stage the child continues to say the theft is wrong, but for different reasons. The theft is now seen as wrong because it breaks the legal and moral code and if everyone broke the code for personal reasons society would face breakdown. In the post conventional stage the adolescent or adult believes the theft may be justified because there are exceptional circumstances where ethical principles must override the legal code. Kohlberg's theory remains controversial and is not fully accepted in all its details by those who work in this field. Nevertheless, he and his associates have collected a good deal of data to show convincingly that children do develop initially a morality based on disapproval and punishment and mature to a more sophisticated morality based on principles of social well-being.

Failure to self-control due to genetic factors and inadequate conditioning by parents

A number of psychologists have taken up Freud's theory that anxiety plays a role in the development of self-control through an association with unacceptable behaviours. This work has been carried out principally in the theoretical tradition of behaviourism initiated by Pavlov in Leningrad and Watson and his successors in the United States. This school emphasises the role of conditioning in the development of behaviour. The leading theorist who has applied conditioning theory to the development of self-control mechanisms involved in moral behaviour is the London-based psychologist H. J. Eysenck.[2]

According to this approach, there are two kinds of conditioning involved in the development of socialised behaviour. The first is known as Pavlovian conditioning because it was first studied extensively in the laboratory by Pavlov. It consists of the development of an association between two stimuli which are presented close together. Pavlov generally worked with presenting a bell and food to dogs, and he found that after some time the dogs could anticipate that when they heard a bell they would shortly receive food. This was shown by the secretion of saliva in anticipation of getting the food.

This initial work was extended to the conditioning of anxiety responses by J. B. Watson and his student, Mary Jones. They presented an infant with a white rabbit and at the same time sounded a loud noise. The noise frightened the infant, and he associated it with the rabbit, so the result was that he became fearful of the rabbit. Eysenck proposes that this is a simple model for the socialisation of children. The theory is that children associate disapproval and punishment with prescribed behaviours. Once this association is formed, anticipatory anxiety acts as a checking mechanism on tendencies to behave in the socially unacceptable ways that have been disapproved of.

This theory suggests that there are two facts involved in the acquisition of moral control mechanisms. The first is the degree to which children feel anxiety when they are punished. Eysenck proposes that there are genetic differences between children in the extent to which they respond to punishment by anxiety. At the extreme there are some children who have minimal anxiety responses to punishment. The result is that punishment has little effect on them. These children fail to acquire the self-control mechanisms that most children acquire and evolve into psychopaths. This explains why psychopaths show little response to punishment and continue to transgress social and legal rules in spite of continual punishments. The theory implies that it should be possible to demonstrate that psychopaths do not readily acquire conditioned anxiety reactions. A number of psychologists have worked on this problem using various forms of conditioning procedure, and by and large the results have shown that this is the case.

Eysenck's theory implies that a further factor involved in the acquisition of moral control will be the effectiveness with which parents apply the requisite conditioning procedures to their children. The study of these parental techniques involves considerable difficulties and convincing evidence has not yet been collected. Nevertheless, it is easy to accept that some parents are poor at providing effective disciplining and training techniques for socialising their children. Others, such as Robert Graves' father, would be much more effective socialisers.

Failure to self-control due to poor adult examples

Freud's theory that the identification of children with their parents as a process by which children come to adopt their parents' moral values has been taken up by Albert Bandwa. In one study Bandwa offered young children a choice between a small candy bar they would be allowed to eat straight-away, and a larger bar they could have in a week's time. This dilemma tests the strength of self-control insofar as the option involving well-developed self-control is to postpone immediate gratification for greater long-term satisfaction. Bandwa had the children observe adults dealing with this dilemma, some of which chose the small candy and others the large. The results showed that the children were influenced in their choices by what they saw the adults doing. The experiment demonstrated that adults act as role models for children and that children adopt the strategies of self-control which they observe in adults.

Failure to self-control due to poor parental socialisation, in turn due to parents with little to lose

The popular image of sociology is of a discipline captured by liberals and leftists for whom the concept of self-control has been devalued and denigrated. Modern sociology, according to this image, teaches that wrongdoing is the fault of society which permits unemployment and inequality. These social ills generate legitimate resentments which frequently and understandably boil over into crime, riot and civil disorder.

There is some justification for this view of contemporary sociology. Nevertheless, there are a number of prominent sociologists who fully recognise the central importance of self-control both for individuals and for a well-ordered society. A leading sociologist who has recently set out this view is James Coleman in his widely acclaimed *Foundations of Social Theory*.[3] Coleman begins his discussion with the sociological concept of norms, i.e., sets of socially endorsed and prescribed modes of behaviour and belief such as telling the truth, behaving honestly and honourably and the like. These norms serve the purpose of controlling the behaviour of individuals whose self-interest sometimes lies in breaking the norms, e.g., by lying in order to escape detection in some misdemeanour. Coleman proposes the existence of what he calls external and internal forms of policing behaviour. External policing is backed up by external sanctions applied to the breaking of norms. Some of these are reinforced by the criminal law and entail legal punishments. Others exert their inhibiting effect through social disapproval, e.g., being late for appointments, rudeness, slackness and so on. Internal policing operates through the conscience. This is developed in the family through the process of socialisation. The object of socialising parents is to get their children to identify with their own norms and incorporate them into a moral system of their own. The advantage of internal policing mechanisms operating through the conscience is that children come to behave in socialised ways in circumstances where there is no possibility of being detected for wrongdoing. This makes internal policing a more efficient process of social control than external policing.

Coleman's general theory of society is based on the axiom of rational choice which states that people act to advance their own interest. Parents socialise their children because it is in their interests to do so. He suggests that this explains why the underclass is relatively ineffective at socialising their children. They have little to lose in terms of loss of social standing and respect if they produce poorly socialised children. The result is that poorly socialised behaviour characterised by high levels of crime, violence, drugs, sexual promiscuity and chronic unemployment have become characteristic of many degraded inner city communities and are transmitted from one generation to the next by parents failing to socialise their children adequately. This theory also explains the decline of moral standards and values which has taken place in North America and Europe over the course of the present century. Growing urbanisation and the weakening of the integrated three generation extended family has had the effect that parents suffer less in terms of social disgrace if they rear poorly socialised children. The result is that parents have been putting less effort into the effective socialisation of their children and public standards of morality have fallen.

Genetic influences on socialisation 59 per cent as opposed to environmental 41 per cent

There is a good deal of evidence that people differ genetically in the strength of their capacity for self-control. This has been generally recognised in the 'black sheep' phenomenon, consisting of the occasional appearance of the psychopath or black sheep in well-socialised families. These individuals have been subject to the right socialisation procedures and exposed to well-socialised role models, yet in spite of this they turn out with psychopathic or poorly socialised behaviour. The most straightforward explanation for these cases is probably that they are born with some deficiency which impairs the development of normal socialisation.

There have been two principal kinds of study designed to investigate the significance of genetic factors for socialised behaviour. These are twin and adoption studies, and criminal records have generally been taken as the criterion of poor socialisation. The twin study method compares the similarity of identical and same sexed non-identical twins. Identical twins have the same genetic constitution and the same environment, and as would be expected, have always been found to be closely similar in every respect. Non-identical twins have only half their genes in common and are therefore genetically dissimilar, although they are reared in similar environments. The amount of similarity between non-identical twins therefore provides a measure of the contribution of genetic constitution to behaviour. The first twin study of this kind was carried out in Denmark by Johannes Lange in the 1920s. He found there was only a 12 per cent similarity between non-identical twins for criminal records, i.e., where one twin had a criminal record the other twin had a criminal record in 12 per cent of cases. This indicates the presence of a strong genetic determination for crime, and in fact Lange called the book in which he published these results *Crime as Destiny.* Ten other studies have been published in a number of countries in Europe, Japan and the United States. All of these indicate that genetic factors play a substantial part in the determination of criminal behaviour. The average of all the studies taken together is a 59 per cent heritability for criminal behaviour, leaving a 41 per cent environmental determination.

The second approach to this problem lies in the study of adopted children. Several studies have shown that adopted children resemble their biological parents in respect of psychopathic behaviour more closely than they resemble their adoptive parents. The major studies of this kind have been carried out in Denmark and Sweden, whose records of the biological parents of adopted children are more readily accessible than in most other countries. The close similarity between adopted children and their biological parents indicates that there must be a substantial genetic factor underlying criminal and psychopathic behaviour.

Conclusions

The problem of the development of self-control is viewed in contemporary psychology as the analysis of how egocentric children normally but not invariably mature into well-socialised adults. There is general consensus that two processes are involved, namely, anxiety about punishment and the development of conscience. Conditioning and identification with role models appear to be the two processes through which control processes over unsocialised behaviour are built up. The genetic constitution of the child is a significant determinant of the effectiveness of the socialisation process.

The scope for reducing social problems due to lack of self-control is centred in the home where so much conditioning, example and socialisation takes place, and in the wider society's use of rules and sanctions.

CHAPTER 9

Fortitude:

The Modern Tendencies to Narcissism and Blaming Others

Adrian Furnham

Bear all inward and outward suffering in silence, complaining only to God.

–L. Gruber

By suffering willingly what we cannot avoid, we secure ourselves vain and immoderate disquiet; we preserve for better purposes that strength which would be unprofitably wasted in wild efforts of desperation, and maintain that circumspection which may enable us to seize every support, and improve every alienation. *–Samuel Johnson*

Fortitute I take to be the quiet possession of a man's self, and an undisturbed doing his duty whatever evils beset, or dangers lie in the way—In itself an essential virtue, it is a guard to every other virtue. *–Locke*

True fortitude is seen in great exploits that justice warrants and that wisdom guides. *–Addison*

The fortitude of the Christian consists in patience, not in enterprise which the poets call heroic and which are commonly the effects of interest, pride and world honour. *–Dryden*

Fortitude—enduring adversity

The diverse troubles of our age—cancer, political persecution, bereavement, natural disasters, a deformed child, racial hatred—have it in common, at least for the unexceptional, that they must be coped with and endured. Fortitude is the name of the virtue concerned. Fortitude, one of the cardinal virtues, means moral strength or courage, particularly unyielding courage in the endurance of pain or adversity. Those with fortitude persevere with the indifference of a stoic. The stoics believed that since the world is the creation of divine wisdom and is governed by divine law, it is man's duty to accept his fate. Fortitude is not synonymous with the acceptance of fate though it may be on occasion. Fortitude is the capacity to endure and cope with adversity. It is a relatively widespread, classless, everyday phenomenon. It is not, like heroism, stoicism or martyrdom: namely, the product of an ideological commitment.

The list of possible synonyms for fortitude could be a list of the names of British 19th-century battleships: Bold; Determined; Endurance; Fearless; Forbearance; Intrepid; Resoluteness; Resolved; Self-controlled; Steadfast; Unwavering. Some of these terms can be found in social science writings, self-controlled, for example, but frequently when they do appear they do so with a pejorative line. Many social scientists see fortitude as stubbornness, inflexibility, dogmatism, and self-control as an outmoded and unhealthy 'coping' mechanism. Indeed it is not always easy to distinguish courage, stubbornness and fortitude. For some it is a matter of the old line: 'I'm firm, you're obstinate, he's pigheaded'. In other words, if people believe that a person is enduring considerable uncontrollable suffering stoically they have fortitude; on the other hand, if they see a person enduring pain, discomfort or humiliation which is stoppable, preventable, even reversible, they may be labelled stubborn, deaf, irrational or worse. Whether this is correct is debatable but it is definitely the case that for fortitude to be seen as a virtue the observer must accept the reactions of the 'sufferer' to an uncontrollable fate.

It would, however, be misleading to argue that there are no accounts of fortitude in the social science literature. For instance, in the literature on death, dying and bereavement there are occasional case studies of those who face the grief of their own or a loved one's death with considerable fortitude.[1] Even more poignant perhaps are the studies on those living under extreme fear or terror such as in concentration camps.[2] Writing by social scientists on the experience of fortitude remains relatively rare: either they write about their personal experiences or observations in total institutions. Those who write most articulately about fortitude tend not to be social scientists. Thus we get theologians, historians and political scientists doing an excellent descriptive and analytic job, but rarely has the social scientist (psychologist, sociologist or whatever) done the necessary conceptual empirical work to elucidate the ideas surrounding the nature of fortitude.

Cynics might argue that social scientists (particularly psychologists) have *not* in fact neglected fortitude: it is far too pervasive and of far too great practical importance. On the contrary, they have made an income out of it; only they call it 'coping mechanism' and charge for training in 'coping strategies'. But this cynical view is not strictly true because fortitude as defined earlier is not really given as a coping mechanism. Even with a changed name and emphasis, the concept does lose something in translation. This chapter will first consider the historical reasons for the disappearance of the concept of fortitude. It will be argued that social forces and cultural change have led to the condemnation of self-realisation and the tendency to blame others and societies' structures for all one's shortcomings. This new values system has no place for fortitude, forbearance and endurance, except perhaps in the competitive world of business and sport. The fact that many social scientists have conspired to hasten the demise of the value and practice of fortitude is greatly lamented.

Fortitude declines as the work ethic is replaced by the leisure and welfare ethic

From various perspectives social science researchers have documented the decline of fortitude and stoicism. Notably the work ethic has been replaced by the leisure and welfare ethic.[3] Many commentators on contemporary culture have attempted to discern trends and patterns that trace the waxing and waning of movements, ethics, cults and social values. One recent and influential analysis of American culture has been that of Lasch, who argues that the dominant American culture of competitive individualism has changed into the pursuit of happiness and a narcissistic preoccupation with self.[4] Fortitude, perseverance, self-control, have given way to self-indulgence.

Central to Lasch's thesis is the decline of the work ethic and what he calls 'changing modes of making it'.

> Until recently the Protestant work ethic stood as one of the most important underpinnings of American culture. According to the myth of capitalist enterprise, thrift and industry held the key to material success and spiritual fulfilment. America's reputation as a land of opportunity rested on its claim that the destruction of hereditary obstacles to advancement had created conditions in which social mobility depended on individual initiative alone. The self-made man, archetypical embodiment of the American dream, owed his advancement to habits of industry, sobriety, fortitude,

moderation, self-discipline, and avoidance of debt. He lived for the future, shunning self-indulgence in favour of patient, painstaking accumulation; and as long as the collective prospect looked on the whole so bright, he found in the deferral of gratification not only his principal satisfaction but an abundant source of profits. In an expanding economy, the value of investments could be expected to multiply with time, as the spokesmen for self-help, for all their celebration of work as its own reward, seldom neglected to point out.[5]

Lasch argued that Puritan values no longer excite enthusiasm or command respect for a variety of reasons: inflation erodes investments/savings; the society is fearfully now—rather than confidently future-oriented; self-preservation has become self-improvement; moral codes have changed. But this change has been graduated over the centuries. For Lasch the Puritan gave way to the Yankee, who secularised the work ethic and stressed self-improvment (instead of socially useful work) that consisted of the cultivation of reason, wisdom and insight as well as money. Wealth was valued because it allowed for a programme of moral self-improvement and was one of the necessary preconditions of moral and intellectual advancement. The 19th century saw the rise of the 'cult of compulsive industry' which was obsessed with the 'art of money-getting' as all values would be expressed or operationalised in money terms. Further, there became more emphasis on competition.

The spirit of self-improvement, according to Lasch, was debased into self-culture—the care and training of the mind and body through reading great books and healthy living. Self-help books taught self-confidence, initiative, and other qualities of success. 'The management of interpersonal relations came to be seen as the essence of self-advancement . . . Young men were told that they had to sell themselves in order to succeed'.[6] The new prophets of positive thinking discarded the moral overtones of Protestantism that were attached to the pursuit of wealth, save that it contributed to the total human good. The pursuit of economic success now accepted the need to exploit and intimidate others and ostentatiously to show the winning image of success.

Envy above esteem

The new ethic meant that people preferred admiration, envy and the excitement of celebration to being respected and esteemed. People were less interested in how people acquired success—defined by riches, fame and power—than in that they had 'made it'. Success had to be ratified and verified by publicity. The quest for a good public image leads to confusion of successful completion of the task with rhetoric that is aimed to impress or persuade others. Thus, impressions overshadow achievements and the images and symbols of success are more important than the actual achievements.

Shifts in emphasis from capitalist production to consumption meant that people had to develop a new pattern of social behaviour. It became important to get on with others; to organise one's life in accordance with the requirements of large organisations; to sell one's own personality; to receive affection and reassurance. The dominant perception was that success depends on the psychological manipulation of one's own and others' positive and negative emotions and social behaviours.

> The growth of bureaucracy, the cult of consumption with its immediate gratification, but above all the severance of the sense of historical continuity have transformed the Protestant ethic while carrying the underlying principles of capitalistic society to their logical conclusion. The pursuit of self-interest, formerly identified with the rational pursuit of gain and the accumulation of wealth, has become a search for pleasure and psychic survival. Social conditions now approximate the version of republican society conceived by the Marquis de Sade at the very outset of the republican epoch.[7]

The cult of narcissism

For Lasch the cult or ethic of narcissism has a number of quite distinct features:

○ The warning of the sense of historical time. The idea that things are coming to an end means that people have a very limited time perspective, neither confidently forward nor romantically backward. The narcissist lives only in, and for, the present.
○ The therapeutic sensibility. Narcissists seek therapy for personal well-being, health and psychic security. The rise in the human potential movement and the decline in self-help tradition has made people dependent upon experts and organisations to validate self-esteem and develop competence. Therapists are used excessively to help develop composure, meaning and health.
○ From politics to self-examination. Political theories, issues and conflicts have been trivialised. The debate has moved from the veridical nature of political propositions to the personal and autobiological factors that lead

141

proponents to make such suppositions.

◦ Confession and anticonfession. Writers and others attempt simple self-disclosure, rather than critical reflection, to gain insight into the pyscho-historical forces that lead to personal development. But these confessions are paradoxical and do not lead to greater, but lesser, insights into the inner life. People disclose not to provide an objective account of reality but to seduce others to give attention, acclaim or sympathy and, by so doing, foster the perpetual, faltering sense of self.

◦ The void within. Without psychological peace, meaning or commitment, people experience an inner emptiness which they try to avoid by living vicariously through the lives of others, or seeking spiritual masters.

◦ The progressive critique of privatism. Self-absorption with dreams of fame, avoidance of failure, and quests for spiritual panacea means that people define social problems as personal ones. The cult suggests a limited investment in love and friendship, avoidance of dependence and living for the moment.

Lasch argues that psychological insights into the narcissistic personality of our time fail to miss the social dimensions of these behaviour patterns such as pseudo self-insight, calculating seductiveness and nervous self-deprecatory humour. This narcissism, or the ethic of self-preservation, appears to many people to be the best way of coping with the tension, vicissitudes and anxieties of modern life. The traits associated with this ethic—charm, pseudo-awareness, promiscous pan-sexuality, hypochondriasis, protective shallowness, avoidance of dependence, inability to mourn, dread of old age and death—are learned in the family, reinforced in the society, but are corruptible and changeable. Ultimately, the paradox of narcissism is that it is the faith of those without faiths, the cult of personal relations for those who are disenchanted with personal relations.

This cynical view of the change of the work ethic into the narcissism ethic is an analysis from a socio-historical view of present-day America. To what extent it is generally or specifically true is uncertain or, indeed, its application to other countries with similar and economic systems. Perhaps because profundity is always associated with pessimism, Lasch's analysis has failed to reveal much good about this narcissistic ethic. While it does seem that some Puritan ideals and virtues have negative consequences for the individual and society that held them, so did some have positive consequences.

Fortitude seen as fatalism

Clearly fortitude is completely antithetical to the cult of narcissism. The idea of enduring pain and adversity is clearly not the spirit of the times. Fortitude in the face of deprivation (relative or absolute) is seen not as desirable, heroic or adaptive, but the opposite. For many, pain, suffering and setbacks are optional, not inevitable. Thus fortitude looks like fatalism or even a sort of sado-masochistic glorification of pain. Lasch's insightful treatment of modern America is probably equally appropriate to modern Europe, with some modification, and goes some way to explaining the decline both in manifestation of, and belief in, the value of fortitude. Like the unfashionable names of one's grandmothers—Constance, Faith, Hope—so the concept of fortitude is unfashionable. Indeed it may have become unfashionable even before modern social science began to have any effect on popular thinking.

Epidemiological and sociological evidence on current inablity to cope with or endure stress

Sociologists working on the topic of adaptation to life stress have come up with a similar analysis. Cochrane and colleagues noted the huge post-war increase in rates of mental hospitalisation, attempted suicide, drug abuse, alcoholism and crime.[8] They argue that the period 1950-1970 saw real and continuing increases in the standard of living in most Western industrial countries including Britain, the diffusion of increased wealth throughout society, and enormous expansion in welfare provision. At the same time, however, deviant behaviour and evidence of psychological disturbance has increased, particularly in the young. Yet this group is the one section of the population that has benefited enormously from increases in material standards of living. Faced with this apparent paradox, Robertson and Cochrane suggested that poor adaptation to stress might be one important explanation. Given that it is probable that the absolute level of daily stress encountered has typically declined, it could be that heightened sensitivity to remaining stresses is related to the above problems. This heightened sensitivity to stress has been brought about by significant changes in values systems that have led people to adopt a particular view of the relationship between themselves and their environment. That is, the way young people distinguish between rights and privileges and their own and others' fault is quite different from that of their parents. Robertson and Cochrane contend that since about the end of World War II, there has taken place a change in popular consciousness, or values, that has had a particular impact on the attitudes and perceptions of everyone in society, but the young in particular. This change has made people much less tolerant of the distressing events which befall most of us.

The emergent value system is organised around two core assumptions. First there has arisen a belief that all human beings are endowed with a set of innate potentials which it is the purpose of life expressly to fulfil. Thus every individual has an intrinsic and equal value to every other, no matter what their station in life, because they have within them great possibilities. This idea is given some support by the contemporary emphasis on psychological growth, self-actualization, subjective experience and self-exploration. The second belief is that the extent to which a person is able to develop and fulful these potentials is contingent upon the social and physical environment within which he finds himself. To invoke a partial analogy the 'potentials' can be seen as a flower which will flourish in a congenial environment but become stunted in an impoverished environment. Further the responsibility for providing the environment means satisfying the needs to express potentials is held to lie in society, not in the individual himself. That is, the state or the government is responsible for making it possible for the person to grow and develop. One of the effects of the interaction between these two beliefs has been to extend the concept of welfare beyond providing minimal material needs to providing for psychological needs. Educational institutions in particular have responded by transforming those elements of schooling held to be inhibiting or constricting personality growth into opportunities for creativity and self-expression.[9]

Self-discovery and self-expression above fortitude

Implicit in this description of the new value system is a contrast with an older system which puts personal achievement, accomplishment and reputation in the place of self-development, and locates responsibility for success or failure in these endeavours firmly within the individual. In the older, rejected value system, fortitude is valued, self-discovery and personal emotional expression played down. Young people in particular who were socialised into the new system of values will have been influenced to much greater extent than those socialised before this era (i.e., pre-war). There is in fact evidence that value systems once formed remain stable and are relatively unaffected by changes in personal circumstances. This goes against the grain of popular thinking which suggests personal values vary over time. It implies, therefore, an older generation schooled in fortitude but a younger one rejecting it.

The decline in influence of religion and the search for an alternative secular basis for morality, and the advent and spread of the welfare state must have played a part in this new value system. It has no doubt been shaped also by an antithetical reaction to the tenets of self-reliance, personal responsibility, and fortitude, and the consumption of goods. The modern age has fostered the development of new attitudes and assumptions, which are appropriate to the notion of consumption, rather than production, as a dominant goal in life.

Turner[10] argues that central to contemporary social movements

> . . . is the view that men have the right to demand assurance of a sense of personal worth from society . . . The novel idea . . . that a lack of a sense of personal worth is not private misfortune, but public injustice, is carried by youth, who are the main constituency for the new movements in the same manner that a rising industrial class and later a rising working class were constituencies in the earlier era.[11]

Robertson and Cochrane used epidemiological evidence on addiction, admission to mental hospitals, conviction, suicide and parasuicide to test their hypotheses about culture change. They

> postulated that an individual with a heightened sense of deprivation will have a diminished threshold of tolerance to stress or frustration. He will feel that he should not be called upon to undergo frustrations to any degree, because these constitute an affront to his expectations about his own freedom to develop and to what he considers are the responsibilities of society. The older value systems might have regarded stresses as something to be borne stoically, or even welcomed as a challenge to character, but this concept is alien to those imbued by the new world-view. When such an individual encounters frustration he is more likely to react to it as intolerable, and resort to one or more types of deviance. This may take the form of escape or withdrawal—as in suicidal behaviour or drug abuse—or an attempt at extracting reparation from society—as in the case of delinquency. In the case of psychiatric disturbance, we would suggest that possessors of the new consciousness will tend to interpret relatively minor feelings of tension, anxiety or depression—perhaps brought on by feelings of deprivation—as evidence of mental disturbance; whereas individuals whose perceptions are governed by the old consciousness will define these

same feelings as 'morbid preoccupation', or as indicating that they need to 'get a grip' of themselves. Individuals in the former group are therefore likely to consult a doctor for less severe levels of disturbance, whereas the latter group will seek treatment only when such symptoms become relatively more serious. It is thus predicted that individuals whose thinking is guided by the new world-view (i.e., the young) and who live in 'objectively' deprived circumstances, will have a higher probability of becoming deviant.[12]

Resenting adversity as 'unjust'

It could be argued that an individual with the 'new value, new age, post-industrial' system will react differently to everyday life stresses than will individuals with the traditional value system who encounter the same stresses. They will be more conscious of, or more sensitive to, such pressures because they view them both as *unjust* because they stem from social rather than personal causes, and as *intolerable* because they tend to obstruct progress towards (and direct attention and energy away from) self-expression and the fulfilment of individual potentials, which is seen as the major purpose of life. There is no room in the new value system for fortitude or fulfilment through suffering which may have moderated the responses to stress of those guided by precepts of self-help, individual initiative and self-denial which are fostered by the old value system. The narcissism of the new-age philosophy has reduced everyday tolerance of stress. They feel that they should not be called upon to undergo frustration and should have freedom to develop. When encountering life stresses such individuals are more likely to resort to one or more forms of deviance and to experience more psychological problems. The possessors of the new value system will tend to interpret relatively minor feelings of tension, anxiety or depression brought about by life stresses as evidence of mental disturbance, whereas individuals whose perceptions are governed by the old value system will define these same feelings as morbid preoccupation or as indicating that they need to 'get a grip' on themselves. Individuals in the former group are therefore predicted to report more symptoms and to be more likely to seek professional help when stressed than are the possessors of the old ethos. Certainly fortitude is central to the old value system and completely lost in the new.

Fortitude scorned: the case of welfare payments

Certainly another major reaction to the complete lack of fortitude of young people may be seen in public opinion surveys of social security or welfare recipiènts. In nearly all countries that established comprehensive welfare systems after the Second World War there is a widespread belief that it is frequently abused and may be in the long term actually bad for the claimant.

In their extensive and scholarly review of press and public attitudes to welfare, Golding and Middleton report considerable evidence from numerous countries of what they call the welfare backlash—namely, negative attitudes to welfare.[13] The document details press exposure of people who abuse the system—in other words, those who believe in, or exploit the welfare ethic. The authors detected a number of themes: the known cases of welfare abuse are just the tip of the iceberg; it is suggested that it is common knowledge that social security/welfare fraud is extremely widespread; that although welfare is a right there is no boundary between the taxpayer and the claimant. Secondly, that the welfare umbrella of the nanny state has extended over too wide a range of clients, at great social, bureaucratic and administrative cost. Thirdly, that many of the recipients of welfare are the undeserving poor or super-scroungers. Fourthly, that the social security/welfare system is failing adequately to control its clientele, that it has become too easy to get, and that welfare benefits have become excessively generous, encouraging indolence and insulting the honest worker.

Most researchers in this area are sociologists who are eager to expose errors in public opinion and consider that excessive 'scrounger-hounding' is unnecessary. It may well be the case that the amount of abuse of the welfare system is grossly over-reported. Nevertheless, it would be equally erroneous to believe that it did not exist.

Taylor-Gooby has pointed out that whereas most people are in favour of some aspects of welfare, they are against others.[14] Many, it seems, make the old-fashioned but obvious distinction between the deserving and undeserving poor. More importantly perhaps, he found evidence for various values associated with welfare payments. These include:

- Reduces self-help—the idea that welfare makes people less willing to look after themselves.
- Increases integration—it makes for a more integrated, caring society.
- Increases the tax burden—that whether it is good or bad, it intolerably

increases tax.
◦ Reduces the work ethic—it saps the will to work, which presumably is extrinsic not intrinsic.
◦ Increases stigma—it makes people who get benefits and services from welfare feel like second-class citizens.
◦ Helps the undeserving—it provides people who do not deserve it with a source of income.
◦ Increases social justice—by being a more compassionate and equally distributed society.
◦ Increases indiscriminate allocation—paradoxically, it tends to help people who do not need help.

Sociologists lament and lambast public opinion for being cruel, unsympathetic and inaccurate. They seem particularly sensitive to the idea that fortitude, self-reliance and independence are virtues not failings.

Encouraging young people to blame everyone except themselves

Pyschologists too have provided two theoretical approaches which are relevant to the issue of fortitude. The first comes from the attribution theory which seeks to explain how, when and why people make moral and causal attributes for everyday events. Many theories exist but there remains a certain amount of agreement about the process. For instance, it has been demonstrated again and again that people have a natural tendency to explain their own success in terms of their effort and natural aptitude while attributing failure to external factors (like society, powerful figures, God, chance or fate).

A number of causes are used to explain success or failure in achievement-related and other everyday contexts. The primary perceived causes of achievement-related outcomes are ability and effort, but the difficulty of the task, luck, mood, and help or hindrance from others are included among the other possible explanations of success and failure. Causes are inferred on the basis of several factors, including specific informational cues (e.g., past success history, social norms, pattern of performance), causal perferences, rules that relate causes to effects (causal schemata, reinforcement history) and communications from others.

The perceived causes of success and failure have been classified within various systems, labelled locus of causality (internal versus external). One of the most interesting, important and powerful distinctions is that of locus of control which divides people into instrumentalists and fatalists, those with internal versus those with external locus of control.

A distinction made by de Charms between 'origin' and 'pawn'[15] is similar to Rotter's differentiation of internal and external control.[16] De Charms states:

> We shall use the terms 'Origin' and 'Pawn' as shorthand terms to connote the distinction between forced and free. An Origin is a person who perceives his behaviour as determined by his own choosing; a Pawn is a person who perceives his behaviour as determined by forces beyond his control . . . Feeling like an Origin has strong effects on behaviour as compared to feeling like a Pawn. The distinction is continuous, not discrete—a person feels more like an Origin under some circumstances and more like a Pawn under others.
>
> The personal aspect is more important motivationally than objective facts. If the person feels he is an Origin, that is more important in predicting his behaviour than any objective indications of coercion. Conversely, if he considers himself a Pawn, his behaviour will be strongly influenced despite any objective evidence that he is free. An Origin has a strong feeling of personal causation, a feeling that the locus of causation of effects in his environment lies within himself. The feedback that reinforces this feeling comes from changes in his environment that are attributed to personal behaviour. This is the crux of the concept of personal causation and it is a powerful motivational force directing further behaviour. A Pawn has a feeling that causal forces beyond his control, or personal forces residing in others, or in the physical environment, determine his behaviour. This constitutes a strong feeling of powerlessness or ineffectiveness.[17]

There is considerable evidence to suggest that being an internal instrumentalist, an Origin, is healthy and adaptive. The belief that one is master of one's fate, captain of one's ship and controller of the environment is desirable because one is less ready to accept and ascribe setbacks and misfortunes to powers beyond one's control. People may accept their fate with stoicism but fortitude is associated with those who persevere in the belief that they can act on their destiny.

In addition to influencing interpersonal evaluation, attributions also affect personal reactions to success and failure. Particular causal attributions are associated with specific emotional reactions. For example, success because of ability promotes feelings of competence; while success attributed to helpful others elicits gratitude; and success from luck generates surprise. For failure, causal ascriptions to a lack of ability promote feelings of incompetence; failure due to others who are perceived as hindering goal attainment elicits aggression; failure due to lack of effort gives rise to feelings of shame and guilt; and so on. The affective consequence of internal versus external attributions appears to be the main functional significance of the perceived locus of causality.

Expectations about the future and emotional reactions are, it is argued, mediated by causal attributions, which also influence the choice, intensity, and persistence of behaviour. Attributions of failure to a lack of ability are particularly debilitating, perhaps because ability is a stable cause (in that it does not change over time) that also generates feelings of incompetence. On the other hand, causal attributions of failure to a lack of effort seem to enhance performance.

In lay terms, blaming yourself—specifically your lack of ability—has been shown to be unhealthy. It leads to shame, depression, hopelessness and helplessness. Depression is seen as the major cause of internal attributions for failure. Psychotherapists and others favour attributional therapy which aims to change people's negative attributions even if they are true, because of their harmful consequences. Instead of recommending fortitude other causes are found. All too frequently people who *have* experienced failure, be it educational, occupational, matrimonial or whatever, find it easier to blame nebulous and often innocent parties or vague concepts like society. Indeed they may be encouraged to do so by psychologists.

We may have socialised young people into an external locus of control (Pawn-think) whereby they find it easier and acceptable to blame their woes on others and society rather than on their own lack of ability and effort. Indeed then, the disappearance or relative neglect of the various symptoms for fortitude may be cited as evidence for this fact. Whereas it is true that people should not be encouraged to attribute personal weakness to various failings beyond their control, it may be even more dangerous to allow or actually encourage ordinary people to believe they, through intelligence, mischief or sloth, are not the prime cause of their plight.

Where fortitude is valued—sport

There do remain, however, certain areas of life where fortitude is valued. One is the sports field where for some there can be 'no gain without pain'. Sportsmen and women need to dedicate their lives to their sport to be successful. Here they learn the meaning of endurance, the importance of fortitude and the benefit of personal effort.

In a very interesting set of observations, Ritzer, Kammeyer and Yelman have implied that the norms that govern sport are not dissimilar from those of the work ethic.[18] Sport is thought of in many countries as an important and healthy socialization experience for young people, and it is assumed that they learn many important lessons, even the virtue of fortitude.

Consider the sporting norms which have 'become a conservative force functioning to maintain and reinforce certain of the traditional American values, beliefs and practices while countering others'.[19] These include:

∘ Sportsmanship—this emphasizes adherence to the rules; acceptance of the decisions of game officials and the desire to uphold the regulations governing the sport. Also a vital aspect of sportsmanship is the concept of magnanimity in victory and the gracious acceptance of defeat.

∘ Competition—social Darwinism is alive and well in the philosophy of sporting enthusiasts. There is consistent legitimization of the idea that competition produces the best players, and those less able to accept their lot with fortitude.

∘ Success—the well-known statement by Lombardi: 'Winning isn't the important thing—it's the only thing'. In other words, it is not exclusively the joy of participation but the possibility of winning that makes athletes. Hence the numerous and consistent ways in which achievement is recognized through prizes and awards.

∘ Universalism—sport is open to all, irrespective of race, class, age, sex, etc., and one is judged entirely and exclusively by the quality of one's athletic performance. In other words, people are to be evaluated according to one criteria—their sporting prowess.

∘ Diligence—the great Puritan virtues of perseverance, fortitude and hard work are to be found in sport. Asceticism pervades all sport with its emphasis on personal sacrifice, long and strenuous preparation and stamina.

∘ Self-discipline—it is frequently held that sporting people need to develop the necessary internal locus of control and personal habits that will enable them to achieve their best possible performance. A life of order, self-discipline and self-control is therefore advocated.

∘ Teamwork—although not true of all sports, this virtue consists of co-operation and unity and is emphasized greatly in team sports.

However, as is quite apparent, some of these values are in conflict with one another: individualism conflicts with teamwork. Nevertheless, the outward portrayal of the sporting ethic which may be seen on sports lockers and in slogans, in post-success sporting speeches, and in sports commentators, is remarkably similar to that of the work ethic. Because of its open and competitive nature, fortitude is a much valued trait among sports-minded people. Indeed, the lack of interest among the young for some more skill-based sports that require considerable dedication and the relatively poor showing of a once great sporting nation (i.e., Great Britain) may in part be attributed to the under-valuation of fortitude and the sport ethic.

The dangers of fortitude

It is true that fortitude can only really be a virtue when it is applied appropriately. Alas, many zealous people show fortitude despite the fact that they are pursuing an irrational, amoral, immoral or emotional cause. Religious bigots, fanatical believers and others of that ilk find it easy to demonstrate fortitude in the face of opposition. Indeed, opposition, contempt, abuse inspire their fortitudous activities much more than apathy. Believing one is right, that God is on one's side or that one had exclusive claims on being just is the ideal spur to fearless endurance, resolute forbearance and determined fortitude.

Equally disturbing may be that pursuance of a goal with fortitude may make people callous and insensitive to the needs of others. In this sense people can become blind to others' rights or arguments.

Psychologists interested in authoritarianism and dogmatism see in the behaviour of some a terrifying fortitude that is rightly not considered admirable. In short, the dangers of fortitude are that it may be applied to an irrational, indeed unnecessary end. The pursuance of this goal with fortitude may blind people's natural scepticism and lead them to create greater evil. Psychologists may argue that distinctions should be made in the cause of personal stress and where the cause is truly beyond one's control fortitude may be an appropriate response, but where the cause is controllable, suitable action should be taken.

Yet enough has been said to indicate that current neglect of fortitude is not without peril

The moral concept of fortitude has practically gone out of everyday language. Where it does occur it has been secularized, psychologically translated and transformed. Reasons for this are socio-historical mass movements, cultural change and significant alterations in people's expectations, outlooks and behaviour. Despite increasing individualism them with fortitude.

To this extent ordinary people seem to prefer sociological rather than psychological explanations for an individual's life adjustment and status. Certainly they strongly reject any moralistic explanations which are perceived in highly pejorative tones. Thus many people are happy to view personal weakness, lack of success, even mental illness and criminal deviance not as personal misfortune that has to be endured, nor the result of lack of fortitude that can be corrected. Rather they are seen as the results of inequality and injustice from a society whose structures in some sense favour the successful over the unsuccessful.

This fact can be observed in the choice of a society's heroes and heroines. Past generations took as their heroes those who had demonstrated considerable fortitude such as Scott of the Antarctic of Florence Nightingale. The outcome of the endeavour was less important than the way people endured adversity. Phlegmatic and stoical in the face of danger and opposition, past generations' heroes stand in strong contrast to those of today.

CHAPTER 10

Honesty, Honour, and Trust:

The Decline of Self-Policing in Society

Robert Grant

Honesty—central among the virtues

On one reckoning, actions can be rated simply according to the desirability of their consequences. Virtue resides, however, neither in the bare action nor in its outcome *per se*, but in the disposition which the desire or intention to secure a certain outcome in performing it displays. In short, virtue is a matter of choice, motive, and character. Virtue, or the virtues collectively, are what we normally call goodness.

It is possible that honesty is central among the virtues: most others have more than a tincture of it; *l'honnête homme*, indeed, is French for the good man. The one virtue with which it does not seem to have a wholly reciprocal relationship is courage. Honesty certainly requires courage but, unless we want to distinguish between kinds of courage (seeing some, for example, as mere insensibility, or as desperation), it will be admitted that the dishonest may also be courageous.

On the other hand, honesty resembles courage more than any other virtue, in that to impugn someone's honesty, just as to accuse him of cowardice, is to thrust at the heart of his whole self-conception (or honour). A man may confess to improvidence, intemperance, or idleness, and be thought little the worse of; he may even boast of his unchastity; but he cannot admit to cowardice or dishonesty, or be detected in them, without shame. His shame will be mitigated only by his still being honest enough actually and visibly to feel it.

There seem to be three kinds, or rather modes, of honesty: honesty towards oneself; honesty towards others; and honesty towards the world ('the world' being understood as reality, or the objective sum of

157

things). The first and third are clearly related since, simple error or others' deception apart, apart also from paranoia or unwarranted sexual jealousy, one's main reason for believing things to be otherwise than they are is that to do so is usually more gratifying, flattering, or comfortable than to face or care about the facts. Self-deception of this kind, like all dishonesty, is a form of selfishness or self-regard (though it involves insufficient regard for the self that really matters, that is, too little self-respect). It amounts to fantasy, or wishing to manipulate reality. And here, of course, the second form of honesty enters in, since others are a part of reality, and dishonesty, which is one way of manipulating them, is a denial of their objective moral claims and (so to speak) existential parity with oneself.

Honesty necessary for society

There are also three justifications of honesty: we may call them the Benthamite, the Kantian and the Aristotelian. A Benthamite or utilitarian justification would say simply that honesty if generally observed works to the general advantage. As we shall see, the assertion is readily confirmed. However, it does not tell me why I should be honest. For, if all are honest but me, I put myself at an enormous advantage.

A Kantian justification, at least of honesty towards others, would rest on two things: on my duty as a rational being to treat them as ends in themselves, and on the absolute value (not to say beauty) of duty performed purely for its own sake, free of all interest. Both considerations have an intuitive plausibility. But neither gives us any immediate reason why we should be honest with ourselves and about the world, except that the alternative is irrational. For that to count, it would have to matter to me whether I was irrational or not.

Both Kant and Bentham reduce the moral agent to an abstraction: in Kant's case, to a transcendent, undifferentiated rational will in stark contrast with the unique empirical persons with whom it has to deal (and which are what human ends-in-themselves must surely be); in Bentham's, simply to one of so many identical utility-receptacles (of which 'each is to count for one, and none for more than one'). Neither takes account of the seeming paradox that we have an interest in our own disinterestedness; an interest which Kant must rule out absolutely, and which for Bentham could scarcely count as one, since it has to do not with the individual's objective, quasi-material 'utility', but with his self-conception as a person. In such matters it is not Kant, much less

Bentham, but Aristotle or Hegel whom we should be consulting.

Without honesty we cannot be ourselves

The self is not given, but made. It is an artefact, created in response to other selves, which, in turn, we recognise as such by analogy with our own dawning selfhood. In his parable of the Master and the Slave, Hegel intimated that true selfhood cannot be achieved except where selves are mutually perspicuous; in other words, except on a basis of honesty. Where the Master holds the Slave in terror, the Slave, to survive, must lie and flatter. So what the Master receives from the Slave is no more than the reflection of his own will. He has denied himself the only authentic confirmation of his selfhood, namely, the unforced, honest regard of another, and he has done so by not according to the Slave the minimal (Kantian) regard due to him as a rational being. It follows that the Master (so long as he remains Master) can never achieve self-knowledge.

Apart from an important political lesson (one re-stated not much later in Shelley's 'Ozymandias'), what emerges is what we knew all along: that knowledge, truth, objective reality and (most importantly) *self*-knowledge are accessible only to honesty. It should be said that in Hegel's fable the Master in fact stands for any subject of consciousness, and the Slave for any object, whether or not personal; so that Hegel's analysis has both an ethical and a general epistemological significance.

This is important, because it bridges the gap between *ought* and is. Of course the subject (or person) has a direct interest in his own honest or undistorted perception of reality, since his safety depends on it (here the Slave has the advantage, for he 'sees' the Master as the Master, having enforced his silence, cannot 'see' him). But it is equally obvious that a person's self-knowledge (in which, unless he is a fool, he must have an interest of sorts) depends upon his renouncing his self-interest sufficiently to be able to concede to the objects of his attention their moral or quasi-moral right to exist independently of his will. However, he cannot do this *in order* to achieve self-knowledge, for those objects then remain instrumental to it. He must do it spontaneously, morally, for its own sake and theirs.

Honesty useful, for instance, in wealth-creation

The utilitarian or pragmatic relation between honesty and self-interest is easily enough illustrated. Without at all subscribing to his general outlook, one might cite Freud's 'reality principle', which not only holds the more primitive 'pleasure principle' in check, but is also, Freud says, its ultimate 'safeguard', in guaranteeing to the organism the maximum quantity of 'pleasure' compatible with its survival.

Again, it is clear that honesty is essential to efficient wealth-creation. Fraud and theft merely transfer wealth from some to others, and, if the element of injury is reckoned in, represent an overall loss of utility rather than a simple constant sum (such as is found in many gambling activities, in which, unlike the victim of dishonesty, no-one is forced to participate). Let us rule out whatever minimum of honest acquisition may actually be a duty (in that it prevents oneself and one's dependents from becoming a charge on others), and assume, arbitrarily, that any further acquisition can be put down to self-interest. Even if that assumption is correct, it appears that honesty is still necessary if all-round utility is to be maximised, in other words, if wealth is to be created.

Importance of trust in business

Modern commercial societies cannot flourish except on a basis of trust, that is, without a well-founded presumption by the transacting parties of each other's honesty. In the City of London, to take an extreme example, billions of pounds' worth of business is done daily on no more security than verbal undertakings. It is neither possible nor necessary to invoke the laws of contract in every one of these myriad transactions. What sustains the arrangement is the extreme moral opprobrium, together with the (purely informal) sanction of exclusion from the market, which attaches to promise-breaking.

But honesty also valuable where 'useless'

Such 'functional' explanations, however, do not fully explain why honesty is valued for its own sake. Those who, to save their lives, have compromised their honesty (told lies or lived them, betrayed the good or the innocent) are frequently haunted thereafter by a sense of guilt; one so extreme, in many cases, as to have led them, in the end, to take the very lives they once sought to save. Honesty may be useful, it may even have an evolutionary, survival-related origin, but its *essential* uselessness has never been better demonstrated than by dissidents in totalitarian societies, who have had the courage—in art, in human relations, in politics, and in academic and scientific endeavour—to challenge the prevailing empire of lies, always at the cost of their own and their families' material welfare, and sometimes even of their lives. What is it that can lead men and women so to bear witness to the truth, either as it is, or as they see it? (So much, by the way, for the Marxist idea that morality reflects the interests of the 'dominant' class.)

Honesty and honour interdependent

The answer, 'honour', is at once clear and obscure, since why should something so contrary to self-interest, and even to survival, be valued? I can suggest only one explanation which the agent himself might reasonably accept as the motive for his actions, which is this: that it is, in an Aristotelian sense, our 'nature' to value honour, and the honesty which both implies and is implied by it. (Such valuations, of course, have to be learned, but there is no paradox here, since self-conscious learning or cultural transmission is natural to human beings.) Our self-respect and self-fulfilment—our identity, in short—depend upon our honour; that is, upon our asserting our freedom to do otherwise than as selfishness dictates.

Selfishness (that is, 'narrow' self-interest) we perceive as a kind of slavery; as a submission to that part of ourselves which we wish to repudiate as ignoble, even though we recognise it as ours, and hence as an occasion of shame (an intuition captured in the concept of original sin). Except fleetingly and superficially, we do not wish to be 'free' of our obligations. We wish, rather, to be free to fulfil them as best we can, and to assert that right (or duty) against all obstacles and counter-compulsions. Honour, like love, is a form of bondage; but one in which we feel ourselves to be free, and in comparison with which mere licence is servitude.

Some existentialists (notably Nietzsche and Sartre) invert this analysis, claiming that to acknowledge obligations is 'inauthentic'. To be inauthentic is to be heteronomous, that is, to be 'compelled' or 'determined' by something outside oneself. Authenticity, therefore, is a peculiarly modern version, or (as Aristotle would say) perversion, of the idea that freedom and honesty are complementary. However, on the view I have been presenting, the self is not so much determined as actually constituted by its moral ties to others. And what could be more like compulsion than one's own egoism, especially when made the object of a novel and bizarre form of obligation? Can it really be called honesty or self-knowledge, let alone honourable, not only to acknowledge my own egoism, but also to vaunt it, even if I disguise it as 'commitment' to some self-chosen, and usually violent or morally repulsive, cause? Come to that, how can I obey the injunction to be authentic if obedience *per se* is inauthentic?

Of course, like the typical Ibsen heroine, one may often have a selfish motive for meeting one's conventional obligations, or even, like Dostoevsky's 'underground man', gloat over one's 'authentic' hypocrisy in meeting them. It is true also that honesty, or bearing witness to the truth, can be made to look like selfishness, as the Communist authorities frequently alleged in their propaganda outbursts against dissidents, and contrived (after a fashion) to make fact by taking their families hostage; true again, that conscience, though it exists and is admirable, is all too often (and as Hegel observed) a form of arrogance or self-display.

But these considerations do no more than complicate the picture. They require only that, before approving any given set of moral demands, we inquire into the kind of society which makes them. There can be no doubt about official Communist society; but 19th-century Norway, and various Puritan communities, even though all may have seemed to make sense to themselves, may also deserve censure, and not merely by the blancmange-like standards of contemporary Western liberalism.

The latter deserve comment, since, although honesty, in some of its guises, is still among them, honour in the old sense is not, and it may be doubted whether honesty, or any other virtue, can long survive without it. Nor can it without trust (of which more shortly). Fortunately what I have called contemporary Western liberalism goes a good deal less deep than the noise made by its spokesmen might suggest.

The denigration of honour

The prevailing cynicism concerning honour, and the consequent fashion for denigrating it, seem to be due mainly to its aristocratic and military connotations. These run counter to 'democratic' values, which (in our, though not in the classical republican, conception of them) are liberal, individualist, egalitarian, hedonistic and rationalist. Traditionally, honour is associated with loyalty to family, school, regiment and country, and implies that the individual is not all-in-all, but depends for his identity on institutions beyond himself (which will be disgraced along with him, should he lapse from the expected standard). There is a kind of parallel here with the connection between a man's honesty and his purchase on external reality.

Even worse, honour is traditionally imputed to some people for no better reason than that their office or rank (the real object of respect in such cases) is imagined to demand it of them. A dustman, simply as a man, is vulnerable to dishonour, but not nearly so much so as a duke. It should be said, however, that if we expect less of a dustman than of a duke, either because he is 'only a dustman' (the traditional view), or because he is in some way 'deprived' (the modern view), we in fact dishonour him. If (as Falstaff says) 'honour is a mere scutcheon', this will not matter; but from a liberal-egalitarian, 'democratic' standpoint, as from a Kantian, it surely ought to matter.

Generally (and as Dr. Johnson ironically observed of prodigies), honourable conduct appears in proportion as it is expected. We say of someone who has behaved badly that we 'would have thought better' of him, and that he has 'let down' not merely us, but himself too. Far from sneering at honour, therefore, we have good reason, if we want to see honesty prevail, to attribute honour to as many people as possible.

Trust essential to honesty

Secondly, trust. Trust is central to honesty. Where it is lacking, one of the motives to honesty, albeit a largely prudential one, is weakened. Your honesty gives me reason to trust you; my trust in you inclines you to think that I must be honest, and therefore gives you reason to trust me. If you distrust me, I may consider you suspiciously familiar with the ways of dishonesty, and may even ask myself why I should deal honestly with you.

Government regulation—a poor substitute when trust breaks down

A prime, if somewhat paradoxical, characteristic of contemporary liberalism is its obsession with regulation. Where honesty breaks down, rather than address ourselves to the reasons for its failure, we instinctively seek to add yet another layer of controls. Yet virtue, though it can be taught, cannot be enforced, any more than belief. Outward conformity to its requirements, however, can, and it might seem that no more were needed. But there is a triple price to be paid: first, the expense of policing conformity; second, the consequent reduction of liberty; and, worst of all, the erosion of virtue itself.

Excessive regulation destroys virtue, since, even if the subject is otherwise disposed to it, the penalties for disobedience make him unsure whether he is really choosing freely. They call his virtue into question where it is most important, in his own eyes. Compulsion also destroys trust; that is, the disposition to believe in another's truth or honesty. The more numerous the possibilities of non-compliance, and the more dangerous its consequences, the less trust there must be, since to inform on deviance or suspected deviance will always be in somebody's interest, and most will accordingly be led to mistrust, and eventually, deceive, their fellows.

Such was the condition of daily life under Communist governments. It would have been the same even if (as in Calvin's Geneva) what they sought to enforce had been virtue, rather than its opposite. The all-pervading atmosphere of suspicion and delation was, in fact, the result less of what they sought to enforce, than of the fact that they sought to enforce it, even at the most private, microscopic or 'capillary' levels of cultural existence. If dishonesty in all its forms could be outlawed, and sanctions against it made effective, we should nevertheless find not dishonesty, but honesty, driven underground.

'Political correctness' destroys both honesty and trust

A more up-to-date example is the attempt in some American universities to impose 'political correctness', or as one might call it, pseudo-virtue. Where 'PC' has taken hold, staff and students alike live in constant fear of denunciation by spokespersons (often merely *ad hoc* spokespersons seeking advancement) for supposedly disadvantaged 'minorities'. (The latter, interestingly, include women, who are actually a majority, not only of the human race, but perhaps also even at some universities.) What PC has done to promote friendly relations between them and the 'majority', or to abate any genuine disadvantages they may chance to suffer, is not hard to imagine. Moreover, PC extends beyond campus manners into teaching and research, so that academic opinions are assessed no longer according to their scientific truth or plausibility, but simply according to whether or not they are PC. Novel pseudo-disciplines, such as 'women's studies', have been designed almost entirely around foregone PC conclusions.

Where truth, objective inquiry, and free intellectual exchange are at an end, so too are honesty (no matter with how much rootless moral urgency its enemies may invest their crusade) and, of course, the university itself. Fortunately, and unlike its totalitarian counterpart, all this nonsense has no power to silence external criticism (it has already made a priceless gift of itself to the satire industry), nor, given the pluralism and substantial autonomy of American higher education, to prevent staff and students from taking themselves elsewhere.

Regulation only becomes necessary once honesty, or honour, is too rare to justify a general expectation of it. Of course some degree of regulation is necessary in any society. But the idea, remarked on earlier, that regulation alone is necessary (and that when it fails, all we need is more of it) is typical of the 'social engineering' approach, according to which every 'problem' must have its external 'explanation' and corresponding external 'solution'.

Crime insoluble by policing alone—a collective self-respect needed

Take crime, which (violence apart) is simply dishonesty writ large. Crime becomes a matter of 'insufficient resources', either for the police or for their notionally 'deprived' quarry, the criminal classes (whose real 'problem', one might have thought, was precisely their existing propensity to live off others' resources). Even the demand for 'stiffer penalties' for the most part addresses only the effects of moral neglect, rather than the thing itself. For what the advocates of 'stiffer penalties' usually mean (in the shape, almost invariably, of longer prison sentences) is either greater deterrence, or a longer isolation of the criminal from his potential victims, whereas what is required, at the very least, and in vivid, morally-meaningful forms, is punishment proper.

Not long ago our culture was marked by a general habit and expectation, which reinforced each other, of honesty in small things. These, taken together, added up to one very big thing, a kind of collective self-respect, continuous at one end with the ordinary citizen's personal honour, and at the other with his unassertive patriotism. There was crime, of course, some of it quite lurid (since our capacity to be shocked was still lively). It was perceived, however, neither as a 'problem' nor as an overwhelming menace, but as what it is, an essentially moral phenomenon.

Punishment as a moral idea

In a free society the level of crime depends far less upon the existing technologies of repression or surveillance, or upon the absolute severity of the penalties incurred (though in some areas that could certainly be increased), than upon the society's overall moral ethos, of which its *conception* of punishment is a part. When that ethos is healthy, morally-intelligible penalties serve to underpin it, being an example to the criminal and the law-abiding alike of what justice is and ought to be.

Penology is not my concern here, but if a snap definition of morally-intelligible (which is to say, effective) punishment is required, it is this: punishment ideally should be swift, probable, cheap, short, proportionate to the crime and also symbolically related to it (so that the criminal is forced to re-live, and hence as far as possible to understand, something like his victim's sufferings), awe-inspiring (and thus, decency permitting, public), and, though maximally unpleasant at the moment of infliction, calculated to cause as little permanent physical harm and as much psychic good to the criminal as are consistent with society's need to see justice vindicated.

The criminal's need (at least, his moral need, of which he will probably require to be convinced) is to find all his inward defiance cowed by the overwhelming force of righteous public outrage. The latter should be moderated solely by his contrition, a thing which, if he does not show it in advance, his punishment must be severe enough to extort. What penalties such a conception of punishment entails cannot be discussed here; but they must obviously differ at almost every point from what currently prevails. To confine a man, whatever his offence, in an academy of boastful, hardened evil-doing for years upon sullen years, and at enormous public cost, does no good to him, or to society, or to his past and future victims.

Moral education

Penal reform notwithstanding, the moral improvement of society, unlike its decline, cannot be 'engineered'. Obviously what is needed is moral education, but that is a trickier business, at least to explain, even than education proper. It is, in fact, previous to education proper, which nobody can acquire unless he already possesses the rudiments of the virtues appropriate to learning: imagination, concentration, perseverance, attentiveness, honesty, and respect, both for his teachers and for his subjects of study.

Just conceivably those virtues might first be acquired at school, and they will certainly wither if the school's ethos (or the home's) is hostile. But they are best acquired in advance, in the home, where they emerge naturally, as part of the day-to-day process of upbringing and growth. One thing is certain, that morality and the virtue on which it depends are not to be instilled formally. Moral sermons or catechisms, the quasi-informational inculcation of precepts, 'rational' appeals to the child's 'self-interest': all alike (to children, who are not fools) are either unintelligible or risible. Ethics may be discussed in the classroom or the lecture-hall; but morality is learned on the job, in the welter of real or imaginative engagements, under the example and influence of one's parents, teachers and fellows, not to mention one's reading-matter.

Morality—the importance of the family

Not only is morality effective primarily at the 'capillary' level, it is also there that it germinates and takes root. That is why New Leftists such as Althusser and Foucault (the author of the 'capillary' image), who rightly see normal morality as an obstacle to their political designs, are obliged to subvert it by vilifying the non-political culture out of which it grows. Althusser even attacks the very notion of 'reality' as 'bourgeois', which raises interesting questions as to what he supposes the basis of his own thought to be, and why, given his outright contempt for intellectual honesty, he should expect anyone to find him persuasive.

Of course moral education should be reinforced in schools, as it will be if they are any good. But, as I have said, the process starts earlier. The only hope of reviving it lies in strengthening the family, and building on parents' surviving moral understanding. This means, among other things, freeing (or if you prefer, protecting) them, first, from 'enlightened' official interference, and secondly, from the influences of the media and so-called 'pop' culture. A few reflections on each may suffice for a conclusion.

Cruelty to children is a great evil. But it is not to be suppressed by forbidding parents to punish them (something which is already on the agenda in Germany). For it is no less cruel, both to children and to those whom they must later encounter, to deprive them of the notions of justice and just conduct. Example apart, these can be instilled by the lightest and most infrequent of disciplinary measures, so long as they comprehend both the child's *mens rea* and his parents' care for his safety and moral development; that is, are understood to be punishments, and not mere arbitrary expressions of his parents' selfish displeasure or inconvenience, or of their frustration at his unwanted existence.

One parent needed at home

Playgroups are an excellent thing. Held for only a few hours a week, and staffed in rotation by the parents (usually mothers) concerned, they simply formalise the spontaneous arrangements for supervised play and temporary child care which have always existed between families in the same neighbourhood. Few things, however, are more likely to convince the pre-school child of his unwantedness than removing him, for virtually the whole of his waking day, from someone with an instinctive, intimate interest in his existence to a child-minder, nursery or creche.

Yet this is exactly what governments encourage in driving both parents out to work. They do so through a combination of parsimonious tax relief and a topping-up of the materialist, feminist and career-oriented propaganda already beamed at parents in vast quantities from other interested sources. It is bad enough if the child is farmed out to private agencies, for, however efficient or conscientious, they are no substitute for a parent; but state nurseries will probably be even worse, in that (at least as things stand) they offer the most priceless opening, at both the practical and the administrative levels, to ideologues fresh from the triumphs of nescience and indiscipline they have already wrought in our schools.

Television, pop culture and morality

Every aspect of this unplanned but systematic destruction of the family, and of the morality which grows from its soil, reinforces the others. Reunited with their offspring, work-exhausted parents commit them to the care of that infallible tranquillizer, television. Most of what children watch is not, in fact, positively pernicious. What is bad is simply its mind-numbing inanity and its truly enormous quantity, which crowds out both the play and the parental contact they need.

No better instrument than television has ever been devised to anaesthetize children's normally lively capacity to discriminate. The scruffiest comic, such as the snootier schools would have banned from their premises a generation back, is a treasure-house of fun, thrills, life-experience, imagination and sound moral sense in comparison. It is instructive, and also heartening (since it shows that all is not lost), to compare children's animated responses at a pantomime with the glazed expression induced by prolonged cathode radiation.

Pop culture, which comes later, and affects parents as well, is simply more of the same, with sex (at a similar level of nullity) thrown in. It is a continuous soap opera, whose characters are half-real, half-fictional, and more imbecile than genuinely depraved. Its heroes are not exemplars of piety, courage, skill, artistry, dedication, charity, ingenuity, enterprise or other virtues, but more or less total nonentities who, at no cost to themselves, and with the reward of additional publicity, espouse the latest ephemeral cause. Its villains die by alcohol or 'hard' drugs (death by promiscuous sodomy, however, is for some reason a badge of heroism); the very worst club seals. Trust and honesty are barely intelligible, though the odd bed-hopper, if the betrayed party is sufficiently famous, or winsome, or simply pregnant, may temporarily qualify as a 'rat'.

Amid all this relentless triviality, the usually sensible advice given in the agony columns of pop magazines to obscure people suffering from real and acute distress (often in consequence of imitating their role-models), seems either hypocritical or, Canute-like, a futile anachronism.

How seriously such matters ought to be taken depends on something it is not easy to discover, namely, how seriously they are taken by their audience. It is conceivable that somewhere beneath all this garbage, the detritus of affluence and security, real honesty and virtue are hibernating, and wait only upon the stroke of misfortune, which visits us all individually sooner or later, for their awakening. But we have a life to live before that, and we are not living it. If we were, we might be better prepared for our inevitable fates, even if we exclude from that category (as we should not) the domestic ruin and the vague, inexplicable unhappiness in the midst of unprecedented comfort which widespread moral indifference, for all its appearance of 'liberation', has brought upon our culture.

For the last few pages I have been speaking of moral virtue generally, and the conditions in which it thrives, but it is plain, as I began by saying, that honesty, or the disposition to seek and testify to the truth, is at the root of it. For the type of all vice is fantasy, or disrespect for reality. That is no more than the belief that the world, and its other inhabitants, can and should be bent to the service of one's selfish pleasure, or that there is any real happiness which does not depend upon a certain degree of personal sacrifice. This belief is both popular and false, and the longer it is persisted in, the greater the revenge which reality will exact. The Gods of the Copybook Headings are not mocked. Or, in the words of the Hussite motto, *magna est veritas, et praevalebit.*

CHAPTER 11

Respect and the Dangers of an Unfettered 'Critical Spirit' in Education

Anthony O'Hear

I said that America no more knew what to do with this black underclass than it knew what to do with its children. It was impossible for it to educate either, or to bind either to life. It was not itself securely attached to life just now. Sensing this, the children attached themselves to the black underclass, achieving a kind of coalescence with the demand-mass. It was not so much the inner city slum that threatened us as the slum of innermost being, of which the inner city was perhaps a material representation.

–Saul Bellow, The Dean's December, *p.201*

A generation unattached

What goes for America doubtless goes, or will go, for Britain too. If what Bellow says is on the right track, it would go some way to explaining the otherwise inexplicable fact that so many young people (and not only students) strive so pathetically to attach themselves to some underclass or other, and continue to chant the outworn mantras of Marxism, feminism, third worldism and anti-capitalism as if that way lay salvation and peace. Any prayer-wheel is better than none, even a wheel which makes but intermittent and eccentric contact with any actual road. But perhaps the blame is not the children's, if it is we who are not securely attached to life just now. Education may be possible only if the educators are bound to life. What might that mean?

The unattached libertarian

Being bound to life would seem to imply that one is not free-floating in one's attitudes and evaluations; that one has a sense of iden-

173

tity and a scale of values by which one guides one's life and against which one measures actions, beliefs and desires. In different ways the attitudes of both the libertarian and the revolutionary are symptomatic of a lack of boundness to life. The libertarian is not bound because for him there is no value which is not dependent on his acts of choosing. His acts of choice are seen as having no source and are constrained by nothing other than his whim.

'I can see us as water-spiders', Keynes wrote in *My Early Beliefs*, 'gracefully skimming, as light and reasonable as air, the surface of the stream without any contact at all with the eddies and currents underneath'. While a few upper-class water spiders can doubtless be tolerated in a society where the majority is grounded in life, the matter becomes rather more problematic when all wish to be spiders. For if we are all skimming over life, without making real contact with it, from where are we to get—or give—the sense that some things, rather than others, are worth spending time and effort on learning?

The unattached revolutionary

The situation of the revolutionary is slightly more complex, often involving commitment to a cause or group far wider in extent than individual choice. Individual whim is sacrificed to collective decision. Nevertheless, the underlying motivation—a desire for wholesale change—certainly manifests a lack of boundness to life as it is. Even though some lives or some forms of life might be better not bound to, the discontent of the revolutionary is psychologically a parlous condition, and often one whose adoption is predicated on the will of the revolutionary, on the revolutionary's refusal or inability to identify with anything higher or better in his present life and society. In this sense, the libertarian's elevation of the individual will can be seen as the source of much current revolutionary commitment; and commitment to a revolutionary cause—any cause, often enough—can in many cases be seen as an attempt on the part of the unbound spirit—the nay-saying spirit—to rebind itself to something more than itself. When this rebinding is predicated on rejection of what is rather than on the humble and loving acceptance of some higher source of value, revolutionary fervour leads inevitably to hate-filled and sectarian violence, a condition captured once and for all by Dostoevsky in *The Devils*.

The fashion for being critical

We are often told—and not only be people with subversive intent—that one of the main aims of education ought to be to instil a critical spirit in the young. There is, of course, criticism and criticism. There is criticism of the sort described by George Orwell in 'Inside the Wale':

> Patriotism, religion, the Empire, the family, the sanctity of marriage, the Old School Tie, birth, breeding, honour, discipline—anyone of ordinary education could turn the whole lot of them inside out in three minutes.

Anyone can raise clever and sophistical arguments against anything good and true; even not so clever and sophistical arguments can always be raised against anything, asking for the criteria on which judgments of value and even of fact are made. The worry implicit in what Orwell says is that education itself can encourage sophistry of this sort. An education which is not itself securely attached to life can all too easily take the form of the cultivation of 'reasoning skills', or something of the sort: an empty and contentless disposition on the part of the young to 'express themselves' in raising questions about whatever topic comes before them. It was for cultivating this sort of attitude without fostering any countervailing reverence for the good, the true and the beautiful that the Sophists were widely reviled in ancient Athens.

Socrates and the critical spirit

Not that, to some of his contemporaries, it was terribly easy to distinguish Socrates himself from the Sophists:

> They sit at the feet of Socrates
> Till they can't distinguish the wood from the trees

And tragedy goes to pot:

> They don't care whether their plays are art
> But only whether the words are smart
> They waste our time with quibbles and quarrels
> Destroying our patience as well as our morals
> And teaching us all to talk rot.

Thus Aristophanes in *The Frogs* (lines 1491-9 of the Penguin translation). From this grew the view of Socrates which was further developed by Nietzsche in *The Birth of Tragedy*: Socrates, the destroyer of all that made Athens great, precisely because of his relentless—essentially plebian—

questioning, questioning to which adherents of the old, aristocratic, Aeschylean morality could provide no answer. The influence of a particular type of philosophy and of education is so pervasive that I imagine that I would be in a small minority in the educated classes were I to follow Peter Geach in speaking of the Socratic fallacy: the fallacy, that is, of thinking that one can properly be said to understand a concept only if one can define its meaning and defend it against dialectical cross-questioning from someone who shows no inclination to submit his own cherished beliefs to a similar examination.

The Euthyphro dialogue

Geach coined the phrase 'the Socratic fallacy' in connection with Socrates's style of argument in the *Euthyphro*, a dialogue represented as taking place when Socrates is actually on his way to the trial which will eventually condemn him. Socrates button-holes Euthyphro, a young man also on the way to the law courts, to press a suit against his father for having brought about the death of a hired hand. This hired hand had been thrown into a ditch by Euthyphro's father after having killed one of the father's slaves; the father had forgotten about the hand, who had subsequently died of exposure and starvation. In reply to Euthyphro's claim that piety demands that he act against his father, Socrates spends a couple of hours in dialectical twisting and turning discovering that Euthyphro cannot define the notion of piety; he concludes that unless Euthyphro had known precisely what was holy and unholy 'it is unthinkable that for a simple hireling you would ever have moved to prosecute your aged sire on a charge of murder'.

Destroying respect for the sources of value and morality

Euthyphro is presented as rather arrogant and complacent, but one cannot help but be struck by the implications of Socrates's conclusion: that only someone who, in Socrates's own terms, knew (i.e., could define) what was holy, would have the audacity to prosecute his own father for the sake of a servant. As I. F. Stone pertinently asked (in *The Trial of Socrates*) 'Did it matter—in the eyes of the law, or of morality—that the dead man was only a servant?' Stone's Socrates is not Aristophanes's or Nietzsche's; he is not a destroyer of aristocratic morality, so much as an impeder of democratic values. Perhaps the truth is that Socrates in a sense was both. To people deeply committed to particular values, Socrates and Socratic questioning can seem, as it did to Stone, not just trivial but destructive. It can destroy respect for the sources of virtue and morality, and, as Stone points out, it can undermine that wider understanding of moral dilemmas that comes only with a degree of pity for those involved in them:

> In the *Euthyphro*, you have to feel compassion for that poor labourer—we are never even told his name—to solve the deadlock in logic on which the dialogue ends. Euthyphro, like Orestes, was caught in a conflict—indeed a maze—of obligations, moral, legal and political. These are unexplored in the arid semantics of the Socratic interrogation.

One could, indeed, say that the Socratic interrogation, which Euthyphro had to undergo, was not securely attached to life. The Socratic fallacy it was based upon is not value-neutral; by its very pretence at objectivity it tends to undermine the hold values have on people, and the respect they have for them. My fear is that too much contemporary educational thought and practice is similarly destructive of practical wisdom, which, though inarticulate, is not the less wise for that.

Rather than encourage ultimately destructive questioning of values, educators should begin by attempting to instil in the young a sense of respect for perennial human values, and open their eyes to the possibility that there are sources of value relating to human life, which transcend individual choice. As what I am talking about—*perennial* human values, *transcendent* sources of value—by definition goes beyond the experience of any specific time or group of individuals, it will be clear that the type of education I seek cannot be child-centred, nor can it be constrained by notions of contemporary relevance. Teachers themselves must have a sense that what they are touching on is greater and more valuable than their own reactions or feelings. They must approach the material in question with respect, seeking to learn from it, rather than to force it into some intellectual mould of their own. And they must seek to convey this sense of respect to their pupils.

The treasures of the arts

What is this material which I am talking about, in which perennial and transcendent values are conveyed?

> Art in its broadest sense provides us with the most remarkable access to some of the essential truths about the meaning and significance of life. Poetry and drama are the forms in which, from the most ancient times,

human values have been expressed, if not created. In every age of our history, poets and painters, musicians and dramatists have transformed crude fact into human meaning . . .

The words are those of the Prince of Wales, and as will already be apparent from my references to Dostoevsky, Aristophanes and Aeschylus, I agree with them completely; while I do not think that literature and philosophy are the same, I do think that literature provides the essential material of human meaning without which philosophy becomes empty and formalistic and misses the human point of things.

For it is in the arts that we receive the most articulate and living expressions and investigations of human meaning, and also, along with the cases of saintly and dedicated lives with which we are all familiar, the most striking refutations of the notion that human life and consciousness are simply the by-products of blind, mechanistic evolutionary processes. Art not only provides us with concrete expressions of the human spirit and the sense that there are demands made on us which cannot be reduced to the narrowly humanistic; it also suggests, again in concrete detail, that there are values which transcend time and place. We can recognise ourselves and our aspirations in transformed form in the heroes of Homer and the tragedies of Aeschylus and the plays of Shakespeare. Art, more than anything else available to us today, can instil in us a sense of perennial and transcendent values.

Aesthetic education—a counter
to the negative rejection of 'criticism'

What I am suggesting here is that we can, through a careful attempt at aesthetic education, find a way to remedy or at least to approach that lack of attachment to life which Bellow deplores in us. In focusing in our education on some of the great works of art which have survived the test of time, we might begin to give our children the wherewithal both to go beyond the fashions of the age and to go beyond the facile and negative rejection of the present which often comes from a felt disgust with present fashion.

Of course, I am assuming that teachers and their pupils will treat the masterpieces of the past with the respect due to them, and this could be problematic, given that respect (as oppose.d to critical enquiry) is a virtue not much spoken about or practised in educational circles today. But perhaps it is this absence of respect for what is greater than us which is conspiring more than anything else to give so many of our children an education which is spiritually less than nourishing. Can an education based on aesthetics, and based on respect, be given today? Sometimes I think that it is the only type of education which can be given. I will end, as I began, with Saul Bellow:

> About *Macbeth* Corde had . . . noted that in a class of black schoolchildren taught by a teacher 'brave enough to ignore instructions from downtown', Shakespeare caused great excitement. The lines 'And pity, like a naked newborn babe, Striding the blast' had pierced those pupils. You could see the power of the babe, how restlessness stopped. And Corde had written that perhaps only poetry had the strength 'to rival the attractions of narcotics, the magnetism of TV, the excitements of sex, or the ecstasies of destruction'.

CHAPTER 12

Diligence Abandoned:

The Dismissal of Traditional Virtues in the School

Dennis O'Keeffe

Educators abandoning morality

In her much admired critique of Piagetian psychology, *Children's Minds*, Margaret Donaldson places her emphasis exclusively on positive questions of cognition and motivation. Neither index nor text has any moral focus. She fixes unerringly, for example, on one of the key discontinuities of education: the tragic loss of enthusiasm between the primary and the secondary stages. Yet she never asks whether this difficulty might have a moral aspect, whether, for example, some moral deficit associated with the earlier stage might engender problems at the later.[1]

The book is well done; but the cognitive paradigm is not up to the job. One cannot investigate moral deficiency via a psychologistic theory in which the idea of learning lacks any moral dimension. Many theorists would find it hard even to countenance the idea of morality as crucial to learning. Where they do talk of morals, they discuss only how children learn them, not how morals help children learn. The reasons for this gap are complex; but at their heart lie the debilitating effects of a movement which in discovering childhood has abandoned virtue.

The child-centred movement in schooling

The origins of this child-centred movement, otherwise to be known as the CCD (Child-Centred Disaster), lie in the 18th-century writings of Rousseau. Progressivism, as it is now called, did not, however, really come into its own until the 1960s. At this time the campaign became very successful in the United States and even more so, especially in relation to young children, in Great Britain.

Progressivism supports the child's 'interests' against academic tradition. It is for play and against drudgery, for personal or group 'topic' work against identical work pursued separately by all children in the class. It favours lots of talking as crucial to children's 'thinking'. The tradition of silence is lost. Whatever is proclaimed, the logic of this relaxing prospectus is a 'fun' curriculum.

Such is the dominant primary ideology today. This chapter deals with its flawed intellectual and moral character and disastrous educational results. It concentrates on primary education, in the belief that subsequent difficulties in secondary and even, at times, higher education, go back largely to the inadequacies of the primary stage. The initial focus is British; but the U.S.A. or anywhere in the English-speaking world would serve equally well.

Economic success and educational failure in Great Britain and the United States

Education is in the news. A steady flow of writing and broadcasting deplores our lamentable standards. Nor is the debate confined to academics or teachers. Worries about school are a staple of popular conversation. After years of complacency, when any voices raised against the educational estate were considered by the 'experts' absurd or extreme, a mood of hostility to prevailing practice has set in. Indeed, both Great Britain and the United States are in the grip of a moral panic about their schools. It is widely believed in both countries that they face a crisis of unprecedented severity. The CCD does exist. Anger and anxiety about what children and students achieve are everywhere apparent.

The question is not whether but why British and American school standards are so low. A voluminous literature shows an average achievement unsatisfactory by international comparison, as well as a vast tail of underachievement. Some contextual comment may thus be worth more than yet another rehearsal of incontrovertible evidence.[2]

First, it must be said that our educational doldrums speak badly for the Republicans in the United States and for the British Conservatives after their long periods in office. Why have they not done more?

The American case is extraordinary. The country with the most successful economy ever, which played a major part in defeating German National Socialism, Japanese Imperialism and now, through its extraordinary high technology, Soviet Communism, has numbers of illiterates running into many millions. The precise facts are contestable; but without doubt millions of souls have passed through the American schools and emerged illiterate. This is one of the most shocking facts of the late twentieth century. The contradiction between great economic and political achievements on the one hand, and the near-moronization of a large minority of Americans on the other, is unbearable as well as bizarre.

In Great Britain too, contradictions abound. The British invented the market economy and political democracy. British scholars have a record of unparalleled intellectual distinction over the last 300 years. But for British courage and ingenuity in the early 1940s, the Nazis or Communists might well control Europe today. Moreover, since then, Great Britain has enjoyed 50 years of increasing affluence, which even severe difficulties like the present recession cannot more than dent for most people. Yet some 10 per cent of British adults are functionally illiterate, and a further 10 per cent functionally innumerate, with a terrible 14 per cent overlap between the two categories.[3]

This is a startling coexistence of wealth/know-how and basic ignorance. Our social order has successfully kept at bay the ancient scourges of famine and primary poverty. Our wealth is now vast and some of it is manifestly available to schools. How then shall we explain why millions languish in such appalling unenlightenment?

Diligence revisited—a school of 1949

To try to uncover an answer, let us change focus, and confining ourselves to the British experience, switch back more than 40 years and fix our imagination or memories on a single room, an imaginary but highly typical classroom. There were thousands like it in the years just after the Second World War. I went to one myself.

It is 1949 or thereabouts. The scene is a classroom in a Catholic elementary school in a working-class suburb of West London. (The specific religious identity is important but not overwhelmingly so; the location is immaterial save that the place is urban and poor.) There are 53 children in the room. They are poorly, drably dressed. The teacher is a nun. There are a few coloured religious representations on the wall. There is also a crucifix. The overall impression of the room, however, is of poverty and bareness.

Silence

The thing which will most amaze the visitor from the 1990s is the silence. The room is extraordinarily silent unless the children have to chant prayers, or multiplication tables or a poem. 'Silence', moreover, also means sitting still and paying attention. Looking behind one or away from the task in hand are infringements of the rule. The prayer-like character of the atmosphere is apparent; there is always silence or official noise. A definite moral order prevails. The desks are in neat rows. The children are all doing the same work, though observably not all with equal competence. Indeed, it is soon apparent that the 'fast' children are bunched together, as are the middle speed pupils and the slow ones.

This separation is one of the few implicit elements in a pedagogic regime whose constituent parts are mostly very explicit. The children understand the performance bunchings; but these are little commented on by the teacher. It emerges, however, that the different seating arrangements for the differentially performing are not connected with pedagogic technique. They do not make the nun's teaching easier by creating pockets of homogeneity. This matters nothing to her, since she does not set the children to work in groups. She teaches them as a whole; she speaks to all of them at once; she gives them all, individually, the same tasks. This is the core of the old pedagogy: collective teaching and individual work. The seating arrangements are rewards and punishments. They reflect different *moral* achievements. They promote a moral hierarchy. This is a world where 'background' never enters the reckoning. Sister Bernadine, as we may call her, would not believe that John Cahill or Mary Devereux cannot manage the work because of their poor homes. All her children come from poor homes.

Fear

The ambience in Sister Bernadine's classroom is very revealing. Mostly it is calm; but there is also a sense of fear, though she rarely raises her voice. When she is moved to wrath it is a formidable spectacle which leaves children trembling. When she is teaching she expects everyone to pay attention; her anger is most easily provoked by infractions of this expectation. This is significant in itself; the moral authority she represents is not up for debate. The children do not doubt it. Few of their parents, be they ever so drunken and shiftless fathers, or inadequate mothers, would dream of challenging that authority. Let us dwell a while, then, on the sister's moral presuppositions.

She has the children grouped by performance; but in practice she does not allow much for different intellectual speeds. It is because she does not take the slower speeds of some for granted that she is more likely to be cross with children of lower ability. She thinks they are idling. Her educational philosophy is not much developed; but it is very clear. She holds that anyone who is not brain-damaged, 'simple' as she would call it in her simple way, can be taught to read, write and master tables. Anyone who sits in her classroom and fails to scale these limited peaks is guilty of idleness. She has not undergone the benefits of modern psychology of education. She is, *avant la lettre*, an egalitarian who, unlike modern egalitarians, has not absorbed the sad news of our differing talents, or at least, the fact is one her moral vocation rejects. She would also reject that environmentalism which sees performance as always governed by background and never by independent human agency. For her, intellectual success springs mostly from diligence, intellectual failure mostly from idleness.

Perseverance, obedience, humility

This moral approach to learning, with technical questions having very secondary significance, falls into easily identifiable elements. Sister Bernadine's favourite reproach is 'bone-idle', an epithet she perhaps confuses with 'unintelligent'. The compensation is her success with very unpromising pupils. For her the virtues which secure learning are rooted in diligence, industry, perseverance, obedience and humility. She works hard; so must the children. She has never let herself be discouraged; her pupils too must be persistent and brave. She took vows of obedience; the children must learn the easier obedience of school. She learned humbly from those who knew more than she; the children likewise must bow before her authority.

If we examine her techniques they are what are now termed 'traditional' and have been excoriated for two centuries by thinkers of the Rousseau/Dewey ascendancy, as stilted and against the developmental interests of children. She teaches reading by first stressing the functions and sounds of individual letters and building these up into syllables and subsequently whole words—the old phonetic approach. But she is something of an eclectic too. English spelling being irregular, she will distinguish between 'though', 'through' and 'rough' by judicious application of 'look-say'. It all adds up, though, to a very demanding regime of spelling, syntax and punctuation.

Given the hard work on which she insists, she would probably make 'look-say' work better than its modern exponents do. But one guesses she would be sceptical of it. As for the bizarre system, fashionable in Great Britain, which holds that children learn to read from the mere proximity of books—the so-called 'real books' method—she would reject it outright. She has probably never heard the term 'category error'; but she knows one when she sees one. Atmosphere and method are two different questions. 'Real books' cannot help in the preliminary enlightenment of those mired in original sin. This shrewd woman would spot such middle-class posturing and affectation a mile off.

Rote

She is keen on tables, without which she thinks arithmetic impossible. She also thinks arithmetic precedes mathematics proper. The modern idea of starting with the deep theory of mathematics, she would reject as nonsensical. Indeed, it is in the teaching of basic arithmetic, and the drumming-in of tables, that the hard slog of her methods is seen at its most unadorned. There is no shortcut. Children must lock number-rules into their memories. This demands diligent repetition. The most familiar sound in her class—apart from prayers—is the chanting of tables, a sound seldom or never heard in primary schools today. It is a slog and a bore, submitting the children to authority in a completely uncompromised way. In other words, it is a moral necessity in the transmission of numeracy and the basic rules of number.

Learning facts

Sister Bernadine's substantive views of history would not appeal today. I remember an embittered Irish romanticism. But her belief in the primacy of facts and chronology in the study of the past seems entirely sound. The progressives have had even more disastrous effects in the study of history than in English or mathematics.[4] True, she would make a better go at the topic-based method than most of its contemporary exponents. But she would deny that history can be studied effectively without a strong factual base.

Sister Bernadine would have despised the contemporary 'de-facting' of geography. In particular she would have been appalled at the dethroning of the sense of *location*. Today, many children and adults do not know where anything is, including themselves. There are millions of people who do not known where the big towns and major rivers of their countries are. Again, she would have taught topic-based geography better than it is usually done today; but it is a path that she would not have followed willingly. Why replace what works; why mend what is not broken?

Today, even the most conservative of educationists might quarrel with her neglect of psychological realities. Sister Bernadine would not count as prepared today. She certainly does not have a degree. She is a daughter of an Irish peasant farmer and was sent by her Order to a Teacher Training College. There is something to be said, though, for her moral egalitarianism, certainly in terms of effects. Whatever preparation she received it throws today's arrangements into doubt. There are, as it happens, no brain-damaged children in her class; and she has not heard of 'special needs'. Consequently, there is no one in her class who cannot read and write and who does not know his tables. The moral hierarchy she maintains is one which draws on and promotes a foundation of accomplishment luxurious compared to what most primary school teachers in the 1990s enjoy.

Though the subject is little researched, there is little doubt that British Catholic schools half a century ago were better than the state schools. This claim will not surprise Americans, given the performance of their parochial schools. A word of caution is in order, though. The state schools too were in those days less tolerant of educational failure and insubstantiality than they are now. The case is not just one of religious conviction. The sense of diligence required for the successful transmission of knowledge was more common in Catholic schools; but it was in fair measure common to most schools. Most teachers then assumed that the child was trying to learn a corpus of desirable knowledge and skills and that this needed moral commitment. Today the differential between Catholic and state schools remains; but both have lost ground, especially in urban areas.

Transformation

Now we may steal away from the intellectual wealth and material poverty of a London school in the 1940s. Sad to say, in a wide experience of modern primary schools, I have never seen one half so good. When we shift our gaze to the present, the picture in British primary classrooms, Catholic or otherwise, is very different. All around we will see evidence of a remarkable material advance. The children do not look poor. The schools are not the drab places of 50 years ago. The walls are covered in bright materials. The furniture is not the old forbidding Victorian functionalism. There are lots of teaching aids, where once there were chalk and blackboards and little else.

Most important of all, we know about the transformation in teacher 'education'. There has been a very large expansion in this field. Once a degree was all you needed; you did not then need formal training. If you were 'trained', on the other hand, you did not need a degree. Now both degree and training are mandatory. Nor can a teacher expect promotion without attending numerous extra courses. The extension of in-service education for teachers has been dramatic. And all this has accompanied an almost continuous fall in the pupil-teacher ratio. There are more teachers than ever before and their preparation is very expensive.

The new educational experts

There has also been an astonishing proliferation of educational advisors and other 'experts', as well as of administrative jobs in local government. According to one leading British economist, the education service now employs as many non-teachers as teachers—just under 400,000 in each case.[5]

In addition there has been a dizzy growth in writings on education, an output so vast no one could command it all, and an equally rapid growth in educational broadcasting. In Great Britain, as in America, if the findings of officialdom, now supplementing those of conservative critics, are true, we are spending much more and getting much less for it.

As we home in on our modern classroom, our presentation is necessarily stylised, but not false. The room is bright. There are interesting wall displays. Sometimes there are no partitions between the classrooms. There are rarely more than 30 children in the room and often 20 or less. The huge classes are gone, along with the uniformity of the desk arrangements. Children sit in bunches of up to five or six at scattered tables. It is impossible for the teacher to see all the children's faces at once; nor can all of them simultaneously observe the teacher.

Noise

The room is rarely quiet and often quite deafening. The children in the various groups do different tasks. Rarely will they be doing the same work. There is, by the standards of the earlier period, astonishingly little all-class teaching. The teacher does not often teach anything in any mainstream curricular fare to the children as a whole. This is the biggest method-shift between the two orders.

The classroom is now very relaxed. Children often walk about freely. They are not frightened as their grandparents often were. What is not clear is that they are learning much. Only occasionally will the visitor find an ability to read, write and number such as would have satisfied Sister Bernadine. Along with visual aids there are often examples of children's work on the walls so incompetent in terms of their authors' ages that she would have been shocked. If this feeble standard is remarked on at all, it will be explained away as due to forces outside the teacher's control. The visitor will be told of the horrendous social problems explaining the poor performance of many children. Individual agency has yielded to material circumstance.

Morality and technique

As Bernstein says, in traditional classrooms the rules governing transmission are mostly explicit, as clear to the pupils as to the teacher, even when some children cannot manage the substantive contents of lessons.[6] Above all, I would add, the moral code is central, if sometimes implicit rather than explicit. The oddity with much modern education writing, by contrast, is its minimal moral content.

Paralleling this evaporation of moral emphasis there has developed a convention to the effect that many complex human activities, hitherto approached via a cautious empiricism, duly informed by traditional moral notions, are really matters of technique. Whether we speak of teaching children, social work or the management of young delinquents or criminals, the representatives of the new middle class 'expertocracy' are at hand, ready to insist that there exist technical solutions to the problems which concern us; and that they are the people who can effect them.

It is not, however, only the moral framework that has vanished with the eclipse of diligence. There has been a parallel loss of clarity. The order of diligence put moral commitment first in the battle against ignorance. Everything else was an also-ran. The very essence of the CCD, by contrast, is its radical incoherence, its mish-mash of technicism, environmental determinism and egalitarian social engineering. One example: though poverty today is negligible compared to the

1940s, social problems are real enough. There is rising divorce and illegitimacy; but the CCD will not even acknowledge their adverse effects, preferring, when it is not asserting the primacy of its own techniques, to chatter about a meaningless 'poverty'. It will not even discuss the idea of education as involving moral commitment by the persons involved. It banks on more resources; it trades in technique and bogus apologetics.

Diligence and technique in reading and mathematics

Where the technical efficiency which divides rival approaches is narrow or problematic, it seems highly likely that it will be the moral commitment which is decisive. The evidence favours phonetic approaches to the teaching of reading, with look-say somewhere behind. Here, Sister Bernadine's moral regime may make the gap closer than the one we observe. Of course, the toughest of moral orders cannot rescue nonsense. Martin Turner has put the real books method entirely outside practical respectability.[7] The whole point, however, is that though the child's diligence is crucial to learning, and the method often secondary, it is precisely the excision of moral imperatives which appeals to progressivism. Throwing out tables, for example, is only secondarily a technical choice. Its true appeal lies in its lightening of life's grim burden. It is a moral cop-out.

The mathematics debate is lost in the kindergarten of soft psychology. It has asserted doubtful claims about the psychology of learning at the expense of mathematical reality. As Colin Coldman has argued, progressive methodology is simply and perversely wrong. Mathematics is not an empirical subject and it is misleading as well as practically disastrous to teach it 'experientially'.[8]

Progressivism persists, against reason and experience, in the fantasy of some quick, technical fix for our educational problems. Where this fails, inevitably, it turns to the pseudo-moral conviction that we should not make children uncomfortable by demanding hard work from them. Maybe we grossly exaggerate the benefits of a return to traditional methods in the absence of any change of moral outlook. In the general revolt against civilisation, key moral rules were abandoned or even derided. Maybe the most traditional and proven commonsense methods will not do the trick in the absence of the appropriate moral assumptions.

Thus technique itself is not the most important consideration for 'progressives', much as they will overstress and misrepresent it. True, in recent educational debate, controversies over 'right' approaches to English and mathematics have tended to fix on purely technical questions. Thus the reading controversy has indeed centred on the technical efficiency of such different approaches as phonetics and look-say. When failure in practice is apparent, however, the ground is shifted quite shamelessly. Commitment to teaching is already attenuated; hence the fulminations against didacticism and factual 'regurgitation'. The central attack on diligence, however, takes the form of an advised rejection of making children work hard.

Progressive education is the flabbiest feature of today's rich societies. The progressives have abandoned work for play, pain for pleasure and stress for comfort. Even if the cultural and intellectual conservative wins the technical arguments—which given the evidence, must be accounted the case—progressive opinion will deny him the moral high ground. It is now alleged that it is immoral to interfere with children's inclinations or local 'culture'. The old calculus turned on diligence. The modern reckoning is primarily hedonic. What counts most is happy children.

The progressive, like the conservative, is an improvising eclectic, but a less coherent one. He persists with the arguments about background and resources. If children achieve little this is because they come from the inner city or from large families, or the government is not spending enough money on them. But failure is really much more to be justified in terms of the proscription on impinging too far on children's personal space. The one possibility never raised is that the teacher/pupil dialectic is fundamentally a moral one in which the child gradually learns to assume the mantle of adulthood. This requires hard work, perseverance and the ability to take the long view. Sister Bernadine would have agreed that such far-seeing commitment was more difficult for poor children than for those from comfortable families. But that they were capable of it was something she and they demonstrated every day.

No wonder there is public anxiety. The general public does not share the anti-work ideology. People know the importance of education for their children. They know that knowledge is the key to success. They know many schools are not good enough. Few people would assert that there was ever an educational 'Golden Age'. But few would doubt that something has gone badly wrong. Schools seem to have been subject, at least for some of their pupils, to historical retrogression. A curricular atavism has been at work.

Moralism and moral confusion

Primary schools differ in their teaching modes. In the advanced societies such approaches fall, we have seen, into two main kinds. The former, standard until the 1960s and still represented by individual teachers and certain schools, we may with stark lack of originality call 'traditional'. The latter, increasingly common since the 1960s, we may, equally unoriginally, call 'progressive'.

Such modes involve different mixes of implicit and explicit moral assumptions and technical methods. It is especially important in this context to distinguish between morality, the advocacy or practice of moral behaviour, and moralism, the advocacy or practice of certain attitudes where there may be a genuine moral component, but where the emphasis is more on emotional commitment or perhaps tokenism; and where reflection is preempted or repudiated. Moral transmission always involves a mixture of morality and moralism; and the purchase which rationality is afforded varies with the subject-matter and the age of the children.

Blind moralism has its place

Moralism should not be interpreted pejoratively. In the values transmitted in childhood, there must be a mechanistic, training element. The prohibitions on stealing, lying and aggression are of this sort. When people are old enough the rules can be rationally scrutinised. One might say that, for very young children, a provisional moralism has to stand in for what will later be articulated as morality.

Because of its lower susceptibility to rational enquiry, however, moralism is always more dangerous than morality. It is more easily tipped over into propaganda, sentimentality or special pleading. This is why moralism is often construed pejoratively and the term itself mostly employed as a booword. This is not entirely helpful. Many important values have a strong moral tinge without constituting morality proper. This is true of such attitudes as patriotism and solidarity, which are quasi-moral values indispensable to social order. Competition is another good example. Successful economic life requires competition; but it is hard to put competitiveness on a moral basis other than a utilitarian one. For example, the testimony of Richard Lynn, who has identified extreme competitiveness in the collective psychology of a nation as greatly to its economic advantage, is no more than utilitarian. Do you want to be rich? Then get competitive: that is his message.[9]

At some point, since the curriculum involves much quasi-moral material, as well as moral notions proper, one has to make value-judgments on what to include and what to reject. Which moralism will accompany the set of true morals, once we have decided what these are? There is bad moralism and good moralism. Thus egalitarianism and multiculturalism are bad moralisms, the first because it lowers intellectual standards and the second because it seeks to compromise or destroy the nation's self-confidence and sense of identity. Patriotism and respect for law are, on the contrary, good moralisms. Nations, like individuals, cannot function without a sense of continuity and togetherness. As for the rule of law, it is the core of civilisation itself.[10]

But moralism and technicism have replaced morality proper

Let us not suppose, however, that schools and the preparation of teachers are no longer morally preoccupied. On the contrary, there is more moral emphasis than ever. But now the stress is increasingly on sub-political moralism. The curriculum itself incorporates greater emphasis on 'equality' in the form of multiculturalism, 'gender' rights and so on. It is the order of diligence which has gone.

All too often, certainly, when we look at the school curriculum, we find that an undesirable moralism has partly ousted moralism of the desirable sort. Traditional moralism was subordinated to morality. The progressivist moralism is subordinated to politics or the pleasure principle. For example, anti-competitiveness has partly pushed out competition. A moralism which destroys economic life replaces one indispensable to it. It is the same when egalitarianism outs excellence as a goal and function of educational practice. In extreme cases, moralism will displace genuine moral discourse totally. This is arguably the case on some teacher education courses both in Great Britain and the United States.[11] There is no real moral discourse. Truth, courage, mercy and magnanimity are discussed no more than the mainly prudential virtues of diligence and perseverance. Even respect for others is diminished as a value by its unhealthy, overcharged predication on questions like race, cultural diversity and 'gender'. The real and incontestably vital morals of conduct are submerged in a glutinous moralism.

To attack competition is to attack hard work and excellence. The fulminations against competition in our schools, which identify it as destructive of social harmony and individual peace of mind, are moralism in the worst sense. They block the way to moral endeavour on the part of children. Affecting to equip them morally, they actually disarm them cognitively, leaving them ill-equipped to deal with the moral hazards of the real world.

Moralism is always much less accessible to ratiocination than is morality. This does not mean that all cases are equally fragile. It does mean we must be very careful over what moralism we build into our practice alongside morality proper. Traditional moralism, the emphasis on family, patriotism and the rule of law, needs reviving. The newer moralisms are hugely accident-prone and need reining back.

The traditional mode of education incorporates strong explicit and implicit morality and moralism realised through systems of reward and punishment, promotion and demotion, praise and condemnation. The highest virtues of courage and mercy coexist with the prudential virtues of care and diligence. Both are deeply embedded in a moral life also favouring strong attachment to family, church and country. The mode also involves notions of industry and perseverance in highly individualised work. The teacher's authority is central to the moral order.

There is little specific reliance on educational theory; and the philosophic roots of the tradition, though ancient and strong, have only indirect application. They are embedded both in the moral values underlying the transmission and in the strong emphasis placed on the discreteness of the subject-matter. The philosophy of centuries informs this curriculum, and its executors, that is the schoolteachers, may have little or no formal knowledge of the intellectual history they represent.

Learning is individual in that it focuses on what one person can do; but it is also impersonal, in that it ignores the psychological disposition or background of learners. It is this intense combination of the individual and the impersonal which permits and requires the endeavour to constitute fundamentally a moral exercise.

Pedagogy and morality: a restoration

The rebirth of pedagogic morality would be the most important restoration. It would also be popular. The notion that education, teaching and learning are essentially moral activities appeals both to everyday expectation and to mainstream philosophical reflection as far back as Plato. The public take it for granted that schools should transmit public morality, and are outraged at evidence that this does not take place. Leading philosophers of education have likewise placed moral considerations at the heart of their concerns, indeed in the titles of their best-known books.[12]

Rather more populist approaches to education in the recent past have suggested the explicit strengthening of the moral dimension in education, proposing that to the three 'R's of tradition another two (right and wrong) be added.[13]

Given this moral background in approaches to education and given the continuing emphasis on the moral component of schooling in the public mind, it is surprising that the CCD could have occurred, that is to say, that so little ordinary moral discussion figures in recent debates on the effectiveness of different educational approaches. There are two main reasons for this absence. First, many of the intellectuals who dominate education are hostile to traditional moral conceptions. Some of this hostility originates within the philosophical estate itself. Across a period of some centuries a moral scepticism has built up among many professional philosophers to the effect that hard and fast ethical systems are based on illusions.[14] This has made its way into schools, universities and institutions of teacher preparation.[15]

Among sociologists, anthropologists and their disciples, on the other hand, there has developed the explicit view that the dominant moral system of Western bourgeois society is an unjustifiable imposition, working against the working class, women and minority races or cultures.[16] There is deep distaste in teacher education and the advisory services for the imposition of middle-class morality. Indeed, this hostility to middle-class virtues reflects a wider hostility to the middle-class ascendancy. Traditional moral ideas have been attacked; but so have patterns of speech, approaches to work and discipline, attitudes to family and country and much else. A 'new middle class' has arisen to rebuke and replace the attitudes of the old.

Interestingly, we can put the moral question in technical language. We have no techniques for the provision of moral guidance. But there is little doubt, though the literature appropriate is either absent or embryonic, that different ideologies have different economic 'production functions', different relationships between inputs and outputs. This must apply to moral inputs also. If you treat diligence as a virtue necessary to learning, you will get a different result from those the progressives secure.

The dislike of differences of talent

The CCD is both the coterm for progressivism and the acronym for its failure. It is a prospectus for moral and intellectual failure, comprising not one but two flawed components. First, it pursues the easy way. This reflects its hatred of the real world. Next comes its related confusion over differentially distributed talent. Where the order of diligence perhaps erred in refusing to admit such differences, the modern 'progressives' are all over the place. Their inconsistencies range from the baroque denial of any such thing as intelligence, via the fanatical desire to prevent its observable registration, to an abject capitulation to 'background' determinism. And along with the obsession about resources goes a mania for children's happiness. All difficulties can be transcended if only we throw in enough fun to back up the increased funding.

The frantic egalitarianism of the new middle class, its desire for converging results, is envy in motion, a version of original sin on the march, marching moreover across that most important and vulnerable of territories, the instruction of the young. Egalitarianism is deficient as a political morality. Those who control its educational application can do so only by replacing traditional moral life with their own inferior moralism. Only by removing diligence can they get downwardly converging performance.

The ideology imposed on primary schools has in part undone them. Since the 1960s they have turned out millions who cannot read, write or calculate. The secondary schools are crippled by this shortfall. Now we see, furthermore, the signs here of an American pattern in higher education as well, where some colleges are forced to teach undergraduates such hitherto taken-for-granted skills as basic essay writing. If the foundations are shaky, the whole edifice is threatened.

Morality is primal and technique secondary. This is not to say, however, that technique does not matter. Indeed, different techniques embody different moralities. The technique may be introduced precisely to enact some moral or political theory. The CCD has specifically attacked the traditional moral regulation of children. Claiming to speak for childhood, it has removed the idea that learning is a moral imperative and has left many millions of people quite unnecessarily incompetent. If we put the matter in economic terms, we may say that the CCD has treated education as a consumption good at the disposal of children. Education is nothing of the kind. It is actually an investment good which in the case of young children is made at the behest of their parents. Progressivism has undermined the very means of education by trying to render it fun-packed and painless. Learning by rote, for example, is hard work and boring. Far from causing the mindlessness the progressives allege, however, it actually cultivates diligence and its accompanying virtues: patience, perseverance and the disposition to defer gratification. Such a morality is the necessary bedrock of real scholarship. It should be restored to its rightful place in the struggle for civilisation.

CHAPTER 13

Discretion:

Quietly Discriminating Between the Deserving and the Undeserving Poor

Mark Almond

Discretion as discrimination between people and as restrained speech

'Discretion' has two meanings, but, like ambivalence itself, both of them have fallen into disfavour today—at least among the dominant circles which form public opinion throughout the West. Neither self-restraint in word or deed is fashionable, nor is the idea of discriminating between people on the basis of their deserts. An unwillingness to speak one's mind on any and every subject is seen as suspicious or lofty. Sparing people's feelings is no longer an honourable motive for silence. Choosing between competing demands for finite resources is regarded as shameful when it affects tax-subsidised welfare or health provision.

Neither fashionable

In an age which has universalised the late 1960s' impulse to let everything hang out, the idea of self-restraint or the silent experience of triumph or distress has disappeared. It is not enough that the public should be told of George Bush's collapse, vomiting into the lap of the Japanese Prime Minister, a poor quality picture must be beamed into every household, not only in the U.S., but throughout the world to confirm it.

A similar phenomenon has occurred with well-known AIDS victims from the worlds of pop, sport, film and the arts. In some cases the maxim appears to be 'if you've got it, flaunt it'!

What the famous sufferers from currently incurable diseases fail to notice is that while they may gain certain psychological comforts from their added distinction of contagion by a socially acceptable, perhaps laudable, pox, their anonymous fellow-sufferers may add to the unhappiness of their condition by contrasting it with the compensations of fame. In any case, sufferers from other less 'sexy' but no less fatal diseases may feel neglected, even despised, in their no less tragic condition. The sight of the famous sick and their healthy hangers-on dancing round the graves of the less chic mortally ill is one of the less attractive trends in the modern world.

Discretion unfashionable in welfare too

In the final analysis, however, the indiscretions of beautiful people are less significant in their social consequences than the lack of discrimination shown by the armies of welfare managers throughout the West. The very idea that welfare workers, whether in their treatment of the poor or the sick, should discriminate will strike some as a modern blasphemy. The welfare mind prefers to see its 'clients' not as normal individuals but as statistical by-products of any anonymous dysfunctional social system. To the social worker the poor are a problem to be managed rather than individuals to be rescued from their plight, preferably by helping them to help themselves. Of course, the poverty of initiative among the poor is one of the last things to be tackled by a welfare system because it suggests that some of the poor might be helpless because they don't want to get out of their condition. The inability of the recipients to imagine life without welfare is compounded by the horror of welfare administrators at the idea of life off the welfare-roll.

So the genuinely unfortunate suffer

Reviving initiative among the recipients of welfare by channelling (part of) it as rewards for good behaviour and a positive approach strikes horror into the minds of welfare administrators. First of all, it requires effort to distinguish between the deserving and the undeserving and, secondly, it risks unpopularity with the 'clients'. So long as the public purse provides an inadequate dole to millions without hinting at any distinction between them, unless it is to prefer the unmarried mother over the childless couple, then all complaints are directed against the 'system', the anonymous universal provider of inadequate welfare cheques to the poor and pay-cheques to the carers. It is depressing enough dealing with those who have drawn short straws in life's great competition without having to distinguish between them yet again.

Yet failing to provide a discretionary element in the welfare system adds to the punishment of the unfortunate without raising up the inveterate claimant.

It is not only advocates of social welfare provision as a weapon in the struggle for an egalitarian society who argue against discretion in the distribution of state as well as private welfare. More powerful voices, usually critical of the nostrums of the Welfare Community, have also spoken out against putting the power to decide who should receive state aid into the hands of the professional carers. John Gray has argued against discretionary grants to welfare claimants on the grounds that in practice they hand over enormous power to malign bureaucratic forces intent on politicising the poor or unwell rather than helping them. Of course, this is all too true of the current welfare dispensation in all Western societies—the only difference being the more indiscriminate welfare payments and services are, the less satisfaction from 'clients' is forthcoming.

The irony—moralising on lifestyle all the rage

A counter-revolution in the mentality of the caring professions (i.e., those who make a living out of what used to be called charity) is required to restore not only fiscal discipline to state-financed welfare organisations, but also to revive their moral purpose. It is an irony of the late twentieth century affluent West that keeping physically fit has become the moralising maxim of society at the same time as the feckless poor have been treated on the same level as the unfortunate recipients of welfare, those who used to be called the 'deserving poor'. As more and more moral energy goes into stamping out smoking and encouraging the middle-aged to risk coronary disaster by running distances hardly suited to healthy twenty year-olds, so little stamina has been left to tackle the question of the moral responsibility of the poor for themselves.

The years of growing state-funded welfare provision since the Second World War have gone a long way to proving that despite taxpayers' largesse, the poor are always with us. The growth in the numbers of 'relatively' poor can be found on either side of the Atlantic—in the U.S. where belated and half-hearted efforts were made to halt the inexorable rise of public welfare, and in Western Europe where the principle of equal access of all the poor to the public purse is still sacrosanct.

Discretion does not necessarily mean inquisitorial means tests

The hostility to allowing discretion in the allocation of state charity is understandable in the context of the history of its normal applications, but it is misconceived. In Britain, for instance, the post-war revulsion against the inquisitorial means tests used to determine whether an unemployed person was entitled to national assistance, and at what rate, was based on the misapplication of the principle of the deserving poor. The means-testers in the 1930s often humiliated decent working folk whose bread-winner had lost his job in the Great Depression by coldly calculating how many chairs or table-settings his family required and obliging him to sell off or pawn the rest before allowing any aid. Naturally such a process hit those poor unemployed who had used their years of labour to provide their families with a modicum of decent living more than their feckless colleagues who had perhaps spent their wages on drink and tobacco.

Any revival of discretionary welfare must be based on the principle of rewarding the hard-working and responsible poor who are dependent on others for their income at a preferential rate compared with those whose lack of employment bears fewer obvious traits of misfortune. In turn, this will require a new type of agent of public charity. The resentment culture fostered by the present system, in the distributors of state aid as well as in the recipients, will have to be banished or at least defied despite the fact that at first it is bound to lead to a raucous uproar.

De-professionalising the distribution of benefits

One important path is to de-professionalise the distribution of aid. So long as welfare is administered by a professional welfare bureaucracy with all the inbuilt tendencies towards a self-serving ethos which affect the best in society, there is little chance that welfare provision of all sorts can be de-politicised. But the de-politicisation of the distribution of welfare is essential to a rational discussion of its purposes. The purposes of welfare or charity cannot be separated from political debate—nor should they be—but the clouding of issues by allowing massive well-funded bureaucracies to pursue their own goals under the guise of representing their clients is a major obstacle to dealing with the central questions of the future. By its nature the competition for effective control of welfare between politicians with many other things on their minds and single-issue professionals is unequal. Even where the public's representatives win the legislative initiative, the implementation of new laws is all too easily perverted to suit the agenda of the professionals rather than the legislators.

Discretion inevitable because ageing population adds to volume of claimants

It does not require a prophet to see an intensification in all developed societies of an already evident problem: as more people live longer than they ever expected to, even the prudent are afflicted by expenses in old age which they can hardly be blamed for not anticipating. Poverty in old age is a peculiarly affecting phenomenon, which requires tact as well as money to alleviate. Precisely because an ageing population will require proportionately more professional nursing and other kinds of assistance, much of it publicly funded, a far more subtle and discriminating direction of policy at the individual and local level will be required. The age of blanket allocations is passing.

The great burden of future medical provision and care for the growing armies of elderly and infirm requires a fundamental reappraisal of all welfare policies. Even a rich society like Germany admitted that its provisions of old-age pensions and medical treatment for the next generation of elderly were inadequate even before it took on the burden of East Germany. Most other Western societies are in a worse position to provide decently for their elderly. A cruel choice will confront democracies as well as individuals before too long: who should come first in the welfare queue—the fit young or the decaying old?

Removing entitlements for young not only efficient but educational

No moral society will hesitate from diverting funds from those able to help themselves to those who cannot. In practice, removing entitlements from the young and able-bodied may be dictated by economic considerations, but it can serve a moral purpose. If young people adapt to a society where assistance is given out according to merit rather than by right, it will at least encourage a great deal more articulacy in the making of demands for the dole than those to which we have recently become accustomed. Of course, this presupposes someone in authority able to distinguish between requests for help. The donor—whether giving from his own resources directly or from a public fund—also benefits from a position of responsibility. Whereas today so many welfare officials have no sense of moral responsibility for the funds they disburse, and sometimes little enforceable legal responsibility either, the placing of the distribution of welfare into the hands of discriminating local people not only provides them with an important function in the community (denied in the welfare state) but also encourages a broader sense of responsibility.

Indiscriminate welfare encourages dependency

After the riots in Los Angeles and other U.S. cities at the beginning of May 1992, the voices of the welfare consensus throughout the West were loud in their demands for more public funds for the poor as the only way to discourage future violence. As ever the consensus overlooked the problem of the responsibility of welfare for stimulating not only the material dependency but also the demoralisation of the poor. The combination of incentives to remaining in dependency with the inherent frustrations which arise from it is likely to foster more crime and mindless violence. A discrete approach to the problem of poverty in general, and to the specific social causes of its prolongation across generations, offers some hope of rescuing many of the poor from the poverty trap and the moral wastelands which so often accompany it.

Social policies which intend to redistribute income to the poor and needy must both offer real assistance to their target individuals and groups without, however, encouraging other people to sink into the class of welfare recipients in the future.

For instance, the correlation between teenage single-parents and poverty is universal throughout the West. How can a subsidised flat be provided for an unmarried mother, who may not even know the identity of her child's father, without seeming to create a link between pregnancy and the availability of a home of one's own?

Of course, this is not to suggest that the virtually automatic provision of a flat to single mothers causes others to engage in a conscious calculation of the pros and cons of unmarried pregnancy as a route to housing. However, there can be little doubt that the daily sight of friends or neighbours who have received a variety of benefits as a result of pregnancy changes the mental and moral climate in which any individual lives. Over two decades, welfare payments to single parents in the United Kingdom rose from 15 million pounds to more than 4,000 million pounds. Even allowing for inflation, this clearly involved a massive increase in the cash available to single parents. And there can be little doubt that the rise in teenage pregnancy was in part promoted by the granting of cash, housing, etc., to pregnant girls as a right.

Little attention has been given to the double problem of how to help a girl in real difficulties, who is unwilling to have an abortion (also at public expense in Britain), without inadvertantly encouraging others to follow the same route. It is the very publicity of the standard universal rights which creates the moral background noise which lowers standards of behaviour. Enormous funds are spent by the British welfare services in promoting public knowledge of individual's rights to welfare benefits. In theory this is supposed to help the needy who may be ignorant of assistance available to them, but in practice it creates a climate of opinion in which the individual is encouraged to seek out what he can get and to behave in a way which will justify receiving benefits.

Loud public statements and quite individualised help

In the days of charity provided primarily through the agency of the churches, the dilemma facing those who wanted to help sinners without rewarding sin was widely understood. The pulpit thundered against anti-social or wicked behaviour, but the clergy were the chief suppliers of aid and comfort to those who had 'fallen'. By setting general standards, encouraging self-reliance and shame at the thought of dependency, the churches discouraged wanton laziness or wilful dependence, but at the same time behind the barrage of moral inculcation, the clergy actively helped those in need, including those whose necessity was the product of breaching its code of ethics. Quiet and discrete aid neither humiliated the recipient nor, however, justified his status as receiver of charity. The obligation to give charitably was invoked rather than the right to receive.

Western progressives dislike what they see as the hypocrisy involved in discrete help. Instead of accepting that some people are poor through no fault of their own while others have chosen—perhaps unthinkingly—patterns of behaviour which end in poverty, the Western welfare consensus prefers to reject both the notion of guilt or responsibility and therefore differential treatment of superficially similar cases of need. Most of all the welfare consensus rejects the idea of preaching to its clients the necessity of mending their ways. Changing people's behaviour even where it is blatantly the cause of their distress is considered arrogant and undemocratic.

Local not universal welfare

By its nature a system of welfare which is discrete and does not advertise universally available benefits must be local. Its agents must be able to draw on knowledge of the individuals in order to determine whether specific forms of aid will help them in their need and to get out of it. It may in fact make some people more dependent on the decisions of others, though much less chronically dependent on social welfare. Already in Switzerland, for example, social workers have a much greater say about the distribution of help to individuals and will often require changes in behaviour before granting it. Monitoring of individual progress is vital to ensure that progress towards independence is rewarded and its lessons understood by all concerned, as well as to avoid waste and misdirected aid.

A renunciation of universal benefits and social rights is an essential step in the progress towards a welfare system which treats individuals as moral persons responsible for themselves and capable of being helped to help themselves. In many ways a reversion to the discrete distribution of welfare will put more demands on social workers—the local agents of the system—but it would reward them with greater authority and sense of achievement. They should be rewarded and respected according to the number of clients whom they help to lift out of poverty rather than on the numerical basis of their clientele.

The restoration of discretion is an important step to the recivilising of society since it is part of liberating adults from the Nanny State. The rhetoric of rights should be replaced by the silence of action. Instead of universal, equal and demeaning welfare, discrimination in public assistance to the less fortunate members of society encourages the human individual to flourish, or at least to recover basic dignity.

CHAPTER 14

Self-Improvement:

And its Neglect by the Contemporary Mainstream Churches

Anthony Flew

Those who suffer poverty and ill health not always helpless victims

There are two very different ways in which we may hope to make the world better. One is through collective action, which in our time is usually the action of the central or the local state. The other is through the spontaneous improvement of ourselves and others as individuals. Both these approaches are essential, they do not have to be mutually exclusive, and they can often be usefully complementary. But on particular occasions and for tackling particular problems one is more relevant, more appropriate and more productive than the other.

Thanks above all to Charles Murray's monumental *Losing Ground*[1] there seems, at least in the U.S., to be an increasing willingness to admit and to explore the policy implications of something which earlier generations scarcely ever overlooked: namely, that those who suffer poverty, ill health, premature death and what in this era of universal, compulsory, tax-financed schooling is euphemistically called (not ignorance but) 'educational underachievement', are not always altogether helpless victims. One straw in a still gentle wind was the conclusion of the Working Seminar on Family and American Welfare established by the American Enterprise Institute:

> The probabilities of remaining involuntarily in poverty are remarkably low for those who, first, complete high school, then, once adult, get and stay married (even if not on the first try) and, finally, stay employed, even at a wage and under conditions below their ultimate aims.[2]

213

Self-improvement once the insistence of the churches

Suppose we make so bold as to assert that there is a great deal which individuals—including victims of supposedly social problems—both can do and ought to do as individuals, both to better themselves and, immediately or ultimately, to benefit other people. Then we might expect to find sympathy and support in the Christian churches, not only for this admission, but also for the sort of policy thinking which grows out of it. Some still living can indeed remember a time when those organisations were forever insisting: both that we are all creatures who can and cannot but make choices; and that we alone, as individuals, are ultimately responsible for the senses in which we make whatever choices may from time to time be open to us. (On occasion then there was even talk of a future life, and perhaps hints on how for every individual the quality of that life would be determined by the senses of his or her most important choices.)

Nowadays, however, expectations of ecclesiastical sympathy and support for such 'individualism' must often be disappointed. Certainly some churches, and many members of all the others, maintain a commitment to individual conversion with consequent transformations in the lives of converts. Those North American churches, for instance, whose missionaries have in Guatemala and other countries of Latin America been making wholesale conversions to a traditional kind of Protestantism, have thereby produced transformations in individual lives, and consequently in entire communities, which are reminiscent of the original impact in 18th- and early 19th-century England and Wales of John Wesley and his preachers.

Mainstream modern churches demand all of governments and nothing from individuals

It is, however, another story altogether with mainstream churches, the churches which in the U.S. belong to the National Council of Churches (NCC) and in the UK to the British Council of Churches (BCC). Especially is this so with those who draft and issue on their behalf an ever-rising torrent of statements about social, political and economic policy. Those people—to borrow the phrase standardly employed by General Lee in speaking of the Union armies—those people appear to be demanding no action by individuals other than efforts to induce government to adopt their own preferred policies.

I propose to examine what is in this respect a representative document, *Faith in the City*, the Report of the Archbishop of Canterbury's Commission for Urban Priority Areas (UPAs).[3] Though bulky, this is a single document. But it came as a climax to a series, and has served as the inspirational prelude to much subsequent action and publication. Nor is it to be dismissed as expressing merely the opinions of 15 Archiepiscopal Commissioners. For their findings were later accepted, apparently without significant reservations, by the Synod—the nearest thing which the Church of England has to a governing body. Again, although that organisation manifestly is, and for many years past has been—in more than one sense—in secular decline, it still remains, at least in England, 'the church by law established'. Finally, although *Faith in the City* speaks directly only for one member church, it is in fact sufficiently representative of the whole BCC. (I must leave it to my American colleagues to say whether it would be equally representative of the NCC.)

Faith in the City is also representative in all the respects for which contributors to *The Kindness that Kills: The Churches' Simplistic Response to Complex Social Issues* faulted that response.[4] The book's editor, Digby Anderson, summed up the findings from studies of 24 pronouncements listed in the name of various church organisations or organisations of churches in two devastating sentences:

> Bluntly, if the Churches are to comment on specific and controversial socio-economic issues, they should work harder at being informed and scrupulously even-handed. Their publications are variously found to be sloppy, ill-thought out, ignorant, one-sided, addicted to secular fashions, uncritical of conventional 'progressive' wisdom, hysterical, unmethodical in their uses of sources and evidence, theologically desiccated and, most deplorable, uncharitable to those who disagree.[5]

It quickly becomes clear that this *Call for Action by Church and Nation* is a call to government, and for substantial, all-round increases in tax-financed expenditure on state-supplied health, education and welfare services. Certainly the authors do at one point bring themselves to concede that 'Individual responsibility and self-reliance are excellent objectives. The nation cannot do without them'.[6] But, having seized upon every previous opportunity not to stress or even mention either the importance or excellence, they proceed to italicize their own conviction, sustained by no deployment of evidence, *'that at present too much emphasis is being given to individualism, and not enough to collective obligation'.*[7]

Judging social policies not by results but intentions: the case of school truancy

While thus refusing to put that heavy emphasis upon individual responsibility which was, and in some places such as rural Guatemala still is, the glory of Protestant Christianity, our Commissioners nevertheless undeviatingly and systematically succumb to what might be dubbed the Moralist's Temptation. This is the temptation to judge public policies as one might quite properly judge an individual agent: by reference, that is, not so much to the actual effects of those polices as to the presumed intentions of their promoters. What, therefore, we lose on the roundabouts, we lose also on the swings.

Both faults can be found in the treatment of education: the first in the failure to say anything about truancy, the rates of which are certainly far higher in poor urban areas than elsewhere.[8] Since knowledge and skills are not substances which can be poured into passive pots it is not sufficient to provide varied and abundant teaching, however excellent in quality. It is necessary also to have pupils willing and able to expose themselves to and to cooperate with that teaching. So it should be obvious that ensuring that exposure and cooperation is a very important thing which individual parents and their individual children 'both could do and ought to do . . . both to better themselves and, immediately or ultimately, to benefit other people'. It is also very much to the present point to add that, if only more children and more parents would in this respect now do what they could do and ought to do, then one most desirable result would be that many children would become more employable than would otherwise be the case, and hence less likely to be numbered among the future unemployed.

The second fault is shown in the Commission's assumptions: that, under the British or any similar system for the public provision of primary and secondary[9] educational services, you get the amount of pupil learning which the taxpayers are paying for; and that any substantial improvements can and will be obtained only by a comparably substantial input of additional resources. These are assumptions which, understandably enough, all the supply side interest groups are concerned to promote. Yet they are also accepted much more widely, and this despite an ever more abundant accumulation of falsifying evidence.[10]

For instance: while the Commission was producing its report the Inner London Education Authority (ILEA) regularly spent more per pupil head than any other—40 to 50 per cent more than the national average—and yet its results were among the worst, if not the worst, in the country, including those in the other UPAs. The person who served as Minister of State at the Department of Education and Science (DES) at that time, and for two or three years both before and after, and who therefore presumably knew what he was talking about, was later to describe the condition of the entire UK (state) maintained system as 'a national catastrophe'.[11]

Affirming school success but not defining it

The Commission's one positive educational suggestion constitutes a paradigm case of addiction to 'secular fashions' and of being 'uncritical of conventional "progressive" wisdom'. For, after noting that the new General Certificate of Secondary Education (GCSE) examinations are supposedly 'designed for only 60 per cent of the year group', and that 'in some UPA schools' this must disqualify considerably more than 40 per cent of the pupils, they conclude: 'The need in such schools is for a curriculum and an assessment system which affirms success rather than records failure'.[12]

The actual need, nationally and not only 'in some UPA schools', was and remains a comprehensive system of independently assessed leaving examinations. This would provide certification of employability, guaranteeing at least a minimum literacy and a minimum numeracy, as well perhaps as embracing whatever other useful skills particular pupils had contrived to acquire. As it is, or was at the time when *Faith in the City* was published, up to half of those leaving ILEA schools at the first legal opportunity were leaving with no such independent evidence showing how if at all they had benefitted from their years of compulsory schooling.[13]

Anyone puzzled by this talk of affirmation should compare the Commissioners' recommendation on what they delicately describe as 'the arrival in our cities of large numbers of adherents to other faiths'. It is that the rest of us should 'affirm other cultures'.[14] Presumably by 'affirm' these *bien-pensants* mean 'adopt a positive attitude towards'—but without on any account pressing the awkward questions whether success actually has been achieved or whether either the Christian faith or another is in fact true. For they are, as should be noted much more widely than it has been, remarkably reluctant to insist upon the truth of propositions traditionally rated essential to the faith in the name of which they labour to promote preferred political prescriptions.

For instance: after much respectful talk of Liberation Theology (always thus, unlike plain old-fashioned theology, accorded genuflectory initial capitals), they nevertheless go on to maintain that, although 'people today' do need something new and of course more relevant, that particular novelty is not right, at any rate for Western Europe. When the Commissioners indicate how the desired new, more relevant theology is to be generated, their specifications escape the dangers perceived only by failing to demand that it be either Christian or even theology. What we need 'would start, not from a conventional academic syllabus of Christian knowledge or Biblical study, but from the personal experience, the modes of perception and the daily concerns of local people themselves'. The Commissioners thus eschew embarrassingly 'divisive' stipulations that the experience and the perceptions should be *of God*.

Neglecting the family's responsibility for its own failure and its effect on other social problems

Once any statement on social policy made on behalf of a church would have insisted on two manifest truths: that families are by far the most important of all institutions promoting health, education and welfare; and that they are formed (or not formed) and preserved (or not preserved) by the congruent choices of two people, one male and one female; and hence that when standard families degenerate into the variant one-parent form, this too now almost always results from a choice made by at least one of the parents, usually the male.[15]

Once . . . but no longer. For when our Commissioners write about marriage and families, which is neither often nor at length, they treat the failure to marry and form families, and the disruption of formed families into one-parent families, as if these were occurrences beyond human control. In such natural disasters as typhoons and hurricanes there is indeed nothing which anyone can do—save try to limit the damage and help the inevitable victims. But this is different. Certainly there are victims needing help—mainly the children. But here there are victimizers as well as victims. And these victimizers are—like us and their victims—agents; who therefore in principle can, and in practice surely should, be held responsible for whatever they have done or failed to do.

The chapter 'Church and City' rates the 'Incidence of marriage and other family problems' both nationally, and still more in the UPAs, as significantly albeit not vastly more serious than 'Level of unemployment' or 'Quality/price of public transport' or 'Number of elderly people'.[16] Yet it seems never to occur to the authors that these marginally top-rated family problems may themselves be prime causes of some of the others. Significantly too they choose to speak of 'marriage breakdown' as if the failure to form marriages or their disruption was, at least immediately, beyond human control.

No one either pretending to have studied or attempting to solve such problems has any business to be unaware of the evidence that the absence of a concerned father makes it much more likely, though of course very far from certain, that the children thus deprived will underachieve educationally and/or become delinquent.[17] Asserting that blacks are disproportionately represented not only among the unemployed but also among both educational underachievers and the prison population, the 'politically correct', knee-jerk reaction of the Commissioners—although they do somewhat prissily allow that a lot of unemployed black youths had 'had fathers living away from home'—is to attribute these disfavoured proportionate over-representations to racism.[18]

Obscuring racial differences

By sometimes although not always following the malicious and obscurantist usage under which all non-whites become brigaded together as blacks, the Commissioners conceal from themselves and their readers both the size, and the likely prime cause, of differences in the track records of our Afro-Caribbeans and our Asians. Researchers for ILEA, which was in the forefront of politically motivated campaigns to encourage all non-whites to see themselves as members of a class chronically victimised by and outcast from white British society, produced performance statistics discrediting the presuppositions of those campaigns.[19] These statistics show that, although there are—as should be expected—substantial performance differences between different subsets of these racial sets, in ILEA schools Asians in general were doing much better than whites; and blacks, or at least those whose parents or grandparents came from the Caribbean, worse.[20] The same statistics also show that, whereas 20 per cent of all the children in these schools came from one-parent families, this is true of 43 per cent of Afro-Caribbeans but of only 5 per cent of Asians.

Uncritically endorsing minimum wage policies

The Low Pay Unit is thanked for submitting written evidence. Both that self-description and its characteristically uncritical acceptance by the Commissioners are significant. For speaking of 'low pay' suggests, as speaking of 'low earnings' would not, that the problem is somehow to increase payments for all the jobs presently accounted low paying. In that case the solution is bound to be collectivist, presumably involving the introduction of minimum wage laws or some equivalent thereto.

There are, however, three very serious objections to the policies thus prejudicially endorsed. First, almost everyone who has ever sincerely sought to discover the actual consequences of introducing minimum wage laws seems to have concluded that they must and do tend to increase unemployment.[21] Yet, surely, low earnings are better than no earnings?

Nor should it be overlooked that increasing a minimum wage is almost bound to provoke demands for the restoration of differentials. To grant these must, all other things being equal, be inflationary. (And if anything deserves to be put down as a social injustice, although in fact it almost never has been, it is the institutionalised robbery and fraud of inflation.) But not to grant such demands reduces the incentives to acquiring skills. We thus have one more occasion to recall what in *Losing Ground* Charles Murray formulated as 'The Law of Unintended Rewards. Any social transfer increases the net value of being in the condition that prompted the transfer';[22] in this case the net value of being unskilled.

The second objection is that low paid jobs, even if not, as they often are, the first steps on a formalised career ladder, can be made, and by many people have been and are being made, the first stages in their own individual advancement. In the U.S.A. before World War II those lacking all special skills could often, by pricing themselves into unskilled jobs, acquire the basic good habits of timekeeping and application needed to make themselves more employable. Minimum wage laws make this sort of self-help impossible. One clear consequence—despite the intervening explosion of civil rights legislation—has been that, whereas in the 1930s the rates of black juvenile unemployment were lower than those for whites, the reverse is now the case.[23]

Thirdly, a great many of the jobs which are accounted low paid are in fact providing some household with its second or even third income; an income which, as an additional income, may well be making all the difference between modest prosperity and actual or at any rate perceived hardship. Minimum wage laws, therefore, by reducing the availability of such modest additional incomes, are likely to hurt a lot of families; just as are laws and regulations which, by requiring employers to provide part-time workers with all the benefits enjoyed by full-timers, similarly reduce the numbers of jobs of a kind ideally suited to mothers with growing children.

A different religious response to social problems: the Chief Rabbi's

Britain's then Chief Rabbi was so disturbed by the teachings of *Faith in the City* that he took what is for a Jewish leader the unusual step of commenting upon a professedly Christian document in a booklet entitled From *Doom to Hope*.[24] Christianity and Judaism, he wrote, both 'raise the relief of want as a precept of the highest religious virtue'. But 'the Jewish work-ethic is rather more positive and demanding . . . Cheap labour is more dignified than a free dole'. So the emphasis is always on both self-help and helping others to help themselves. For Judaism the best of charity is that which helps the poor to dispense with charity and to escape dependency. It is, said Rabbi Moses ben Maimon (Maimonides):

> . . . that of the person who assists the poor man by providing him with a gift or loan, or by accepting him into a business partnership, or by helping him find employment—in a word, by putting him where he can dispense with other people's aid.[25]

The persistent confusion of injustice and inequality (of outcome)

In the nearly 200 pages of part III, 'Challenge to the Nation', the Commissioners, although ever ready to dismiss opposition as 'dogmatic', never once name or quote any opponent. The nearest that they themselves ever get to entertaining and attempting to meet argued objections is in an aside. Without actually citing—perhaps never having read—the heretical book quoted above,[26] they protest that 'the original provision of sewerage and piped water in our cities could clearly not be called "a kindness that kills" '.[27]

Indeed, it could not. But then it never has been—least of all by the authors of that unmentionable book.

Guided, or misguided, by the 'Black Report' the Commissioners attend mainly if not only to *Inequalities in Health*,[28] while giving, characteristically, no consideration whatsoever to any possibilities of self-improvement. Here too, as elsewhere, they are entirely uncritical clients of the fashionable assumption that justice is to be identified with equality

of outcome.[29] This explains their commitment to 'people-oriented policies which *promote justice by mitigating inequalities wherever they are found*'
(emphasis added).

But a system of criminal justice treating the convicted in exactly
the same way as the innocent would, as Kant might have protested, contradict itself. The truth is that the rules of justice, like all rules, require
only that we always treat in the same way, not all cases, but only all rele-
vantly like cases. If and insofar as 'social justice' requires the enforcement of an equality of outcome it is no more a sort of without prefix
or suffix justice than People's Democracy is a kind of democracy or positive freedom a kind of freedom. 'Three minutes thought would suffice
to find this out; but thought is irksome, and three minutes is a long
time'.[30]

Here, as always when reference is made to the putative demands
of justice, we need to recall the traditional definition. The *Institutes* of
Justinian makes the criterion of just dealing a constant and perpetual
will *sum cuique tribuere* (to yield to each their own). Ulpian prefaced that
with two further clauses: *Honest vivere, reminem laedere, suum cuique tribuere*
(To live honestly, to injure no one, to yield to each their own); what is
properly our own in the present context being our deserts—such as due
punishment for our crimes—and our entitlements—above all to have and
to hold in our possession our properties, honestly acquired.

Presumably it is their misguided identification of inequality with
injustice, and their failure to distinguish supposed imperatives of 'social'
justice from the mandates of old-fashioned without prefix or suffix justice, which together explain the confidence with which the Commissioners agree with the Bishop of Liverpool's dogmatic denial: 'It is not charity when the powerful help the poor . . . it is justice'.[31]

Misunderstanding the Good Samaritan

Apart from quoting the three words 'remember the poor' from
Galatians II, 3, a quotation backed by reference to II *Corinthians*, VIII-IX,
the sole Scriptural support supplied by the Commissioners, either for
this denial or for any of the many recommendations which they would
presumably claim to be making 'as Christians', is a mere mention of the
Parable of the Good Samaritan—without, perhaps significantly, the reference (*Luke*, X, 25-37). Consultation with that by some seemingly only
half-remembered passage reveals, however, that its citation here is egre-
giously inept: both because the Samaritan tended the traveller with his

own hands and paid the innkeeper out of his own purse; and because his deeds of charity (of love) constituted a fulfilling—not simply obedience to but a substantial going beyond—the minimal requirements of the law (of justice).[32]

Since taxation is necessarily the extraction of resources, whether in cash or in kind, under the threat of force, the appropriate model for a 'redistributing' Chancellor of the Exchequer is Robin Hood rather than the Good Samaritan. So there is a peculiar problem of justifying such 'redistributive' exactions, in the more particular sense of showing that they are just. For it is one thing, and comparatively easy, to develop that kind of justification for those exactions which constitute, in effect, payments for services received: they can be seen as (a forced) repayment of debts. But it is quite another to demonstrate the justice of the legalised robbery of Peters and Petras in order to finance handouts to Pauls and Paulas. For to do that you would, surely, need to show that what is taken from those Peters and Petras never was honestly acquired and justly theirs?

No doubt most of us—quite apart from any selfish desires for more for ourselves—would like to see the good things of this world differently distributed. We cannot, however, be equally sure that whether we would or ever could all agree upon one and the same distribution as our single, shared ideal. Everyone eager for the state to enforce the realisation of their own personal ideal is, therefore, almost irresistibly tempted to maintain that that realisation is mandated by a kind of justice. If true this would equip them with an adequate answer to the challenge: 'By what right are you attempting to realise such an ideal by force?' For, as Adam Smith remarked in his less familiar masterpiece, the just man is one who 'does everything which his equals can with propriety force him to do, or which they can punish him for not doing'.[33]

The consequences of the confusion of injustice and inequality of outcome suppose that we were to endorse the Commissioners' 'people-oriented policies which promote justice by mitigating inequalities wherever they are found'. Then we would need to notice two further logical consequences of the assumption that inequalities are necessarily injustices. First, if justice does indeed demand an equality of outcome, then those presently possessing above average capitals or enjoying above average incomes must be possessing and enjoying more than is justly theirs. If such people maintain this conception of justice, then they should be seen as—on their own terms, and morally speaking—thieves; and, worse still, thieves in possession of the property of others worse off than themselves.[34]

The second further and more immediate relevant consequence is that, if handouts to the beneficiaries of the welfare state are mandated by a sort of justice, then their provision necessarily becomes a moral right possessed by the morally entitled beneficiaries. But if that were so, then there could, presumably, be no moral obligation upon any of us to exercise our utmost efforts to avoid succumbing to (or, should we be so unfortunate as to succumb, to emancipate ourselves from) any of the conditions entitling us to such benefits.

The nub of the matter: social conditionings and social necessitations

'Philosophy', the Commissioners report, 'has moved far beyond Descartes and has finally exorcised "the ghost in the machine"'. Not noticing—or perhaps not caring—that that exorcism must threaten all doctrines of a future life,[35] they go on to tell us that 'Modern social scientists insist' upon social and economic conditioning and determination. The Commissioners never reveal exactly what such conditioning and determination is supposed to involve, or how far it extends. But clearly they believe it goes a very long way towards removing any warrant for holding individuals responsible for what they choose to do or not to do—at least if those individuals are resident in UPAs.

Perhaps, therefore, the most useful way to conclude the present chapter is by deploying one or two of the crucial distinctions needed to show how much or how little findings from the social sciences can reasonably undermine traditional and—let it be said, even if it is left to the unbeliever to say it—Biblical ideas of individual responsibility.

The first essential is to distinguish two fundamentally different senses of the word 'cause', and of all such semantic associates as 'determine' and 'condition'.[36] In one of these—let us call it the physical—the sense in which we speak of the causes of everything except human actions—causes physically necessitate their effects. Given the total cause no power within the universe can prevent the occurrence of the effect. It is with this concept of causation in mind that J. Q. Wilson, in his commendably fresh and open-minded *Thinking about Crime*, argues that 'if causal theories explain why a criminal acts as he does, they also explain why he *must* act as he does'.[37]

In the physical sense of the word 'cause', this is perfectly correct.

But that is not the sense in which social scientists and others discover the causes of human actions. Consider, for example, the case of someone who, by announcing splendid news, causes others to celebrate. By thus providing them with what they may themselves choose to adopt as their reason for celebration (choose to make a cause for celebration) that someone certainly makes it more likely, even perhaps reliably predictable, that they will in fact celebrate. If this happens to be, or to involve their doing, something which they ought not to do, then perhaps it will be right and proper to allow that the announcement made it much more difficult for them to obey the Categorical Imperative. But what is most certainly not true is that those who were thus caused were by this sort of causing physically necessitated to celebrate; necessitated in a way which must completely excuse behaviour which was, by the hypothesis, delinquent. Let us, taking a hint from Hume, label causes of this second sort 'moral'.[38]

'He had no choice'

Frequently, in concluding from the presence of powerfully explanatory motivation to an inexorably necessitating and hence completely exculpatory determinism, a lot is made of two massively misleading idioms: 'he had no choice'; and 'she could not have done otherwise'. The crux is that the correct application for those common idioms is to cases where it is not to be denied, but taken for granted, that in a profounder sense, agents did have a choice, and could have done otherwise.

'Here I stand. I can no other. So help me God'. These most famous words of the archetypal Protestant hero are not to be interpreted, as the French would say if only they spoke English, at the foot of the letter. For Luther was not claiming to have fallen victim to a sudden general paralysis—God help him! For to say, in the everyday sense of 'could have done otherwise', that I could not have done otherwise is not merely inconsistent with, it actually presupposes the truth of the assumption that, in a more fundamental sense, I could. What, as really we all know, Luther meant—and indeed said—was: not that he was afflicted with general paralysis, and hence unable to withdraw; but that none of the alternative courses of action open to him were, to him, acceptable.

Again, consider people who, unlike Luther before the Diet of Worms, act not of their own free will but under compulsion. It may be the bank manager who opens the safe and hands out its contents in the face of menacing guns. Or it may be a small girl who says something rude to her teacher because a horrid boy threatened to spoil her pretty new frock if she did not.

The excuse that they acted under compulsion does not imply that there was no alternative possible course of action which they could have chosen. There was in each case a very obvious alternative available. It is precisely that alternative to which their respective excuses refer. The point is: not that the agent had no alternative; but that the obvious alternative was one which that agent could not properly be blamed or punished for not choosing.

Both the person who does something of his own free will, and the person who does the same thing under compulsion, act. Both, that is to say, rather than the former only, have and are exercising free will—in the confused and confusing theologico-philosophical understanding of that expression. There therefore must have been some possible alternative which they might have chosen. It is for this reason, and for this reason only, reasonable that we should—as we do—require more formidable alternatives to excuse more serious offences. Had our bank manager been able to plead only that the villains had threatened to spoil his, the manager's, natty executive suit, then even in our soft and permissive period, that excuse would scarcely have been acceptable.

Such differentiation would be unwarranted and unintelligible if those pleading that they acted only under compulsion had in truth not acted at all; if really, in the more fundamental senses, they had had no choice and could not have acted otherwise—or, more strictly speaking, could not have acted at all. By contrast, when we utter these words in their less fundamental everyday senses, what we are saying is that the agents in question could not reasonably have been expected to do other than they did—in either the descriptive or the prescriptive construal of the word 'expect'.[39]

There is no doubt but that cases where people act, or refrain from acting, under compulsion are totally different from cases where they do not act at all. Suppose that I am overpowered by a team of skilful strong-arm men, who throw me willy-nilly out of the window. Suppose too that in consequence I fall through the roof of your greenhouse, and that your treasured orchids are ruined by that fall. Then, however, excusable in the excitement of the moment, it would be incorrect for you to demand to know why I did such damage to those precious orchids, or for me to explain that I only acted under compulsion. For there is no conduct of mine to be explained or excused. I did not do or refrain from doing anything. I did not act under compulsion. I did not act at all. The responsible agents were the defenestrators. I was simply a missile victim.

To have free will in the theologico-philosophical understanding just now explained, that is to say to be an agent and therefore both be able and have to make choices, is a part, and a large part, of what it is to be a human being. It is, therefore, a truth which ought never to be forgotten in any discussions of social problems and social policies—least of all by persons pretending to respect the human dignity of the far from passive subjects of those problems and those policies.

CHAPTER 15

Making People Good—Again:

The Role of Authority, Fear and Example

David Martin

Goodness is still widely approved of

A lot of people, probably most, would like most people to be good, or at least better. I assume this entirely from persistent hearsay because although pollsters have asked people if they are happy, no pollster, at least to my knowledge has asked:

Would you like mankind to be better?
Very much better? Perfect?
What would be your response to more goodness? Dismay? Modest approval? Passionate enthusiasm?

We lack this information mainly because calls for more evil and larger legions of unashamed malefactors are so infrequent. The current balance of good and evil seems to be such that nobody demands a more robust and invigorating tilt in favour of evil or feels it would be so much nicer if people were nastier. Presumably that is why, when George Bush called for a kinder, gentler world no enterprising columnist nailed him for misjudging public sentiment. The case for more brutishness and nastiness goes unmade and the reaction in favour of evil fails to materialise. Everyone stays on board the coalition against sin. *Nemo contendere.*

That must mean there is the largest possible market for any proposal about whatever makes people good. Yet one observes with tremulous astonishment that the market is virtually empty. Clearly we have an insatiable, universal demand for a good, perhaps indeed for *the* good. Here is an uncontested want, constantly stoked up by fresh supplies of vileness, abuse, exploitation and malignancy. And no countervailing proposal presents itself. I for one find it extremely difficult to imagine a TV advertisement for the *National Review* which intones 'Do you suffer from greed, malice, pride, concupiscence and all uncharitableness? In yourself? In others? Read the *National Review* for a modest proposal'.

But why not? What is it about goodness that there are virtually no proposals for its augmentation? The answer lies in two false ideas. One is that virtue is a 'natural good' snuffed out by any attempt at assiduous cultivation and efforts to provide favourable conditions. Once you assist virtue it ceases to be all that good. For example, if investigation showed people would be better were they sufficiently frightened of what happened when they were bad, then a policy based on that finding would only 'damage the goods'. They just would not be as good as when they just came good naturally.

Proponents of this false idea are united in rejecting any policy which might assist good in the contest with evil. To speak publicly, let alone organise in favour of virtue, undermines that spontaneous and unprompted embrace of the good which shows virtue at its very best. Indeed, officious preference for virtue and its public promotion can get you labelled an agent of social control (presumed to be inherently bad) or roundly accused of suffering secret psychic diseases. In other words protagonists of virtue will be placed under the surveillance of sociology or psychology and arraigned accordingly. No wonder then that good is left to fend for itself.

The other false idea condemning virtue to flounder unassisted is the supposed disagreement about what is good. People say we have entered an era of moral anarchy and warring moral preferences. Yet the evidence of sociology and commonsense is quite the contrary. According to the International Values Survey we are mostly agreed about good and bad. Setting aside the unabated *practice* of false witness etc., etc., the *belief* in goodness is well-nigh uniform. As the French say, people are *croyant* even if *non-pratiquant*, and it may even be that the lack of practice spurs on the will to believe. People are, it seems, adamantly opposed to lying, stealing, cheating, coveting, killing, and dishonouring their parents. The same goes for the moral details. Just imagine responses to the following questions. Grinding the faces of the poor, the widowed, and the fatherless is reprehensible/admirable? Drinking and driving is irresponsible/responsible? Causing a little child to stumble is perverse/life-enhancing? Taking your share of the chores is wicked/virtuous? Poking a sharp shard in another person's eye is revolting/entertaining?

Though it has been partially relativised and detached from action, there is still a concern for goodness

Of course, there are dilemmas about how to reconcile acknowledged goods. Peace and justice, for example. And selective indignation ensures we exculpate some groups and excoriate others. But a consistent moral relativist is hard to find. People are unwilling to evaluate each and every way of life from imperialism to societies sanctioning female infanticide as part of the charming and morally indifferent variety of culture. You can't get very far with an argument based on alternative life-stances when it comes to infibulation. Indeed, in liberal company where tolerance and moral relativism are supposed to be the order of the day you are continually confronted by a noble rage about the delinquent condition of the world. Here is little else but moral passion for purity: pure jokes, pure speech, pure earth, sky, and sea, pure food and pure bodies, even undiluted equality.

On the other hand, liberals do entertain certain notions which divert attention from 'what makes people good' and even render suspect proposals for the encouragement of virtue. According to one notion, goodness is primarily inhibited by social structures, and will be naturally exhibited when these are reformed or overturned. Goodness, so to speak, is a dependent variable, and politically doesn't 'do much good'. Nowadays this half-truth may be on its way out, especially after Eastern European regimes have so convincingly illustrated the state organisation of lies and mistrust and have had to look elsewhere, even to churches, for the independent generation of virtue. Vaclav Havel, after prolonged suffering under a regime of organised and principled lying, has even dared to espouse truthfulness as central to his political programme. But the implications of this restoration of virtue for moral education in the West are slow to sink in. Because, how exactly do you encourage truthfulness if it neither comes naturally nor is generated by the abolition of bourgeois society?

The possibility of making people better somewhat obstructed by the obsession with victims

The other notion blocking proposals to help make people good is a secular version of Christianity. It takes off in thoroughly amiable fashion from an attempt to reverse the balance of denunciation in favour of the victims of history and society, both groups and individuals. As a result you are not 'saved' and 'justified' *by* a victim as in orthodox

Christianity, but by *being* yourself a victim. Victimage opens up an un-limited credit line absolving you of all responsibility for the past or for the future. Indeed, in some versions this theology holds that the *only* re-sponsible and guilty people are the rulers of the present American em-pire or the descendants of the British ex-empire. It follows that you can only express a moral opinion provided you first certify your status as a qualified victim or bow before all approved victims in silent humility.

This is very serious because it encourages liberal moral education to turn away from the demanding disciplines of virtue or hard thinking about the world, to the seductively easy acquisition of nice attitudes, es-pecially attitudes to victimage. After all, the vast majority of humankind has a claim to victimage and so to non-responsibility and the unlimited credit line. We all hasten to claim so seductive a status which is espe-cially useful if we are about to set up as oppressors on our own account. The history (and misleading name) of Liberia is a terrible warning. As for the consequences for whatever it is 'makes people good' these are pretty clear. We can face down the requirements of virtue by citing our status as victims and telling our hard luck story. Even Saddam Hussein tried it.

But what might increase goodness?
The firm exercise of authority and the deployment of fear

But supposing we repudiate the moral licence granted by this credit line, and also know perfectly well that goodness doesn't come nat-urally or even in any straightforward way by social rearrangements, how do we devise a modest proposal for its modest encouragement? Modest, of course, it has to be, since 'we must never go beyond the marginal improvement of the average sensual man', sanctity and heroism must be left to heaven. To help make people good, or (better) to help *them* to 'make good', is first of all to diminish any gross advantages accruing to greed and malice and to discourage the deleterious inclinations of uni-versal egoism and self-aggrandisement. That requires, as a necessary *though far from sufficient* condition, the firm exercise of authority and the deployment of fear—that is, sanctions. No civil or civilised society signif-icantly larger than Tristan da Cunha can exist without the exercise of authority, meaning by that a graduated distribution of executive power.

In one sense this is too obvious to mention, but it is necessary to do so because the obvious is strictly unmentionable according to the contemporary Index of Prohibited Concepts and Words. Even if everyone in civilised society knows that civilised society and decency depend on authority and sanctions, civilised society does not allow this to be said. This is a serious restriction (and a patent misuse of authority and sanctions) because it encourages social science to avoid serious analyses of taboo areas, and because what is not allowed to be said often hamstrings what has to be done, or ensures what is done comes too little and too late.

Not too much authority and fear, but still some

The underlying problem is the high-minded feeling that these necessary conditions for people to 'make good' are not good enough. There must be a better way to make good. Put it another way, since authority has in the past been appallingly abused and has been an engine to promote every kind of abomination and oppression, it is somehow impolite to notice that it is also an unavoidable requirement for the promotion of goodness. The goods of liberty and equality, for instance, are specifically dependent on the exercise of authority, and indeed the protagonists of equality demand deployments of authority and fear far beyond what is proposed here. The logical extension of their aims is Hoxha's Albania where even clothing was equalised and made 'uniform' by fiat. What I propose is only a limited but secure exercise of authority in home, school or society, to ensure an open social space for the disposition to good and a more restricted space for the disposition to ill.

This is the minimum costing of whatever it is makes people good. If you think you can get it more cheaply, and so preserve your access to nice words, nice concepts and appealing stances, reality will exact an even higher price, often not at your expense but at the expense of others less well privileged and protected, and at the expense of society and future generations.

Good order protects the weak, fosters
good habits and restrains appetite

The case for authority and sanctions is a case for the enforcement of rules in particular to protect the vulnerable, and to allow free space for the exercise of good will. Good order offers room to foster good habits, and for the uninhibited activity of the well-disposed. Goodness is more achievable where good habits rest on good order and clear expectations. Chaos is an enemy of the *practice* of virtue and confusion a breeding ground of cumulative evil. That does not imply that we should, as Hilaire Belloc satirically put it:

Hold tight to nurse
For fear of something worse.

But the 'peaceable commerce' of human beings one with another does depend on 'degree', that is, on graduated authority. Otherwise we are all prey to 'appetite', the 'universal wolf'. Only God can allow Satan to 'go up and down upon the earth' wreaking what havoc he or she will. Only God can advance innocently towards evil to pay the cost of good directly in His own person. To imitate the innocent divine victim cannot be a matter of social policy, though it remains open to individual heroism at a particular exemplary moment. Indeed that exemplary moment is the most moving of all human demonstrations of the good, but it is not in the cognisance or remit of Caesar or society.

Anyone will recognise the menace of 'appetite' and disorder who has had a child cruelly exposed in a playground where authority refuses to pre-empt the issue of bad behaviour. Once accord a freedom to ill-will properly accorded to goodwill and goodwill begins to pass out of currency. It is not that people can or should be forced to be good, but that authority has to provide an opportunity or window for the good. Otherwise the decent are damaged and reduced to doubtful defensive strategies or practices, while the indecent are confirmed in their indecency.

Virtue, then, is a reinforced practice, within the self and society. A good school is inevitably also a 'school of goodness', recognised by the steady contented murmur of children doing what has become habitual and accepted without demur. This desirability of habit is universal precisely because goodness flourishes where spaces and times are marked out for the regular practice of habitual, fraternal, and inoffensive activity. Only when this has been achieved can authority retire into the background to allow what is securely established to run on its own momentum. This is so obvious that it could only be ignored where people are afraid of fear, and authority unnerved by the label 'authoritarian'.

Authority inimical to goodness when arbitrary

Of course authority can also be inimical to the good, and this is above all the case where government is arbitrary. Arbitrary government often neglects moral language and allows good and bad to be displaced by deviance and conformity or adjustment and maladjustment. 'Maladjustment' looks nonjudgemental, even coolly scientific, but is a tool of naked and improper power. Once judgements are medical rather than moral it either happens that 'pathological' is employed as a covert and sneaky form of moral disapproval, or the human being is treated as an object. The most deadly aspect of psychological techniques for securing control is their evacuation of moral language, because once moral language goes out of common circulation, there is no ground for complaint. Dismiss justice as meaningless and there is no court of appeal. This means that the promotion of goodness requires us to appeal as far as possible in moral language because it simultaneously controls the one appealed to and the one who appeals. Adjustment and control must be subordinate to decency and mutuality.

The importance of moral language . . .

I once attended a group called together by the British Secretary of State for Home Affairs to consider 'what makes people good', though it wasn't phrased quite like that. A psychologist put up a proposal more designed (I thought) to make people perform than to enable them to be better. It *made* them good in a way that really did destroy the value and meaning of goodness. The psychologist remarked that the nervous system varied from person to person in its responsiveness to conditioning. Some people responded to a little, while others required a lot, before they would exhibit the required 'behaviours'. (A degradation of language usually accompanies the degradation of people.) The trick therefore was to test the variable response to conditioning at an early age and make sure those with poor responses received an adequate dose. It made one think of certain problems of implementation and the cost of employing an adequate army of trained conditioners. And indeed the whole idea was morally objectionable.

. . . Especially guilt

At the heart of moral language is guilt, and guilt is to be firmly encouraged in any humane moral psychology. Guilt does not mean a kind of brooding disablement but simply a recognition that our actions have consequences, and could have been otherwise and better. People cannot 'make good' unless they have been encouraged to recognise they are guilty. Those who devalue guilt deny freedom and responsibility. Guilt is moral truthfulness about the self, undeterred by excuses, especially the kind of excuse made available by popular psychology. To espouse guilt is to reject reliance on mechanistic talk of need and instinct in favour of recollection, evaluation, and scrutiny. It is also to reject, at least for oneself, the projection of blame elsewhere, on society or parents or circumstance. Of course, there are circumstances and there are needs to be taken into account, but 'making good' depends on the recognition of fault and the possession of moral being.

It follows that the cure for guilt is not an explanation enabling the self to excuse actions in terms of a blind machine jerking and manipulating an irresponsible sprite, but by confession and absolution (or telling and being released). Of course you have to be very careful whom you tell because confession invites blackmail. As for absolution, it may come from the self, by inner compassionate pardon, but it comes best from authoritative pronouncement 'speaking for' the impaired and fractured good. This means that people need first to be told they are free and then they have to be set free. Or rather we need to be spoken to and addressed as free beings existing in a necessary and utterly familiar entanglement, from which we can in principle be released. This 'address' simultaneously restores the person and the moral universe. It is part of a profound dynamic of ravage and restoration.

Stories promoting moral understanding

The best way to convey a world adequately stocked with good and evil is a story. A good story is the means of making a good person. People cast and recast themselves as they follow narratives and fables. I have now to admit that you can have too much of a good thing. As a child I browsed without proper restraint in my mother's Edwardian Sunday School prizes and came out sprayed with morality from head to foot. Even today when I read Mrs. Gaskell or George Eliot or Jane Austen I recall that relentless spray and start like a guilty thing. Moral tone can be just too high, precise, sensitive, and persistent to allow '*l'homme moyen sensuel*' to get out from under. The same is true of *The Pilgrim's Progress*. Life can be too obviously framed between the rival powers of Vanity Fair and the Delectable Mountains, and the journey altogether too purposefully located 'between this world and the next'. But too exclusive a diet of *Pilgrim's Progress* is not today a frequent problem.

For those of tender years the best stories about the good are secretive and insinuating. Tolkein and C. S. Lewis create landscapes of threat and promise full of winding journeys and circuitous paths. The mountains and islands, human and animal figures, are alive with luminous attraction or repulsive menace, and also contain unstable human-like compounds who have 'good in them'. Once these imaginative worlds are implanted it doesn't matter so much what philosophy children eventually come to espouse, because the point of reference stays secure in the original garden of the soul. The wounding of Aslan is never forgotten. This is where the moral sympathies permanently reside and retain their primitive power and influence. Of course these are first approximations, initial intimations of a kind of firm world found also in Dickens. But it is from this necessary and beneficent ground that ambiguity can take off and amusement and irony become possible.

The need for moral examples—a hunger for heaven

The big problem for 'making good' in the contemporary world lies with finding moral examples for emulation. There may well be a hunger for heroes but all candidates for moral emulation seem disqualified in one way or another. This is odd since in all the really serious activities, like baseball, rock music or war, people achieve excellence by identifying with the finest practitioners. In the past emulation and discipleship were clearly part of the pursuit of the good. Virtue was furthered by the imitation of the morally attractive.

So what has happened now? Perhaps the idea of *the* good woman and *the* good man has splintered into myriad fragments, leaving a row of empty plinths where once the examples stood. Certainly the historical figures filling my mother's Sunday School prizes are now either unknown, like David Livingstone and Mary Slessor, or debunked. Of course many of them were heroes of empire or missionary enterprise, though no less heroic for that. The change has occurred in my own lifetime since I have never asked my own children to emulate the examples set up for me by books and teachers and parents. There is now a pervasive fear of falsely idealising past heroes or creating a fixed national (and nationalistic) pantheon.

We are so afraid of dismissive and knowing gestures and ironic insinuation that we do not admit anyone is admirable or steadfast and generous. The very words make us recoil defensively and we even feel relief when another noble being is 'deconstructed' and diminished. The finest words in the language like prudence and probity are reserved for liturgies or obituaries.

This backing away from the exemplary may prove a costly cowardice because worth and integrity are embodied in people more than they are conveyed in ideas; and any good society needs publicly to recognise goodness. Everyday citizens don't find their way forward just by stumbling around in a state of pure directionless being and raw humanity. It should be possible openly to acknowledge integrity and speak of people doing at least some good things, whatever dubieties investigative journalism may uncover. Of course, in a way people like Martin Luther King and Andrei Sakharov are there, in place, but mainly because modern media maintain a spotlight on the heroic victim under trial or threat. Sheer goodness on its own has a poor press, and it is revealingly difficult to think of names. Irina Ratushinskaya, imprisoned by the KGB for writing poems, is one of the most luminously admirable people I have ever encountered. But, unhappily, she too is a victim. It so happens that Prince Charles is a good man, marked by nothing more and nothing less than persistent decent concern and desire to discover his duty. But I'm not sure I can propose him. Admiration for good examples of the species should not really be that difficult. It is an important element in 'what makes people good'.

Goodness for sensual men

The author of such a chapter as this had better write a concluding unethical postscript. He is the 'average sensual man' referred to earlier and he has no claims either to goodness or to victimage. But speaking now for that 'average sensual man' it seems necessary to admix the rigours of ethics with the relaxations of entertainment and play.

One way to do this is by reading novels and stories about venial sin and moral micro-climates. E. F. Benson's novels about the rivalry of Miss Mapp and Lucia are accounts of fads, foibles, and fallibilities which provide the right mix of entertainment and warning. Kenneth Grahame's *The Wind in the Willows* is another marvellous entertainment which also introduces a moral micro-climate. The reader is adopted by the unformed childlike view of Mole as he is introduced to the ways of the world by the wise and knowledgeable Ratty. On the one side Mole encounters the immediate terror of the spiteful weasels and on the other the awesome authority of Badger. At the centre of the action is the whirligig charisma of Toad the Trickster, who is nevertheless dependent on the resentful solidarity of his faithful friends. This mixture of threat and awe, wise induction and irrational but somehow fascinating disorder, just about summarises the human condition.

Apart from such entertainments and their amusing instruction some other thing is needed. For me it is music. For other people it may be dancing, or arranging flowers, or enticing shapes out of the grain of wood or stone, or watching birds, or simply ordering and reordering a room until it is pleasurable to the eye. Encouraging growth, observing orders, responding to or making graceful motion, delighting in powerful or delicate lines, juxtaposing masses and colours are all kinds of well-being. If people are to 'make good' they also need 'well-being'. In any 'school of goodness' there needs to be plenty of room for making and listening, watching and playing.

Notes
&
References

Chapter One

1. See Shirley Foster Hartley, *Illegitimacy*, University of California Press, 1975, pp. 39-40; and Peter Laslett, *Family Life and Illicit Love in Earlier Generations*, Cambridge University Press, 1979, p. 113 and p. 123.
2. See Christie Davies, *Permissive Britain*, Pitman, 1975, pp. 140-2 and pp. 150-6.
3. Quoted in Sir Leon Radzinowicz and Joan King, *The Growth of Crime*, Penguin, 1979, p.15.
4. Ibid, pp. 15-6.
5. *Criminal Statistics England and Wales*, volumes for 1980 and 1989, HMSO (Cmnd 8376 and 1322 respectively). These later statistics are not strictly comparable with those for earlier years, but for our present purposes this does not matter. They are simply cited to show that the rise in crime has continued.
6. *Criminal Statistics England and Wales 1989*, p. 21; and see also Pat Mayhew, David Elliott and Lizanne Dowds, *The 1988 British Crime Survey*, HMSO, 1989.
7. In some cases the crime surveys have indicated that the increase in crime in some areas and for some crimes is even more rapid than the official statistics of recorded crime indicate. See Stephen Davies, 'Towards the Remoralization of Society', in Martin Loney *et. al.* (eds.) *The State or the Market*, Sage, 1987, pp. 174-5.
8. Ibid, p. 175.
9. V. A. C. Gatrell and T. B. Hadden, 'Criminal Statistics and their Interpretation', in E. A. Wrigley (ed), *Nineteenth Century: Essays in the Use of*

Quantitative Methods for the Study of Social Data, Cambridge University Press, 1972, pp. 373-7. See also V. A. C. Gatrell, 'The decline of theft and violence in Victorian and Edwardian England', in V. A. C. Gatrell (ed), *Crime and the Law: the Social History of Crime in Western Europe since 1500*, Europa, 1980.

10. Gatrell and Hadden, *op cit*, p. 374.

11. Christie Davies, 'Crime, Bureaucracy and Equality', in *Policy Review*, Vol 23, Winter 1983, pp. 89-105.

12. Stephen Davies, *op cit*.

13. Jerzy Sarnecki, 'Some Mechanisms of the Growth of Crime in Sweden', in *Archiwum Kryminologii*, T.XII, p. 203 and p. 208; see also Christie Davies, 1983, *op cit*, p. 91.

14. See A. E. Dingle, 'Drink and Working Class Living Standards in Britain 1870-1914', in Derek Oddy and Derek Miller (eds), *The Making of the Modern British Diet*, Croom Helm, 1975, pp. 118-121 and p. 131; and Christie Davies, 1975, *op cit*, p. 166.

15. See Eric Dunning, Patrick Murphy and John Williams, 'Spectator Violence at Football Matches: Towards a Sociological Explanation', in Norbet Elias and Eric Dunning (eds), *Quest for Excitement: Sport and Leisure in the Civilizing Process*, Basil Blackwell, 1986, p. 261.

16. It is always easy to make out a shallow and meaningless case of this kind by selectively collecting the shocked reactions of the middle-aged at some contemporary enormity and showing that in their own youth there had been similar bursts of outrage at the wickedness of the times. For such an enterprise to have any meaning, the researcher must be equally diligent in collecting the sentiments expressed by those who have emphasised the improvements in popular behaviour and manners that have taken place in a particular era and then try to balance the two. For an example of the latter, that has not been noted by the anti-golden age school, see for instance Dean E. B. Ramsay, *Reminiscences of Scottish Life and Character*, Gall and Inglis, 1873, pp. 101-126 on the remarkable decline of drunkenness in polite society in Scotland in his life-time. In some quarters the beginning of the anti-rot had set in even earlier, see for instance William Makepeace Thackeray writing in the *Quarterly Review*, December 1854, p. 78.

17. George Orwell, *The English People*, (1944), in Sonia Orwell and Ian Angus (eds), *The Collected Essays, Journalism and Letters of George Orwell*, Vol III, *As I Please 1943-45*, Secker and Warburg, 1968, pp. 2-3.

18. Ibid, pp. 6-7.

19. Geoffrey Gorer, *Exploring English Character*, Cresset, 1955, p. 16.

20. Ibid, p. 16.

21. See, for example, Christie Davies, 1983, *op cit*, pp. 98-100; and Sarnecki, 1985, *op cit.*

22. See Marshall B. Clinard, *Cities with Little Crime: The Case of Switzerland*, Cambridge University Press, 1978; Ralph Segalman, *The Swiss Way of Welfare, Lessons for the Western World*, Praeger, 1986; Christie Davies, 1983, *op cit*, pp. 101-5; and Hartley, 1975, *op cit*, pp. 39-43.

23. See Bryan R. Wilson, 'Morality in the Evolution of the Modern Social System', *British Journal of Sociology*, Vol 36, September 1985, pp. 315-332.

24. Hans Jurgen Eysenck, *Crime and Personality*, Paladin, 1970, p. 50.

25. Ibid.

26. Ibid, p. 53 and p. 56.

27. See Richard Lynn and S. L. Hampson, 'Fluctuations in National Levels of Neuroticism and Extroversion 1935-1970', *British Journal of Social and Clinical Psychology*, No. 16, 1977, pp. 131-8; and 'National Differences in Extroversion and Neuroticism', *British Journal of Social and Clinical Psychology*, No. 14, 1975, pp. 223-40.

28. Gorer, *op cit*, p. 194.

29. The figures are taken from Table 21 in Thomas Walter Laqueur, *Religion and Respectability, Sunday Schools and Working Class Culture 1780-1850*, Yale UP, 1976, p. 246. (Like the author, I have resisted the temptation to round them.) See also David Martin, *A Sociology of English Religion*, Heinemann, 1967, pp. 41-2.

30. Alan Wilkinson, *The Church of England and the First World War*, SPCK, 1978, p. 7.

31. Martin, *op cit*, p. 42.

32. See Olive Anderson, *Suicide in Victorian and Edwardian England*, Clarendon, 1987, pp. 100-10; and David W. Howell, *Land and People in Nineteenth Century Wales*, Routledge and Kegan Paul, 1977, p. 156.

Chapter Four

1. Versions of parts of this chapter first appeared in *The Sunday Telegraph* and the *Sunday Times* and were subsequently extended and published as *The Unmentionable Face of Poverty in the Nineties: domestic incompetence, improvidence and male irresponsiblity in low income families*, Social Affairs Unit, 1991.

2. Jonathan Bradshaw and Hilary Holmes, *Living on the Edge*, CPAG, 1989.

3. Jane Ritchie, *Thirty Families: Their Living Standards in Unemployment*, HMSO, 1990.

4. All these and following U.S. figures from Edward Lucas in *The Independent*, 30 January, 1991.

5. IEA Health and Welfare Unit Conference, 20 November, 1990.

6. Ritchie, *op cit.*

7. Ibid, p. 29.

8. Ibid, p. 37.

9. Ibid, p. 64.

10. Jan Pahl, *Money and Marriage*, Macmillan, 1989.

11. Ibid, p. 1.

12. Loc cit.

13. Ibid, p. 68.

14. Ibid, p. 139.

15. Ibid, p. 149.

16. Gail Wilson, *Money in the Family*, Avebury, 1987.

17. Ibid, p. 123.

18. Ibid, p. 129.

19. Ibid, p. 132.

20. Pahl, *op cit*, p. 1.

21. Bradshaw and Holmes, *op cit.*

22. Ibid, p. 89.

23. Ibid, p. 97.

24. Ibid, p. 45.

25. Chief Rabbi's Office, 1985.

26. Samuel Smiles, *Self Help: with Illustrations of Conduct and Perseverance*, John Murray, 1889, p. 291.

27. Faith Press, 1935.

28. Odhams, 1952.

29. Thomas Childers, *The Information-Poor in America*, The Scarecrow Press, 1975.

30. Jeremy Seabrook, *Working Class Childhood*, Victor Gollancz, 1982, p. 72.

31. Janice Winship, *Inside Women's Magazines*, Pandora, 1987.

32. Digby Anderson, *Imperative Cooking*, Harrap, 1987.

Chapter Six

1. C. Moskos, *A Call to Civic Service: National Service for Country and Community*, Free Press/Macmillan, 1988.

2. B. S. Turner, *Outline of a Theory of Citizenship Sociology*, 1990, Ch. 24, pp. 189-217.

3. Moskos, *op cit*, p. 5.

4. A. Giddens, *Capitalism and Modern Social Theory*, Cambridge University Press, 1971, p. 117.

5. Ibid, p. 118.

6. E. Durkheim, *The Division of Labour in Society*, Free Press/Macmillan, 1968, p. 227.

7. Ibid, p. 228.

8. Moskos, *op cit*, p. 2.

9. Ibid, p. 165.

10. Ibid, p. 166.

11. S. Cohen, *Visions of Social Control*, Polity Press, 1985, pp. 236-272.

12. J. Burk, 'National Attachments and the Decline of Mass Armed Force', *Journal of Political and Military Sociology*, No. 17, Spring 1989, pp. 65-81; I have also drawn on an unpublished paper by Burk on the decline of mass armed force and national variations in this and the following paragraphs.

13. On these issues see also P. Manigart, 'The Decline of the Mass Armed Force in Belgium', *Sozialwissenschaftliches Institut der Bundeswehr*, 1990, Forum 9, pp. 37-64.

14. B. Boene, 'The Non-Military Functions of the Military in a Democratic State: The French Case', delivered to a conference on 'The Military in the Service of Society and Democracy' organised by the Israeli Institute for Military Studies and sponsored by the Konrad Adenauer Foundation, December 1991.

15. H. Kohr and J. Kuhlmann, 'Conscription Forever—or General Voluntary Civic Service? Some Utopian Perspectives and Theses', paper delivered to the international conference 'The Armed Forces in Democratic States', Moscow, 25-28 November, 1991.

16. Moskos, *op cit*, p. 111.

17. Durkheim, *op cit*, p. 197.

18. A. Giddens, *Capitalism and Modern Social Theory*, Cambridge University Press, 1971, p. 117.

19. Durkheim, *op cit*, p. 211.

20. Ibid, p. 214.

21. Ibid.

22. Moskos, *op cit*.

Chapter Seven

1. Meyer Fortes, *Rules and the Emergence of Human Society*, Royal Anthropological Institute of Great Britain, Occasional Paper No. 39, 1983, p. 28.

2. Ibid, p. 20.

3. Jonathan Sacks, 'Social and Moral Concerns We Share: A Jewish Perspective', unpublished paper, June 1987, p. 13.

4. Ibid, p. 20.

5. Fortes, *op cit*, p. 27.

6. Ibid, p. 24.

7. Ibid.

8. Bronislaw Malinowski, *Sex and Repression in Savage Society*, Routledge and Kegan Paul, 1960 (first published 1927).

9. Michael Gordon and Susan J. Creighton, 'Natal and Non-natal fathers as Sexual Abusers in the United Kingdom: A Comparative Analysis', *Journal of Marriage and the Family*, No. 50, 1988, pp. 99-105.

10. Judith A. Seltzer, 'Relationships between Fathers and Children who Live Apart: The Father's Roles After Separation', *Journal of Marriage and the Family*, No. 53, 1991, pp. 79-101.

11. Judith S. Wallerstein and Sandra Blakeslee, *Second Chances*, Tickner and Enright, 1989, p. 143, p. 158 and p. 144.

12. Malinowski, *op cit*.

13. Fortes, *op cit*, pp. 23-4.

14. Roger Scruton, *The Meaning of Conservatism*, Pelican, 1981, pp. 32-3.

15. Joseph R. Peden and Fred R. Glahe, *The American Family and the State*, Pacific Research Institute for Public Policy, reviewing work of Gabriel Marcel, 1986, p. 4.

16. Ibid, p. 23.

17. Fortes, *op cit*, p. 28.

18. Scruton, *op cit*, p. 33.

19. Alan Macfarlane, *Marriage and Love in England*, Basil Blackwell, 1986.

20. Fortes, *op cit*.

21. John R. Gillis, *For Better, for Worse*, Oxford University Press, 1985, p. 101.

22. Faith Robertson Elliott, *Family Change or Continuity*, Macmillan, 1986, p. 144.

23. Simon Schema, *An Embarrassment of Riches*, Collins, 1987, p. 386.

24. Ibid.

25. Carl N. Degler, *At Odds*, Oxford University Press, 1980.

26. Allan C. Carlson, 'The Family and Liberal Capitalism', *Modern Age*, Vol. 26, Pt 3-4, 1982, p. 366; and 'Taxes and Families', *The Human Life Review*, Pt 1, 1983, pp. 38-45.

27. Michael Novak, *The Spirit of Democratic Capitalism*, IEA Health and Welfare Unit, 1991, p. 182 (first published 1982).

28. Ibid, pp. 156-7.

29. Carlson, *op cit*, p. 369.

30. Eugene Steuerle, 'The Tax Treatment of Households of Different Size', in Rudolph G. Penner (ed), *Taxing the Family*, American Enterprise Institute for Public Policy Research, 1981.

31. J. S. Mill, *Essay on Liberty*, Everyman Edition, p. 159-60.

32. Fortes, *op cit*.

33. Minutes of evidence, Royal Commission on Marriage and Divorce, 16th - 17th days, p. 428.

34. Barbara Wootton, 'Holiness or Happiness', *Twentieth Century*, November 1955, p. 407.

35. O. R. McGregor, *Divorce in England*, Heinemann, 1957, p. x.

36. Wootton, *op cit*.

37. Roger Smith, *Trial by Medicine*, Edin, 1981.

38. Brigette Berger and Peter L. Berger, *The War Over the Family*, Hutchinson, 1983, p. 145.

39. Gillis, *op cit*, p. 303.

40. Allan Bloom, *The Closing of the American Mind*, Simon and Schuster, 1987, p. 175.

41. Ibid.

42. *Putting Asunder*, report of a group appointed by the Archbishop of Canterbury in January 1964, SPCK, 1966, p. 41.

43. Ibid, p. 38; see also Thomas B. Marvell, 'Divorce Rates and the Fault Requirement', *Law and Society Review*, Vol 23, No 4, 1989, pp. 543-565.

44. McGregor, *op cit*, p. 161.

45. George Brown, *Finding Fault in Divorce*, Social Affairs Unit, 1989, p. 4.

46. Basil Mitchell, *Why Social Policy Cannot be Morally Neutral*, Social Affairs Unit, 1989, p. 17.

47. Elliot, *op cit*, p. 144.

48. Mitchell, *op cit*, p. 13.

49. Bloom, *op cit*.

50. Lawrence Stone, *Road to Divorce*, Oxford University Press, 1991, p. 422.

51. Law Commission and the Scottish Law Commission discussion papers on the Ground for Divorce, Nos 170 and 176, HMSO, May 1988.

52. McGregor, *op cit.*

53. Judith S. Wallerstein and Joan Berlin Kelly, *Surviving the Breakup: How Parents and Children Cope with Divorce*, Basic Books, 1980.

54. Ann Mitchell, *Children in the Middle*, Macmillan, 1985, p. 103.

55. J. T. Landis, 'The trauma of children when parents divorce', *Marriage and Family Living*, 22, 1960, pp. 7-13.

56. Wallerstein and Kelly, *op cit*; and Wallerstein and Blakeslee, *op cit.*

57. Wallerstein and Kelly, *op cit.*

58. M. P. Richards and Michael Dyson, *Separation, Divorce and the Development of Children*, Cambridge Child Care and Development Group, 1982.

59. Wallerstein and Kelly, *op cit*, p. 14.

60. Ibid, p. 33.

61. Ibid.

62. Bloom, *op cit*, p. 118.

63. Wallerstein and Kelly, *op cit.*

64. Wallerstein and Blakeslee, *op cit*, p. 29.

65. Scruton, *op cit*, p. 32.

66. Bloom, *op cit*, p. 115.

67. Wallerstein and Blakeslee, *op cit*, p. 307.

68. Peter Berger and Hansfield Kellner, 'Marriage and the Construction of Reality', *Diogenes*, Summer 1964; and Berger and Berger, *op cit.*

69. Brown, *op cit*, p. 4.

70. G. Davis and M. Murch, *Grounds for Divorce*, Clarendon Press, 1988.

71. Wallerstein and Blakeslee, *op cit*, pp. 6-7; Eleanor R. Maccoby, Charlne E. Depner and Robert H. Mnookin, 'Coparenting in the second year after divorce', *Journal of Marriage and the Family*, No. 52, 1990, pp. 141-155.

72. Ibid, p. 7.

73. Jack Dominian, Penny Mansfield, Duncan Dormer and Fiona McAllister, *Marital Breakdown and the Health of the Nation*, One plus One, 1991.

74. Midge Decter, 'For the Family', *Policy Review*, No. 27, 1984, p. 44.

75. Bloom, *op cit*, p. 119.

76. Adrienne Burgess, 'Long Live the New Family', *Cosmopolitan*, September 1991.

77. Helen Franks, *Mummy Does not Live Here Anymore—why women leave their children*, Doubleday, 1990.

78. Annette Lawson, *Adultery*, Basil Blackwell, 1989.

79. Lesley Garner, 'Happy Families: Just a game or an ideal way for us to live?', *Sunday Telegraph*, 21 January, 1990.

80. Robert Chester, 'The Myth of the Disappearing Nuclear Family' in Digby Anderson and Graham Dawson (eds), *Family Portraits*, Social Affairs Unit, 1986. 81. Garner, *op cit*.

82. C. C. Harris, *The Family and Industrial Society*, George Allen and Unwin, 1982, p. 216.

83. William J. Gribbin, 'Courting Disaster: Welfare and the Federal Judiciary', in James S. Denton (ed), *Welfare Reform: Consensus or Conflict*, 1991.

84. Scruton, *op cit*, p. 145.

85. Decter, *op cit*, p. 44.

86. Kenneth Minogue, *Alien Powers*, Weidenfeld and Nicolson, 1985.

87. For example, Mark Poster, *Critical Theory of the Family*, Seabury Press, 1978; and Shulamith Firestone, *The Dialectic of Sex*, The Women's Press, 1979.

88. David Cooper, *The Death of the Family*, Allen Lane: Penguin Press, 1971.

89. Scruton, *op cit*, p. 120.

90. Carlson, *op cit*, p. 371.

91. Christopher Lasch, *Haven in a Heartless World*, Basic Books, 1977, p. 177.

92. Mitchell, *op cit*, p. 13.

Chapter Eight

1. S. Modgil and C. Modgil, *Lawrence Kholberg: Consensus and Controversy*, Falmer Press, 1986.

2. H. J. Eysenck and G. Gudjonsson, *The Causes and Cures of Criminality*, Plenum Press, 1989.

3. J. S. Coleman, *Foundations of Social Theory*, Harvard University Press, 1990.

Chapter Nine

1. C. Parkes, *Bereavement: Studies of Grief in Adult Life*, Harmondsworth, 1975.

2. B. Bettelheim, *The Informed Heart*, Penguin, 1986.

3. A. Furnham, *The Protestant Work Ethic*, Routledge, 1990.

4. C. Lasch, *The Culture of Narcissism*, Collus, 1985.

5. Ibid, pp. 52-3.

6. Ibid, p. 58.

7. Ibid, p. 69.

8. A. Roberts and R. Cochrane, 'Attempted suicide and cultural change: an empirical investigation', *Human Relations*, 9, 1976, pp. 863-883; A. Roberts and R. Cochrane, 'Deviance and cultural change: attempted suicide as a case study', *International Journal of Social Psychiatry*, 22, 1976, pp. 1-6; R. Cochrane and M. Sobel, 'Life stresses and psychological consequences', in P. Feldman and J. Orford (eds), *Social Psychology of Psychological Problems*, Wiley, 1980.

9. Cochrane and Sobel, *op cit*, p. 165.

10. R. Turner, 'The themes of contemporary social movement', *British Journal of Sociology*, No. 20, 1969, pp. 390-405.

11. Ibid, p. 394.

12. Roberts and Cochrane, *op cit.*

13. P. Golding and S. Middleton, *Images of Welfare*, Martin Robertson, 1983.

14. P. Taylor-Gooby, 'Legitimation deficit, public opinion and the welfare state', *Sociology*, No. 17, 1983, pp. 165-184.

15. R. de Charms, *Personal Causation*, Academic Press, 1968.

16. J. Rotter, 'Generalised expectancies for internals vs. externals control of reinforcement', *Psychological Mongraph 80*, No. 609, 1966.

17. de Charms, *op cit,*, pp. 273-4.

18. G. Ritzer, C. Kammeyer and N. Yelman, *Sociology: Experiencing a Changing Society*, Allyn & Bacon, 1982.

19. Ibid, p. 18.

Chapter Twelve

1. Margaret Donaldson, *Children's Minds*, Fontana/Croom Helm, 1978.

2. But see Richard Lynn, *Educational Achievement in Japan: Lessons for the West*, Macmillan/Social Affairs Unit, 1988.

3. Adult Literacy and Basic Skills Unit (ALBSU), *Literacy, Numeracy and Adults*, 1987.

4. Geoffrey Partington, 'History Rewritten to Ideological Fashion', in D. O'Keeffe (ed), *The Wayward Curriculum*, Social Affairs Unit, 1986; Alan Bloom, *The Closing of the American Mind*, Simon and Schuster, 1987; E. D. Hirsch, *Cultural Literacy*, Houghton and Mifflin, 1987.

5. Lord Harris of High Cross, letter to *The Times*, April 4, 1992.

6. Basil Bernstein, *Class, Codes and Control*, Routledge and Kegan Paul, 1978.

7. Martin Turner, *Sponsored Reading Failure*, IPSET, 1990.

8. Colin Coldman, 'Maths in a Muddle', in Stewart Deuchar (ed), *What is Wrong with our Schools?*, Campaign for Real Education, 1990.

9. Richard Lynn, *The Secret of the Miracle Economy*, Social Affairs Unit, 1991.

10. For a lengthy discussion, see D. O'Keeffe, *The Wayward Elite*, Adam Smith Institute, 1990.

11. Rita Kramer, *Ed School Follies: The Miseducation of America's Teachers*, The Free Press, 1990.

12. R. S. Peters, *Ethics and Education*, Allen and Unwin, 1966.

13. Nick Seaton (ed), *Higher Standards and More Choice: A Manifesto for our Schools*, Campaign for Real Education, 1991.

14. Alasdair MacIntyre, *After Virtue*, University of Notre Dame Press, 1984.

15. Bloom, *op cit*; O'Keeffe, 1990, *op cit*; Kramer, *op cit.*

16. Len Barton, *Ideology and the School Curriculum*, Falmer, 1981.

Chapter Fourteen

1. C. Murray, *Losing Ground: American Social Policy 1950-1980*, Basic Books, 1984; compare also *The Pursuit of Happiness and Good Government*, Simon and Schuster, 1988, in which the same author himself enquires into these implications.

2. *The New Consensus on Family and Welfare: A Community of Self-Reliance*, American Enterprise Institute and Marquette University Press, 1987, p. 5.

3. *Faith in the City: A Call for Action by Church and Nation*, Church House Publishing, 1985.

4. D. Anderson (ed), *The Kindness that Kills: The Churches' Simplistic Response to Complex Social Problems*, SPCK, 1984.

5. Ibid, p. 2.

6. *Faith in the City*, *op cit*, p. 208.

7. Ibid.

8. Precise and reliable statistics, taking account of actual unlicensed absence after morning register has been taken, are not available. The Department of Education and Science has not encouraged investigation of the phenomenon of Post Registration Truancy, presumably anxious lest the findings of such research should be recognised as casting some discredit upon its stewardship. It is easy to locate, in the words of England's most formidable political thinker, 'The benefit that proceedeth from

such darkness and to whom it accrueth' (Thomas Hobbes, *Leviathan*, Ch XLVII).

9. Roughly speaking, Elementary and High School.

10. It is most abundant for and from the U.S. system which, despite the many differences, is perhaps more like that of the UK than that of any other NATO country. See, for instance, J. E. Chubb and T. M. Moe, *Politics, Markets and America's Schools*, Brookings Institution, 1990; also Myron Lieberman, *Public Education: An Autopsy*, forthcoming.

11. *House of Lords Debates* for 18 April 1988, Column 1263. U.S. readers will naturally compare this statement with the comparably alarming verdict upon their system in *A Nation at Risk*.

12. *Faith in the City, op cit*, p. 295.

13. One rarely noticed consequence of this deficiency is that official committees established to make recommendations about illiteracy or innumeracy have to begin their deliberations by scratching around for evidence of the extent of the problem. The flip side of the same deficiency is that there is at present no means of determining the total output of this large and exceptionally important industry.

14. *Faith in the City, op cit*, p. 306.

15. For a recent British attempt to restore these emphases, see D. Anderson (ed), *Full Circle: Bringing up Children in the Post-permissive Society*, Social Affairs Unit, 1988.

16. *Faith in the City, op cit*, pp. 39-60.

17. See for instance, P. Morgan, 'For the sake of the children?' in *Full Circle, op cit*; and compare N. Davidson, 'Life without Father: America's Greatest Social Catastrophe', *Policy Review*, No. 91, Winter 1990.

18. *Faith in the City, op cit*, p. 17, pp. 302-3 and p. 327.

19. See my 'Education against Racism', in D. O'Keeffe (ed), *The Wayward Curriculum*, Social Affairs Unit, 1986; and compare F. Palmer (ed), *Anti-Racism: An Assault on Education and Value*, Sherwood, 1986, *passim*.

20. This will surely surprise students of Thomas Sowell. For he has often pointed out that in the U.S. immigrants and the immediate descendants of immigrants from the Caribeean tend to be in every way significantly more successful than native-born blacks. The parents of General Colin Powell, for instance, emigrated from Jamaica.

21. See, for instance, Walter Williams, *The State Against Blacks*, McGraw Hill, 1982, Ch. 3.

22. *Losing Ground, op cit*, p. 212.

23. Compare, again, Williams, *op cit*; also the Report of the Lay Commis-

sion on Catholic Social Teaching, *Toward the Future*, American Catholic Committee, 1984, p. 41: 'Ray Kroc, who in his later years invented the concepts on which McDonalds is based, gave more employment to teen-aged youths than all the programs of the federal government put together, costing the government not a penny and paying taxes for the privilege'.

24. Chief Rabbi's Office, *From Doom to Hope*, 1985; my several quotations from this booklet are borrowed from an examination of *Faith in the City* by Julius Gould in *Encounter*, 1986.

25. I borrow this quotation from Jonathan Sacks, *Wealth and Poverty: A Jewish Analysis*, Social Affairs Unit, 1985, p. 16. Sacks, himself now Chief Rabbi, there insisted 'that the one thing Judaism rules out *ab initio*, by specific Biblical command, is a bias to the poor; "You shall not favour a poor man in his cause" (Exodus XII, 3; and compare *Leviticus* LXI, 15)'. This remark constitutes a decisive put-down for the Bishop of Liverpool, David Sheppard, who was both an active member of the Archbishop's Commission and the author of an influencial book entitled *Bias to the Poor* (Hodder & Stoughton, 1983).

26. *The Kindness that Kills*, *op cit*.

27. *Faith in the City*, *op cit*, p. 212.

28. *Inequalities in Health*, Department of Health and Social Security, 1988.

29. For a more extensive treatment of this identification, and of 'social' justice generally, compare A. Flew, *The Politics of Procrustes: Contradictions of Enforced Equality*, Prometheus, 1981, Chs. I-IV.

30. A. E. Housman, *Juvenalis Saturae*, Cambridge University Press, Revised Edition, 1931, p. xi.

31. *Faith in the City*, *op cit*, p. 169.

32. Perhaps, in what Wittgenstein delighted to call 'the darkness of these times', it is worth noting that the Greek 'agapee', standardly rendered in Latin 'caritas', from which we derive the English 'charity', is the word now usually translated 'love'. This sort of love is by instructed Christians favourably compared with the Greek 'eroos' (Eros!) which is typically, but not necessarily, sexual desire.

33. Adam Smith, *The Theory of Moral Sentiments*, II (ii) I.

34. It is one thing, and by no means discreditable, to refuse to pay what would admittedly be your fair share of the costs of some public good until and unless others are forced to do the same. No one is morally obliged to be a sucker. But it is quite another to steal, especially from

others worse off than yourself.

35. Because it denies that the mind or soul can be a substance, in the sense of something which can significantly be said to exist separately and in its own right. Nor can this objection be avoided by insisting that Christians assert, or used to assert, not the immortality of the soul, but the resurrection of the flesh. For unless there is some substance to provide continuity, a reconstructed Flew would not be the author of *The Logic of Mortality* (Basil Blackwell, 1987) but a custom built replica.

36. For more, much more, on this compare A. Flew, *Thinking about Social Thinking*, Harper Collins/Fontana, Revised Edition, 1992.

37. J. Q. Wilson, *Thinking about Crime*, Vintage, 1977, p. 63; emphasis in original.

38. See D. Hume, 'Of National Characters', in *Essays, Moral, Political and Literary*, edited by E. F. Miller, Liberty Press, 1985, p. 198; 'By *moral* causes I mean all circumstances, which are fitted to work on the mind as motives or reasons . . . By *physical* causes I mean those qualities of the air and climate, which are supposed to work insensibly on the temper, by altering the tone and habit of the body . . . '

39. When before the decisive Battle of Trafalgar, the British naval hero, Lord Nelson, issued the signal 'England expects every man will do his duty' he was, of course, playing on this ambiguity.